Constantin Stanislavski

BUILDING
A CHARACTER

Translated by
ELIZABETH REYNOLDS
HAPGOOD

A Theatre Arts Book
ROUTLEDGE
NEW YORK

Published by Routledge/Theatre Arts Books
A Division of Routledge, Chapman and Hall, Inc.
29 West 35th Street, New York, N.Y. 10001

Twenty-third hardback printing, 1994
Fifth paperback printing, 1994

Hardback ISBN 0-87830-012-0
Paperback ISBN 0-87830-982-9

PRINTED IN THE UNITED STATES OF AMERICA

CONTENTS

An Actor must work all his life, cultivate his mind, train his talents systematically, develop his character; he may never despair and never relinquish this main purpose—to love his art with all his strength and love it unselfishly.

CONSTANTIN STANISLAVSKI

EXPLANATORY NOTE
BY THE TRANSLATOR

AS FAR back as 1924 my husband, Norman Hapgood, and I discussed with Stanislavski the possibility of publishing the results of his experience as an actor and trainer of actors in the foremost acting company of this century. But in the years immediately following this first conversation various matters contributed to prevent this great innovator from carrying out his desire. He was too absorbed by the responsibilities of his work in the Moscow Art Theatre, of which he was not only co-founder and co-director, with Nemirovich-Danchenko, but also one of the principal actors. His own Opera Studio, where he was working out the application of his acting techniques to operatic performance with the object of achieving a complete union of the music, the words and the action, also took much of his time and energy. A third inhibiting factor was Stanislavski's own temperament. His creative and artistic genius was never fully satisfied; it urged him on to the very day of his death to search for, to test, to choose new approaches to the art of acting, so that he hesitated to sum up any conclusions as final. He always hoped to find a better path to his high goal. Moreover he was fearful lest his written record might assume the aspect of some unalterable grammar, of rigid rules, of a kind of Bible. The thing that finally persuaded him to share his results by means of the printed word with artists throughout the world was the argument that others might receive some stimulus from them to strike out into new paths of their own.

So in 1930, when Stanislavski, after a serious illness in Russia, had come to Southern France on a leave of absence from the Art Theatre to be near my husband and me, the time came to cast into final form the long prepared book.

At that stage Norman Hapgood, who had been both an editor and a drama critic, urged him to put into one volume both aspects of his method—the inner preparations of an actor and the external technical means of bringing a character to life before an audience. In the first drafts worked out on the Riviera the two parts were side by side.

Subsequently Stanislavski returned to Russia to take up his work once more. He was no longer able to act, but he continued to direct new productions and he went on with his writing. Many months later he sent me a manuscript of book length. Because he had lacked the time and strength to edit all his material, and also because he believed its inclusion in one volume would further delay the book as well as make it too bulky, he had decided to limit it to the inner preparations of an actor—or of any artist dealing with the creation of a character. It was published by Theatre Arts, Inc., under the title *An Actor Prepares* in 1936—two years before it even appeared in Russia.

In letters to me and in the course of a visit to him in 1937 Stanislavski told me about the sequel to *An Actor Prepares* which is this present book. It would include, he said, the chapters drafted in Southern France and others which he showed me. He also let me look at his *Promptbook for Othello,* which he had written out in France in order to guide a production at the Art Theatre he was prevented from overseeing personally. He felt that this manuscript might likewise be of interest to the English-speaking theatre.

But neither of these manuscripts was at that time in a form satisfactory to him. He continued to work on them until his death the following year. Shortly afterward the Second World War intervened, making communications more difficult even before Russia became involved in 1940. Although his family cabled me that manuscripts were on their way, only fragments appeared and it wasn't until considerably after the war was over that I received a bulk of the material in this volume. Last autumn Robert M. MacGregor, who had acquired the book publishing department of Theatre Arts which he formerly managed, planned to publish *Building a Character* as a part of the commemoration of the fiftieth Anniversary of the founding of the Moscow Art Theatre and the tenth of Stanislavski's death, but the news that more material and later versions were on their way caused him to delay publication. The postponement also allowed further editing which consisted mainly of choosing among the various versions of given chapters which had come to hand.

In this continuation of *An Actor Prepares*, the scene is again the same dramatic school with its own auditorium and stage, a part of a permanently established theatre. Here are the same students, who represent a characteristic group of young actors—that argumentative young fellow Grisha; Sonya, who is both pretty and vain about it; her admirer, the clowning Vanya; Maria, with her woman's intuition; the introspective pair, Nicholas and Dasha; the well-co-ordinated, acrobatic Vasya; and above all Kostya, the ex-stenographer who because he knows shorthand can make a detailed record of the lessons in a sort of actor's diary. Ever searching, ever throwing himself ardently into any project that shows promise of further development, he is possibly a picture of Stanislavski himself many years before. The teacher is of course Stanislavski, the mature actor, thinly disguised as Tortsov, the director of the school and the theatre. He is assisted by Rakhmanov, who is full of inventiveness in driving home the points made by Tortsov, in divising visual aids, in conducting drill.

The emphasis in this book, as in Stanislavski's *My Life in Art* (now also published by Mr. MacGregor) and *An Actor Prepares*, is on acting as an art and art as the highest expression of human nature. His continual return to the study of human nature is the Antean touch which distinguishes what has come to be known as the Stanislavski "system". It is the basis of all his theories and the reason they were always being modified slightly; with each return to the study of human beings something new was learned. As he says of his method in this book: "It is not a hand-me-down suit that you can put on and walk off in; or a cook book where all you need to find is the page and there is your recipe. No, it is a whole way of life."

Stanislavski makes no claim to have more than set down the principles all great actors have used consciously or unconsciously. He never intended that his statements be taken as rigid rules or his exercises be considered literally applicable to all situations or usable by all persons. In questions of diction and speech particularly, he wanted it understood that the primary purpose of the exercises was to challenge the imagination of the student of acting, to arouse in him a realization of his own needs, of the potentialities of the technical tools of his art.

The overall objective, however, is always the same. It is to help an actor to develop all his capacities—intellectual, physical, spiritual, emotional—so that he will be enabled to fill out his roles to the proportions of whole human beings, characters who will have the power to move the public to laughter, to tears, to unforgettable emotions.

ELIZABETH REYNOLDS HAPGOOD

I

TOWARD A PHYSICAL CHARACTERIZATION

AT THE beginning of our lesson I told Tortsov, the Director of our school and theatre, that I could comprehend with my mind the process of planting and training within myself the elements necessary to create character, but that it was still unclear to me how to achieve the building of that character in physical terms. Because, if you do not use your body, your voice, a manner of speaking, walking, moving, if you do not find a form of characterization which corresponds to the image, you probably cannot convey to others its inner, living spirit.

"Yes," agreed Tortsov, "without an external form neither your inner characterization nor the spirit of your image will reach the public. The external characterization explains and illustrates and thereby conveys to your spectators the inner pattern of your part."

"That's it!" Paul and I exclaimed.

"But how do we achieve that external, physical characterization?" I asked.

"Most frequently, especially among talented actors, the physical materialization of a character to be created emerges of its own accord once the right inner values have been established," explained Tortsov. "In *My Life in Art* there are many examples of this. One is the case of the part of Dr. Stockman in *An Enemy of the People* by Ibsen. As soon as the right spiritual form was fixed, as the right inner characterization was woven out of all the elements germane to the image, there appeared, no one knows from where,

Stockman's nervous intensity, his jerky gait, his neck thrust forward and two jutting fingers, all earmarks of a man of action."

"But if we are not lucky enough to have such a spontaneous accident? What do you do then?" I asked Tortsov.

"What do you do? Do you remember in Ostrovski's play, *The Forest*, how Peter explains to Aksyusha the way to act so that the two will not be recognized on their flight? He says to her, 'You drop one lid—and it makes a squint-eyed person!'"

"Externally it is not difficult to disguise yourself. I once had something of the sort happen to me; I had an acquaintance I knew very well. He talked with a deep bass voice, wore his hair long, had a heavy beard and bushy moustache. Suddenly he had his hair cut and shaved off his whiskers. From underneath there emerged rather small features, a receding chin and ears that stuck out. I met him in this new guise at a family dinner, at the house of some friends. We sat across the table from one another and carried on a conversation. Whom does he remind me of? I kept saying to myself, never suspecting that he was reminding me of himself. In order to disguise his bass voice my friend used only high tones in speaking. This went on for half the meal and I talked with him as though he were a stranger.

"And here is another case. A very beautiful woman I knew was stung in the mouth by a bee. Her lip was swollen and her whole mouth was distorted. This not only changed her appearance so as to make her unrecognizable, it also altered her pronunciation. I met her accidentally and talked to her for several minutes before I realized that she was one of my close friends."

As Tortsov was describing these personal experiences he squinted one eye almost imperceptibly, as though he were bothered with an incipient sty. Meantime he opened his other eye wide and raised the brow above it. All this was done so that it could be scarcely noticed even by those standing close to him. Yet even this slight change produced a strange effect. He was of course still Tortsov but he was different and you no longer had confidence in him. You sensed knavery, slyness, grossness, all qualities little related to his real self. It was only when he stopped acting with his eyes that he became once more our nice old Tortsov. But let him squint one eye—and there again was that mean little slyness, changing his whole personality.

"Are you aware," he explained to us, "that inwardly I remain the same and speak in my own person regardless of whether my eye is squinted or open, whether my eyebrow is raised or lowered? If I were to acquire a twitch and that were causing my eye to squint I should also have remained unchanged in personality and continued normal and natural. Why should I change inwardly because of a slight squint in my eye? I am the same whether my eye is open or shut, whether my eyebrow is raised or lowered.

"Or, let us suppose, I am stung by a bee as was my beautiful friend and my mouth is distorted."

Here Tortsov, with extraordinary realism, pulled his mouth to the right side so that his speech was completely altered.

"Does this external distortion not only of my face but of my speech," he went on in his radically changed method of pronunciation, "impinge on my personality and natural reactions? Must I cease to be myself? Neither the sting of the bee nor the artificial distortion of my mouth should influence my inner life as a human being. And what about lameness (Here Tortsov limped) or paralysis of the arms (Instantly he lost all control over them) or a humped shoulder (His spine reacted correspondingly) or an exaggerated way of turning your feet in or out (Tortsov walked first one way and then the other)? Or an incorrect position of the hands and arms holding them too far forward or too far back (He illustrated this)? Can all these external trifles have any bearing on my feelings, my relations to others or the physical aspect of my part?"

It was amazing with what ease, simplicity and naturalness

Tortsov instantly demonstrated all the physical shortcomings he was describing—a limp, paralysis, a hump, various postures of legs and arms.

"And what remarkable external tricks, which completely transform the person playing a part, can be accomplished with the voice, with speech and pronunciation, especially of consonants! To be sure your voice has to be well placed and trained if you are to change it, for otherwise you cannot, for any length of time, speak either with your highest or your lowest tones. As for altering your pronunciation, especially that of consonants, this is done very simply: pull your tongue back, shorten it (Tortsov did it as he was speaking) and a special manner of speech, rather reminiscent of the English way of handling consonants, will result. Or lengthen your tongue, pushing it a little in advance of your teeth (Again he did what he was describing) and you will have an inane lisp, which with proper elaboration would be suitable for a role like that of the Idiot.

"Or else, try putting your mouth into unusual positions and you will get still other ways of talking. For example, take an Englishman who has a short upper lip and very long, rodent-like front teeth. Give yourself a short upper lip and show your teeth more."

"But how can you do that?" I said, trying it out on myself without success.

"How do I do it? Very simply," answered Tortsov, pulling a handkerchief out of his pocket and rubbing his upper teeth and the inside of his upper lip until they were quite dry. Then under cover of his handkerchief he tucked in his upper lip which remained stuck to his dry gums, so that when he took his hand from his face we were amazed at the shortness of his upper lip and sharpness of his teeth.

This external artifice hid from us his ordinary, familiar personality; in front of us there stood the Englishman he had just mentioned. We were under the impression that everything about Tortsov was changed; his pronunciation, his voice were different, as well as his carriage, his walk, his hands and legs. Nor was that all. His whole psychology seemed transformed. And yet Tortsov had made nó inner adjustment. In another second he had abandoned the trick with his upper lip and continued to speak in his own person, until he again put the handkerchief in his mouth, dried his lip and gums and, when he dropped his hand with the handkerchief, was at once changed again into his Englishman.

This happened intuitively. It was only when we worked it out and confirmed it that Tortsov admitted the phenomenon. It was not he who explained it to us but we who told him, how all the characteristics which intuitively came to the surface were appropriate to and filled out the portrait of the gentleman with a short upper lip and long teeth—and all the result of a simple external artifice.

After digging down into his own thoughts and taking account of what went on inside himself Tortsov remarked that even in his own psychology in spite of himself there had been an imperceptible impulse which he found difficult immediately to analyse.

It was, however, an undoubted fact that his inner faculties responded to the external image he had created, and adjusted to it, since the words he pronounced were not his words, although the thoughts he expressed were his very own.

In this lesson then Tortsov vividly demonstrated that external characterization can be achieved intuitively and also by means of purely technical, mechanical, simple external tricks.

But how to find the right trick? Here was a fresh problem to intrigue and disturb me. Is this something to be learned, to be imagined, to be taken from life, or found accidentally, in books, by studying anatomy?

"The answer is—in all those ways," explained Tortsov. "Each person evolves an external characterization out of himself, from others, takes it from real or imaginary life, according to his intuition, his observation of himself and others. He draws it from his own experience of life or that of his friends, from pictures, engravings, drawings, books, stories, novels, or from some simple incident—it makes no difference. The only proviso is that while he is making this external research he must not lose his inner self. Now I'll tell you what we shall do. For our next lesson we'll have a masquerade."

This proposal produced general astonishment.

"Each student will prepare an external characterization and mask himself in it."

"A masquerade? An external characterization of what kind?"

"No matter what kind. Choose anything you like—a merchant, a Persian, a soldier, a Spaniard, an aristocrat, a mosquito, a frog—whatever and whoever appeals to you. The costumes and the make-up facilities of the theatre will be at your disposal. Go and choose clothes, wigs, make-up."

His announcement at first caused consternation, then discussion and curiosity, and finally general interest and excitement. Each one of us began to think of something, to imagine something, make notes, secret drawings, preparing his choice of a portrait, costume and make-up.

Only Grisha remained, as usual, indifferent and cool to the whole idea.

2

DRESSING A CHARACTER

TO-DAY our whole class went to the great costume store-rooms of the theatre, one of which is up above the foyer and the other in the basement under the auditorium.

In less than fifteen minutes Grisha had chosen what he wanted and left. Some of the others, too, did not take long. Only Sonya and I could not arrive at a definite choice.

Being a flirtatious young woman, she found her eyes distracted and her head in a whirl from seeing so many lovely gowns. As for me, I still was uncertain about what I wanted to portray and was trusting to a lucky inspiration.

In examining carefully everything that was shown me I hoped to happen on a costume which would suggest an appealing image to me.

My attention was drawn to a simple old morning coat. It was made of some remarkable material I had never seen before—a kind of sand-coloured, greenish, greyish stuff, which seemed faded and covered with spots and dust mixed with ashes. I had the feeling that a man dressed in that coat would look like a ghost. An almost imperceptible squeamishness but at the same time a slightly terrifying sense of fatefulness stirred in me as I gazed at that old morning coat.

If one matched it with a hat, gloves, dusty foot-gear, and prepared a make-up and wig in the same colour and tones as the material—all greyish, yellowish, greenish, faded and shadowy, one would get a sinister, yet somehow familiar effect. Exactly what that effect was I could not yet determine.

The wardrobe attendants laid aside the coat I had chosen and promised to look for accessories to match—shoes, gloves, a high hat, as well as a wig and beard. But I was not satisfied and went on hunting up to the very last minute when the amiable mistress of the wardrobe finally told me that she had to get ready for the evening performance.

There was nothing for me to do but leave without having arrived at a definite decision and with only the spotted morning coat held in reserve for me.

Excited, disturbed, I left the costume rooms carrying away with me the riddle: what was the personality I should put on when I dressed myself in that decayed old morning coat?

From that moment on and right up to the time of the masquerade, which was set for three days later, something was going on inside of me: I was not I, in the sense of my usual consciousness of myself. Or, to be more precise, I was not alone but with someone whom I sought in myself and could not find.

I existed, I went on with my usual life, yet something inhibited me from giving myself up to it fully; something was disturbing my usual existence. I seemed divided in two. Although I looked at whatever caught my attention I did not see it to its fullest extent, but only in vague terms, without plumbing its depths. I did some thinking but without thinking things through, I listened but with only half an ear, I smelled things but only partially. Half of my energy and human capability had somehow vanished and that loss sapped my strength and power and attention. I did not finish anything I undertook. I felt that it was necessary for me to accomplish something of the utmost importance. But then a cloud settled on my consciousness, I no longer understood the next step, I was distracted and divided. It was a fatiguing and tormenting state in which to be! It never left me for three whole days and in the course of that time the question of whom I was to play at the masquerade remained unanswered.

Finally in the night I suddenly woke up and everything was clear. That second life which I had been leading parallel to my usual one was a secret, subconscious life. In it there was going on the work of searching for that mildewed man whose clothes I had accidentally found.

However, the clarification did not last long. It melted away again and I tossed around in my bed sleepless and irresolute. It was as though I had forgotten something, could neither recall nor find it. It was a painful state and yet if a magician had offered to blot it out I am not at all sure that I should have let him.

And here is another strange thing that I noted in myself: I seemed convinced that I should not find the image of the person I sought. Nevertheless the search went on. It was not in vain that during those days I never passed by a photographer's shop without examining the portraits in the window and attempting to understand who the originals were. You may ask: Why did I not walk into the shop and examine the stacks of photographs lying around there? At a second-hand dealer's one might find even greater piles of grimy, dusty old photos. Why did I not make use of that material? Why did I not go through it all? But I indolently looked over only the smallest packet of them and nonchalantly ignored the rest for fear of soiling my hands.

What was the matter? How can one explain this inertia or this sense of a split personality? I think that it came from an unconscious but firm conviction inside me that the dusty gentleman with the mildewed clothes would sooner or later come to life and rescue me. "It's no use looking, it's better not to find the mildewed man"—was probably the unconscious prompting of an inner voice.

And then there were strange moments which repeated themselves two or three times: I would be walking along the street and everything would suddenly be clear to me, I would stop short in order to try to grasp to the fullest extent what had happened to me . . . one second passed, then another and I seemed able to fathom some depths . . .

then seconds passed and what had risen to the surface in me plunged out of sight again and I found myself once more filled with perplexity.

Another time I caught myself walking in an uncertain, unrhythmic gait, quite foreign to me, and of which I could not immediately rid myself.

And at night, when I was sleepless, I began to rub my palms together in a peculiar way. "Who rubs his hands like that?" I asked myself but could not recall. I only know that whoever does it has little, narrow, cold, perspiring hands but red, red palms. It is most unpleasant to shake a hand of this kind, all mushy and boneless. . . . Who is he? Who is he?

I was still in this state of inner division, uncertainty and ceaseless search for something I could not find, when I went into the general dressing-room where we would all have to put on our costumes and make-up together instead of by ourselves. The buzz and racket of the conversation made it difficult to concentrate. And yet I felt that this moment of my first investiture in that mildewed morning coat, as well as the putting on of the yellowish grey wig, beard, and the rest, was one of extreme importance to me. Only those material things could prompt me to find what I had subconsciously been searching for. On this moment I had pinned my last hope.

But everything around me was disturbing. Grisha, who sat next to me, was already made up as Mephistopheles. He had already dressed himself in a gorgeous black Spanish costume and was causing groans of envy on the part of all who saw him. Others were doubled up with laughter as they looked at Vanya, who, in order to turn himself into an old man, had covered his child-like face with so many lines and dots that it looked like a map. Paul riled me inwardly because he had been content to put on the banal costume and general appearance of a dandy.

To be sure the result was surprising because no one had hitherto suspected that inside his customarily baggy clothes he hid a well-shaped figure with fine straight legs. Leo amused us by his new attempt to make an aristocrat out of himself. Of course he was not able to do it this time either but one could not fail to give him credit for his perseverance. His make-up, with a carefully trimmed beard, his shoes with high heels, increasing his stature, made him appear slimmer and gave him an impressive air. His careful gait, resulting no doubt from the high heels, lent a grace not usual to him in ordinary life. Vasya also made us laugh and won our approval by his unexpected boldness. He, the agile acrobat, the ballet dancer, the operatic orator, had conceived the idea of concealing his personality under the long skirted coat of a Moscow merchant, with broad lapels, flowered waistcoat, rotund belly, his beard and hair cut "à la russe".

Our dressing-room resounded with exclamations, just as though the occasion were some ordinary amateur performance.

"Why, I'd never know you!"—"Don't tell me that's you?"—"Amazing!"—"Good work, I didn't think you had it in you!"—and so on indefinitely.

These exclamations drove me wild, and the remarks, tinged with doubt and dissatisfaction which fell to my share, quite disheartened me.

"Something is wrong . . . I don't know just what it is . . . who is he?" "I don't understand, who are you supposed to be?"

How awful it was for me to listen to these remarks and questions when I had nothing to reply!

Who was I trying to represent? How did I know? If I had been able to guess I should have been the first to tell who I was.

And I heartily wished the make-up man in the nether regions. Until he had come along and transformed my face into that of a routine pallid theatrical blond I had felt that I was on the track of discovering my secret identity. A light shiver went through me as I slowly dressed myself in the old suit, fitted the wig and pasted on the beard and moustache. Had I been alone in the room, away from all the distracting surroundings, I should surely have understood who the mysterious stranger inside me was. But the hum and chatter prevented my withdrawing into myself and kept me from penetrating that inscrutable thing going on inside me.

Finally they all went off to the school stage to be inspected by Tortsov. I sat alone in the dressing-room, completely prostrated, helplessly gazing in the mirror at my featureless theatrical face. Inwardly I was already convinced of my failure. I decided not to present myself to the Director but to take off my costume and remove my make-up with the aid of some horrid looking greenish cream which stood before me. I had already put one finger in it and begun to rub it on my face. And . . . I went on rubbing. All the other colours blurred, like water-colour which has fallen into some liquid. My face turned greenish-greyish-yellowish, like some counterpart to my costume. It was difficult to distinguish where my nose was, or my eyes, or my lips. I smeared some of the same cream on my beard and moustache and then finally all over my wig. Some of the hair clotted into lumps . . . and then, almost as though I were in some delirium, I trembled, my heart pounded, I did away with my eyebrows, powdered myself at random, smeared the back of my hands with a greenish colour and the palms with light pink. I straightened my coat, and gave a tug to my cravat. I did this all with a quick, sure touch, for this time I knew who I was representing and what kind of a fellow he was!

With my high hat on at a slightly rakish angle I was suddenly aware of the style of my full-cut and once stylish trousers, which were now so worn and threadbare. I made my legs fit the crease which had formed in them by turning my toes sharply in. This gave me ridiculous legs. Have you ever noticed how ridiculous the legs of some people are? I have always had a sense of aversion towards such people.

As a result of this unusual posture of my legs, I seemed shorter and my gait was quite changed. For some reason my whole body was slightly inclined to the right side. All I needed was a cane. One was lying near-by so I picked it up although it did not exactly fit the picture of what I had in mind. Now all I lacked was a quill pen to stick behind my ear or hold in my teeth. I sent a call boy for one and while waiting for his return paced up and down the room, feeling how all the parts of my body, features, facial lines, fell into their proper places and established themselves. After walking around the room two or three times, with an uncertain, uneven gait I glanced in the mirror and did not recognize myself. Since I had looked into it the last time a fresh transformation had taken place in me.

"It is he, it is he!" I exclaimed, unable to repress the joy that was suffocating me. If only that quill would come, then I could go up to the stage.

I heard footsteps in the corridor. Evidently it was the call boy bringing me the quill. I rushed to meet him and at the door ran straight into Rakhmanov.

"What a fright you gave me!" burst from him. "My dear fellow, who on earth is this? What a get-up! Is it Dostoyevski? The Eternal Husband? Can it be you—Kostya? What are you supposed to be?"

"A critic!" I answered in a hoarse voice, and with sharp diction.

"What critic, my boy?" Rakhmanov continued his query, somewhat taken aback by my bold and penetrating glance.

I felt like a leech clinging to him.

"What critic?" I retorted with obvious intent to insult him. "The fault-finding critic who lives inside of Kostya Nazvanov. I live in him in order to interfere with his work. That is my great joy. That is the purpose of my existence."

I was myself amazed at the brazen, unpleasant tone and the fixed, cynical, rude stare which accompanied it, and with which I addressed Rakhmanov. My tone of voice and self-confidence upset him. He did not know how to find a new angle of approach and therefore was at a loss to know what to say to me. He was quite disconcerted.

"Let's go," he finally said rather uncertainly. "The others have long since begun."

"Let's go, then, since they have long since begun," I mimicked his words and did not budge but continued to stare brazenly at my disconcerted instructor.

An awkward pause ensued. Neither of us moved. It was obvious that Rakhmanov wanted to get this incident over with as quickly as possible but did not know how to go about it. Fortunately for him at this moment the call boy came running in with the goose quill. I snatched it from his hand and stuck it between my lips. This narrowed my mouth into a straight, angry line. The sharpened point on one side of my lips and the broad flare of feathers on the other underscored the corrosive expression of my face.

"Let's go," repeated Rakhmanov in a low, almost shy voice.

"Let's go!" My mimicking tone was caustic and brazen.

We walked onto the stage but meantime Rakhmanov tried to avoid meeting my look. To begin with I kept out of sight behind the large grey tile stove, a part of the set that happened to be on the stage, only occasionally allowing my top hat to come into view, or my profile.

During this time Tortsov was trying out Leo and Paul—the aristocrat and the dandy—who had just been "introduced" to each other and were talking nonsense because there was little else, given the intellectual calibre of the characters they represented, that they could talk.

"What's that? Who's that?" I suddenly heard Tortsov exclaim. "I seem to have the impression someone is sitting around back of the stove? Who the devil is it . . . I've already seen all of you, who is this? . . . Kostya? No, it isn't."

"Who are you?" Tortsov addressed me directly and was obviously much intrigued.

"I am the Critic," I introduced myself and came forward,

As I did this, quite unexpectedly my twisted leg came out in advance of me and this threw my body more to the right. I removed my top hat with careful exaggeration and executed a polite bow. After which I again retired to my seat partly out of sight behind the stove which my clothing matched in faded colouring.

"The Critic?" said Tortsov, somewhat bewildered.

"Yes, and a mean one," I explained in a rasping voice. "See this quill? It's all chewed . . . from my being in a rage. . . . I bite it like this, in the middle, it cracks and quivers."

Here to my complete surprise I let out a shrill squeak instead of a guffaw. I was quite taken aback myself, it was so unexpected. Evidently too it had quite an effect on Tortsov.

"What the—" he began to exclaim, then added, "You come over here, closer to the footlights."

I moved over in a sinister, ambling gait.

"What critic are you?" asked Tortsov, probing me with his eyes as if he did not recognize me. "Critic of what?"

"Of the person I live with," I rasped.

"Who is that?" pursued Tortsov.

"Kostya," I said.

"Have you gotten under his skin?" Tortsov knew just the right cues to give me.

"Indeed, yes!"

"Who let you do it?"

"He did."

At that my squeaking laugh again began to choke me. I had to get myself under control before I could continue:

"He did. Actors like the people who praise them. But a Critic. . . ."

A fresh outburst of shrill sniggering interrupted me. I dropped to one knee so that I could look straight at Tortsov.

"Whom can you criticize? You're nothing but an ignoramus," objected Tortsov.

"Ignoramuses are the ones who do criticize most," I retorted.

"You don't understand anything and you don't know how to do anything," Tortsov continued to provoke me.

"It's the very person who does not know anything himself who teaches," said I as I mincingly sat down on the floor of the stage by the footlights beyond which Tortsov was standing.

"It's not true that you are a critic—you're just a fault-finder! A leech, a louse! Your bite is not dangerous, but it makes life unbearable."

"I'll wear you down . . . by degrees . . . unrelentingly . . . ," I rasped.

"You vermin!" exploded Tortsov with frank annoyance.

"Dear me, what a way to talk!" I leaned low over the footlights, angling for Tortsov's attention. "What lack of self-control!"

"You filthy vermin!" Tortsov was almost bellowing now.

"Good, good, very good!" I gleefully pressed my insinuations now relentlessly. "You can't brush off a leech. Where there's a leech there's a lake . . . and in lakes there are more leeches. . . . You can't get rid of them . . . nor of me. . . ."

After a moment's hesitation Tortsov suddenly reached across the footlights and gave me an affectionate hug.

"Good work, young man!"

Whereupon, realizing that I had smeared him with the grease paint dripping from my face, I added:

"Oh, mind what you're doing! Now you certainly can't brush me off!"

The others rushed to repair the damage but I was in such a state of ecstasy over having thus been given a token of the Director's approval that I jumped up, cut a few capers and then, to the clamour of general applause, ran off the stage in my normal gait.

As I turned I saw Tortsov, handkerchief in hand, stop cleaning off the grease paint long enough to follow me at a distance with admiration.

I was truly happy. But my state was not that of any

ordinary satisfaction. It was a joy which stemmed directly from creative, artistic achievement.

As I walked home I caught myself repeating the gestures and gait of the character whose image I had created.

But that was not all. During dinner with my landlady and the other boarders I was captious, scoffing and irritable —unlike myself but very like my carping Critic. Even my landlady noticed this.

"What's the matter with you to-day?" she remarked. "Aren't you being rather overbearing . . .?"

This delighted me.

I was happy because I had realized how to live another person's life, what it meant to immerse myself in a characterization.

This is a most important asset for an actor.

As I was taking my bath I recalled the fact that while I was playing the part of the Critic I still did not lose the sense of being myself. The reason, I concluded, was that while I was acting I felt exceptionally pleased as I followed my own transformation. Actually I was my own observer at the same time that another part of me was being a fault-finding, critical creature.

Yet can I really say that that creature is not a part of me? I derived him from my own nature. I divided myself, as it were, into two personalities. One continued as an actor, the other was an observer.

Strangely enough this duality not only did not impede, it actually promoted my creative work. It encouraged and lent impetus to it.

3

CHARACTERS AND TYPES

OUR work to-day was devoted to a critical analysis of our "masquerade" performance.

Tortsov turned to Sonya and said:

"There are actors and especially actresses who do not feel the need of preparing characterizations or transforming themselves into other characters because they adapt all roles to their own personal appeal. They build all their success exclusively on that quality. Without it they are as helpless as Samson shorn of his locks.

"There is a great difference between searching for and choosing in oneself emotions related to a part and altering the part to suit one's more facile resources.

"Anything that might screen their own human, native individualities from their audience seems to alarm such actors.

"If their good looks affect their public they parade them. If their charm lies in their eyes, face, voice, mannerisms, they beam it to the audience the way you, Sonya, did.

"Why should we change into another character when we shall be less attractive in it than in real life? You see, you really love yourself in the part more than you love the part in yourself. That is a mistake. You have capabilities. You can show not only yourself but a role created by you.

"There are many actors who believe in and rely on their charm. They show that to their audience. Take Dasha and Nicholas. They believe that their attraction lies in the depth of their feelings and the nervous intensity with which they experience them. They do each part on that basis, larding it with their own strongest, native attributes.

"Whereas you, Sonya, are in love with your own external attributes, the other two are not indifferent to their inner qualities.

"Why bother with costumes and make-up—they are only in your way!

"This too is a mistake from which you must free yourselves. Learn to love your role in yourself. You have the creative capacities to build it.

"Now there are actors of still another type. Do not look around. You have not had the time to develop into this kind. These actors hold the public through their original ways, their finely wrought special variety of acting clichés. They appear on the stage for the sole purpose of exhibiting them to their spectators. Why should they bother to transform themselves into other characters since this would not give them the opportunity to show off their forte?

"A third category of false actors are the ones who are strong in technique and clichés but who did not work these out for themselves, they merely have acquired them from other actors of other times and countries. These characterizations are based on a highly conventional ritual. They know how every role in a world-embracing repertory should be played. For such actors all roles have been permanently cut in an accepted stencil. Were it not for this they could never play nearly three hundred and sixty-five roles a year, each one after a single rehearsal, as is done in some cities in the provinces.

"I trust that those of you who feel inclined to follow this dangerous path of least resistance will be warned in time.

"Take your case, Grisha. Do not think that by a careful choice of make-up and costume for our last lesson you created an image of Mephistopheles, that you transformed yourself into him or even hid inside him. No, that was your mistake. You remained the same good-looking fellow that you are. You merely took on a new exterior and a fresh set of ready-made mannerisms, this time culled from the list of Gothic or Medieval character clichés, as we call them in our jargon.

"In *The Taming of the Shrew* we saw you in the very same outfit, except that it was adapted to comic rather than tragic purposes.

"We know, too, your modern-dress routine for contemporary comedies, for dramas in verse or prose. But no matter what the make-up on your face or the costume on your body, no matter what mannerisms or habits you put on you cannot get away from 'Grisha Govorkov, the Actor' while you are on the stage. On the contrary, all the methods you use only bring you back to him more closely.

"Yet—and this is not altogether true—your stereotyped ways do not blind you to 'Grisha Govorkov, the Actor' but to all actors of all times of the same type.

"You may think that your gestures, your way of walking, and talking are your own. But they're not, they are universal, generalized mannerisms cast in iron-clad permanent form by actors who have exchanged art for business. Now if it would ever occur to you to show us on the stage something we have never seen, if you would show us yourself as you are in real life—not the 'actor' Grisha Govorkov but the man—that would be splendid because the human being that you are is far more interesting and talented than the actor. Let us see him because the actor Govorkov is someone we have seen all our lives in all theatres.

"It is my conviction that Grisha the man will be the father of a whole generation of character parts. But the actor Grisha will never bring forth anything because the gamut of rubber-stamp business on the stage is astonishingly limited and worn down to the last layer."

After Grisha, Tortsov took up Vanya's performance. It is obvious that the Director is growing increasingly severe with him. No doubt he does this in order to break him of his slovenly habits, and this is both healthy and good for him.

"What you offered us," said Tortsov, "was not an image

but a misunderstanding. It was neither a man nor a monkey but a chimney sweep. He had no face, only a dirty rag to wipe brushes on.

"And what of your manners, movements, actions? What were they, a kind of St. Vitus' dance? You wished to conceal yourself behind the external characterization of an old man but you did not succeed. On the contrary, you revealed more obviously and vividly than ever the actor Vanya Vyuntsov because all your antics were typical, not of the old man you were supposed to portray but only of yourself.

"Your method of overacting only brought you yourself more powerfully into evidence; it belonged only to you and at no point did it reflect the old man you wished to portray.

"Such a characterization is not a true mutation! It only betrays you and offers an opportunity for contortions.

"You do not like the idea of true characterization, of putting yourself into your character's skin. You do not even know what it is or feel the need of it, and one can scarcely discuss seriously what you offered us in its stead. It was something that never under any circumstances should be seen on any stage.

"It is to be hoped that this failure on your part will bring you to your senses and oblige you at last to reconsider your frivolous attitude towards what I tell you and towards your work here in the school. Otherwise you will fare badly!"

Unfortunately, our work was interrupted at this point because Tortsov was called away unexpectedly so we continued with some of Rakhmanov's drill.

2

To-day Tortsov continued his criticism of our "masquerade".

"I have already spoken to you of the actors who avoid and detest a characterization of a part which constitutes a complete change from their own personality.

"Now I shall speak of other types of actors who, in contrast, and for various reasons make an effort on the whole in the direction of characterization. They do this because they are not exceptionally endowed with good looks, with the power to enthrall an audience either by their outer or inner gifts. Indeed, as individuals their personalities are not theatric and this forces them to hide inside of characterizations and to try to find in them the appeal they lack in themselves.

"To accomplish this they need a highly refined technique and also a great sense of artistry. Unfortunately this excellent but extremely precious gift is rarely to be met with, yet without it an actor is easily misled into the false paths of clichés and overacting.

"To illustrate more clearly which are the true and which the false paths to the creation of a character I shall give you a brief outline of the variety of the facets of an actor with which we are already familiar. In so doing however I shall refer you to what you yourselves presented to me in the way of costumes and make-up rather than give you further illustrations.

"It is possible to portray on the stage a character in general terms—a merchant, a soldier, an aristocrat, a peasant, etc. for the purpose of superficial observation of a series of categories into which people were formerly divided, it is not difficult to work out striking mannerisms, and types of carriage. For example, a professional soldier as a general rule holds himself stiffly erect, marches around instead of walking like a normal person, wiggles his shoulders to show off his epaulettes, clicks his heels together to make his spurs ring, speaks in a loud, barking tone out of habit. A peasant spits, blows his nose without a handkerchief, walks awkwardly, speaks in a disjointed manner, wipes his mouth on the tail of his sheepskin coat. An aristocrat always carries a top hat, wears gloves and a monocle, his speech is affected, he likes to play with his watch chain or the ribbon of his monocle. These are all generalized clichés supposed to portray characters. They are taken from life, they actually exist. But they do not contain the essence of a character and they are not individualized.

"It was in this over-simplified manner that Vasya approached his problem. He gave us everything that sometimes passes for a portrait of a certain merchant but it was not the character of the part. Nor was it a simple merchant but a 'merchant' in quotation marks.

"The same must be said of Leo. His aristocrat was a generalization. It was not something prepared by him for ordinary life but specifically for the stage.

"Both of these were traditional, lifeless, hackneyed portrayals, what actors are 'supposed to do' in most theatres. They were not live people but figures in a ritual.

"Other actors, who possess more acute powers of observation are able to choose sub-divisions in the general categories of stock figures. They can make distinctions among military men, between a member of an ordinary and a guard's regiment, between infantry and cavalry, they know soldiers, officers, generals. Among merchants they distinguish small shop-keepers, traders, department-store owners. They know what reveals the identity of an aristocrat and tells whether he belongs in the capital, in the provinces, is of Russian or foreign extraction. They endow the representatives of these various groups with features which are characteristic for them.

"In this field Paul did a good job. Of all the generalized military types shown in the masquerade he alone was able to convey certain elemental and typical features. This made his character not a military man in general but a regular soldier.

"In the third category of character actors we find a still more heightened, detailed sense of observation. We now have a soldier with a name, Ivan Ivanovich Ivanov, and with features not duplicated in any other soldier. Such a person is undoubtedly still a military figure in general, but he is as indubitably a plain soldier and, in addition, he possesses an individual name.

"From this point of view of creating an individual personality only Kostya was successful.

"What he gave us was a bold, artistic creation and therefore, it should be discussed in detail.

"I shall ask Kostya to tell us in detail the history of the evolution of his Critic. It will be interesting for us to know what the creative process was which helped him to live his part."

I did as Tortsov asked and recalled step by step everything I had written down in my diary concerning the maturing inside me of the man in the mildewed coat. After listening to me attentively the Director then asked me to go further.

"Now try to remember what you experienced when you felt yourself firmly established in the image of that man."

"I had a sense of special satisfaction, quite unlike anything else I ever felt," was my enthusiastic rejoinder. "Unless it was comparable in considerable degree to that one moment in our first student performance when I played the Othello scene with Iago. At other times, I felt this only in flashes in the course of various exercises."

"Can you give us a more precise verbal definition of what you mean?"

"First of all I believed fully and sincerely in the reality of what I was doing and feeling; out of this there emerged a sense of confidence in myself and in the rightness of the image I had created, in the sincerity of his actions. This was not the self-confidence of a person absorbed in himself, a self-conscious actor; it was something of a quite different nature, akin to a conviction of its own integrity.

"Just think how I bore myself in relation to you! My sense of respect and admiration for you is extremely keen. In ordinary life I am inhibited from freely expressing myself, I cannot forget that I am speaking to the Director. I am utterly unable to let go, to unbridle my emotions. But as soon as I was in this other man's skin my attitude towards you underwent a radical change. I even had the sensation that it was not I conversing with you but someone entirely different, and that you and I were both observing him. That was why your nearness to me, your look directed straight into the core of my being not only did not embarrass me but, on the contrary, egged me on. I enjoyed looking you full in the face in a brazen way and at the same time felt I had the right to do it without fear. Yet do you believe I could ever have done this in my own person? Never under any circumstances! In that other person's skin I went as far as I liked, and if I dared do that face to face with you I should have no compunction in treating the audience across the footlights in the same way."

"Yes, but what did you feel when faced with the black hole of the proscenium arch?" asked one of the other students.

"I never even noticed it. I was so taken up with something far more interesting which absorbed my whole being."

"Therefore," Tortsov concluded in a summary of what I had said, "Kostya really did live in the image of his disagreeable Critic. So, as you see, one can use one's own emotions, sensations, instincts, even when one is inside another character, for Kostya's feelings while in his part were his own.

"Now the question is: Would he dare show us those same emotions without masking himself in a created image? Perhaps down in the depths of his being lie the seeds from which another repellent personality might grow? Suppose we have him show us that here and now, without make-up or costume. Do you think he will dare do it?"

Tortsov said this last in a challenging tone.

"Why not?" I retorted. "After all I often attempted to play the part without any make-up."

"But you used the appropriate facial expressions, gestures and way of walking?" Tortsov pressed the point.

"Naturally," I replied.

"Well then, that was the equivalent of a make-up. That's not the important part. One can produce the mask even without the make-up. No, what I want you to do is to show us your own traits, no matter what they are, good or bad, but your most intimate and secret ones, and in your own person, not hiding behind any image," Tortsov insisted.

"I'd be ashamed to do that," I confessed.

"But if you hid yourself behind the image of a character, would you still be embarrassed?"

"No, then I should be able to do what you ask."

"There, you see!" Tortsov exclaimed with delight. "This is the same thing that happened at the masquerade. We have seen how a modest youth, who would scarcely even speak to a woman, suddenly becomes insolent and from behind a mask exposes his most intimately secret instincts and features—things he would not dream of mentioning even in a whisper to anyone in ordinary life.

"What makes him so bold? The mask and costume behind which he hides. In his own person he would never dare to speak as he does in the character of this other personality for whose words he does not feel himself responsible.

"Thus a characterization is the mask which hides the actor-individual. Protected by it he can lay bare his soul down to the last intimate detail. This is an important attribute or feature of characterization.

"Have you ever noticed that those actors and especially actresses who are not keen on transposing themselves into other characters, who always play themselves, like to appear on the stage as beautiful, high born, kindhearted, sentimental creatures? And also the converse, that character actors like to play scoundrels, deformed, grotesque individuals because in them they find scope for sharper outlines, more colourful patterns, bolder and more vivid modelling of an image—all of which is theatrically more effective and leaves deeper traces in the memory of the public?

"Characterization, when accompanied by a real transposition, a sort of re-incarnation, is a great thing. And since an actor is called upon to create an image while he is on the stage and not just show himself off to the public, it is something that becomes a necessity for all of us. In other words all actors who are artists, the creators of images, should make use of characterizations which enable them to become 'incarnate' in their parts."

3

When Tortsov arrived on the school stage to-day he entered with his arm around Vanya, whose eyes were red and who seemed obviously upset.

Continuing their conversation the Director said to him: "Go and try it."

A minute later Vanya was hobbling around the room all doubled up as though he had had a stroke.

"No," said Tortsov stopping him, "that's not a human being, that is a cuttlefish, or some kind of a monster. Don't exaggerate."

In another minute Vanya was hobbling around with youthful speed.

"Now that is too boisterous!" said Tortsov, again checking him. "Your mistake lies in the fact that you follow the line of least resistance: you indulge in purely external imitation. But copies are not created works. That is a bad line to follow. It would be better for you to begin by studying the nature of old age. That would make clear to you what you should search for in your own nature.

"Why can a young man instantly jump up, turn around, run, sit down, stand up without any preliminary preparation whereas an old man is deprived of such possibilities?"

"Because he's old, that's all!" said Vanya.

"That is no explanation. There are other purely physical reasons."

"What, for instance?"

"Thanks to the sedimentation of salts and to the hardening of muscles and other reasons which undermine the human constitution as time passes the joints of an old man are not well-oiled. They rasp and squeak like rusty iron. This lessens the breadth of his gestures, it reduces the angles of flexibility of his torso, his head. He is obliged to break up his larger motions into a series of smaller ones and each has to be prepared before he makes it.

"Whereas a young man can make fifty- and sixty-degree turns with his hips with speed and ease, as he gets older these will be cut down to angles of twenty degrees and will not be effected quickly but in several sections and with delay. That is why the tempo and rhythm of motions among the old is so slow, so flaccid.

"All these tempering factors become, for those of you who are playing parts, integrally bound up with the 'given circumstances' the 'magic if' of the plot of a play. Now begin, but be persistent in watching your every movement. Bear in mind exactly what an old person is or is not capable of doing."

Not only Vanya but all the rest of us started right off to act like old people in the 'given circumstances' explained by Tortsov. The place was transformed at once into a home for the aged.

In doing this the important point was to feel: I am operating within the framework of the definite limitations associated with an aged person's physical condition; I am not just play-acting and mimicking.

Nevertheless both Tortsov and Rakhmanov were obliged to catch us up, one after the other, on lack of precision or inaccuracies, whenever we permitted ourselves gestures that were too free, too rapid, or other physically illogical actions.

In the end, by a concerted effort of attention, we did succeed after a fashion.

"Now you are falling into the opposite extreme," said Tortsov by way of correction. "You are keeping constantly to the same slow rhythm and pace as you walk and to an exaggerated caution in your gestures. Old people are not like that. To illustrate what I mean here is an incident out of my own experience.

"I once knew a lady a hundred years old who could run the length of this room. She had to collect herself for some time in advance, stamping her feet, exercising her legs, trying short steps to begin with. At this point she gave the impression of a year-old child, who with great concentration of thought and attention is getting ready to take his first steps.

"Now when the old lady's legs were limbered up and in working order, her movements acquired a kind of momentum which she could not restrain. She would move forward faster and faster until she would practically break into a run. As she neared her objective it was difficult for her to stop. Yet once there, she stood still and was like an engine without steam.

"Before she undertook her next and most difficult task, that of returning, she would rest for a long time. Then again came the long preparations on the one spot, the worried expression on the face, all the precautions. Finally the return trip would be accomplished at the slowest possible tempo. Then the whole manœuvre would start over again."

After this explanation we all began fresh experiments. We ran forward with short steps as far as the wall and then turned around very slowly.

I felt that at first I did not achieve the right action in the given circumstances of old age. All I did was reproduce an external copy of a hundred-year-old woman and her motions as described by Tortsov. In the end, however, I did set myself going and decided even to try sitting down like an old person, presumably because I was tired out.

Here Tortsov checked me and said that I had been guilty of an endless number of errors.

"What sort of errors?" I asked.

"Only young people sit down like that," explained Tortsov. "You decided you wanted to sit down so you promptly did so, without further consideration or preparation.

"Moreover," he continued, "check for yourself the angle at which you bent your knees as you sat down. Was it almost fifty degrees? Yet, as an old man, you could not possibly be able to bend them more than twenty degrees. No, no, that's much too much! Less than that . . . still less . . . much less. There you have it. Now sit down."

I leaned back and fell off the chair like a sack of oats from a cart.

"There, you see, your old man is broken in two or else he has an attack of lumbago!"

I began to try in every way to adjust myself to sitting down without bending my knees. To do this I was forced to bend my hip joints, and have recourse to the use of my hands as auxiliary aids. By putting my weight on them and taking hold of the arms of the chair I could bend my elbows, and let my body down with care into the seat.

"Slower, slower . . . carefully!" Tortsov said as he watched me. "Don't forget that a really old man is half blind. Before he puts his hands on the chair arm he has to notice where he is placing them and what he is leaning on. That's right. Now, go slowly, or you'll get another crick in your back. Don't forget that your joints are all rusty and gnarled. Still more slowly now. . . . There you are!"

"Stop, stop! What are you thinking of! You can't do that all at once," Tortsov objected, because I had no sooner seated myself than I immediately leaned back in the chair.

"One must rest," he explained to me, "give one's circulation time to get around. Little is done rapidly in old age. That's the way. Now lean slowly back. Good! Take one hand, now the other, put them on your knees. Let yourself rest. Now you've done it.

"Yet why are you so cautious now? You have accomplished the most difficult part. Now you can at once grow young again, you can be more active, energetic, lithe; change your pace, your rhythm, move more boldly, bend over, put more vigour into your actions, almost like a young man. But . . . do it all only within the limits of fifteen to twenty degrees of your normal movements. Do not exceed those limits from now on, or if you do, be extremely cautious or else—you'll get cramps.

"If a youthful impersonator of an elderly role will put his mind on how to absorb and handle the component phases of difficult and more extensive action, if he will begin to act conscientiously, honestly, consistently, without over-emphasis, while keeping himself within the confines of the character, of the play, of the 'given circumstances' which surround an old person, then the actor will succeed in putting himself into analogous circumstances, will assimilate the external features, the rhythm and pace of an old person—all of which plays a great and indeed preponderating part in presenting such a portrayal on the stage.

"It is difficult to realize and to discover what the 'given circumstances' of old age are. But once found it is not difficult to retain them by means of technique."

4

MAKING THE BODY
EXPRESSIVE

I

THERE had been rumours that the closed doors in the school corridor led to a room that was being converted into a museum and which would also be a lecture hall. Someone had heard that photographs of the best painting and sculpture from all over the world were being assembled, as well as reproductions and original art objects; another that there would be scene designs and pictures of actors in their greatest roles. The theory was that by being surrounded by these things for the better part of our hours in school we could not help but develop some standard of beauty.

There was also the rumour that our instructors planned a smaller exhibition of false art. Among other things this would include photographs of the most hackneyed and cluttered stage settings, of actors in over-theatrical costumes, with exaggerated make-up, displaying grimaces and artificial gestures—all those things which we hoped to avoid in ourselves. This collection, we heard, was to be housed next door in Rakhmanov's office. Ordinarily it would be hidden by a curtain and only shown us to drive home some point of contrast. Both enterprises were of course evidences of Rakhmanov's pedagogical zeal; and it was because of his excitement and pride that the rumours had leaked out in such detail.

To-day the closed doors of the mysterious room were opened to us. But the "museum" proved far from ready. Plaster statues, large and small, a few paintings, framed photographs and others half mounted in mattings, large, richly bound volumes on art, on costumes and scene design, on the ballet and modern dance, were scattered about on chairs, tables, window sills, even on the floor. In his anxiety to make the exhibition as full and effective as possible, Rakhmanov had not left enough time for its installation!

On one wall I noticed a placard listing all the museums and points of artistic interest in and around Moscow together with the days and hours when they were open. From the pencilled numbers against the list and the names of authorities written in, I guessed that we were to have a systematic tour of these places co-ordinated with lectures on the arts allied to our art, acting.

In a corner was a veritable arsenal of swords, rapiers, daggers, fencing foils, masks and plastrons, boxing gloves, as well as ballet slippers and gymnastic equipment. Our new course in body training, I surmised, was likewise to be considered an art.

2

To-day Tortsov came for the first time to our class in Swedish gymnastics. He watched us and about half-way through the usual hour he interrupted and led us to our new museum-classroom where he talked to us.

"People generally do not know how to make use of the physical apparatus with which nature has endowed us," he began. "They neither know how to develop this apparatus nor keep it in order. Flabby muscles, poor posture, sagging chests, these things we see around us continually. They show insufficient training and an inept use of this physical instrument.

"Maybe a body with bulges in the wrong places, legs so spindly that their owner has to totter, shoulders hunched almost into a deformity do not matter in ordinary life. In fact we become so accustomed to these and other defects that we accept them as normal phenomena.

"But when we step on the stage many lesser physical

shortcomings attract immediate attention. There the actor is scrutinized by thousands of onlookers as through a magnifying lens. Unless it is his intention to show a character with a physical defect, in which case he should be able to display it in just the proper degree, he should move in an easy manner which adds to rather than distracts from the impression he creates. To do this he must have a healthy body in good working order, capable of extraordinary control.

"Already you have come a long way since this class began. The regular daily exercises have started to limber up not only the muscles and joints you use in ordinary life but others you did not know existed. Without exercise all muscles wither away, and by reviving their functions, toning them up, we have come to make new movements, to experience new sensations, to create subtle possibilities for action and expression. The exercises contribute toward making your physical apparatus more mobile, flexible, expressive and even more sensitive.

"The time has come to consider another, an even more important thing to be brought about through your exercises. . . ."

After a brief pause Tortsov asked, "Do you admire the physique of a circus strong man? For my part I know nothing more repellent than a man with shoulders that more rightly belong on a bull, with muscles that form great Gordian knots all over him. And have you seen these strong men, after their own weight-lifting demonstrations, come out in dress suits leading beautiful horses in the parade? In some ways they are as comical looking as the clowns. Can you imagine these bodies squeezed into the form-fitting costumes of medieval Venice or the snug Renaissance doublet and hose generally worn by the men in *Romeo and Juliet?* How absurd they would look!

"It is not my province to judge to what extent this physical culture is required in the realm of sport. My only duty is to warn you that the acquisition of such over-development is ordinarily unacceptable in the theatre. We need strong, powerful bodies, developed in good proportions, well set up, but without any unnatural excess. The purpose of our gymnastics is to correct and not to swell out the body.

"Now you are at the cross-roads. What direction will you take? Proceed along the line of the muscular development of a weight lifter, or follow the requirements of our art? Naturally I must direct you along this latter line.

"We now add sculptural requirements to your gymnastic training. Just as the artist with the chisel seeks the right line, the beautiful proportions in the balance of the parts of the statues he creates out of stone, the teacher of gymnastics must try to achieve the same results with living bodies. There is no such thing as ideal human structure. It has to be made. To that end one must first study the body and understand the proportions of its various parts. When the defects have been found they must be corrected; what nature has left undone must be developed, so that the muscles of the shoulders and chest can be expanded. Others, however, have broad shoulders and a barrel chest. Why let these defects increase with exercise, is it not better to leave them alone and concentrate more attention on the legs if they are disproportionately slight? By increasing the muscular structure there a proper overall form can be established. For such purposes athletic exercises can be of help. The rest can be remedied by a designer, costumier, a good tailor and shoe-maker."

3

Tortsov brought a famous circus clown along to our gym class to-day. In welcoming him he said:

"To-day we are adding tumbling to our activities. Although this may seem strange it helps an actor in his great moments of highest exaltation and for his creative inspiration. Is that astonishing? The reason is that acrobatics aid in developing the quality of decisiveness.

"It would be too disastrous for an acrobat to go off wool gathering just before he performs a *salto mortale* or other neck-risking stunt! In such moments there is no room for indecision; he must, without stopping to reflect, give himself into the hands of chance and his skill. He must jump, come what may.

"This is exactly what an actor must do when he comes up to the culminating point of his part. In such moments as when Hamlet says 'Why, let the stricken deer go weep' or Othello cries 'Oh, blood, blood, blood!' the actor cannot stop to think, to doubt, to weigh considerations, to make ready and test himself. He must act, he must clear the jump at full gallop. Yet the majority of actors have an entirely different attitude about this. They dread the big moments, and long in advance they painstakingly try to prepare for them. This produces nervousness and pressures which prevent their letting themselves go at the high points, when they need to give themselves completely to their parts.

"At times you may get a bruise or a bump on your forehead. Your instructor will see to it that it will not be too big. But a slight injury for the sake of knowledge cannot harm you much. It will teach you to make your try next time without extra thought, without shilly-shallying, with manly decision, using your physical intuition and inspiration.

"When you have developed will-power in your bodily movements and actions it will be easier for you to carry it over into living your role and you will learn how, without thinking, to surrender yourself instantly and utterly into the power of intuition and inspiration. There are difficult places of this sort in every part, so let acrobatics, to the extent that they can do so, help you over them.

"Besides, acrobatics can render you another service. They will help you to become more agile, more physically efficient, on the stage when you get up, bend over, turn, run and when you make a variety of difficult and rapid moves. They will teach you to act in a quick rhythm and tempo impossible for an untrained body. I wish you luck!"

As soon as Tortsov left the room we were asked to try somersaults on the bare floor. I was the first to volunteer, as his words had made the deepest impression on me. Who, if not I, longed to rid himself of the difficulties inherent in the tragic moments of a part!

Without stopping long to think about it I went head over heels with a resounding bang. A large lump on the top of my head was my reward. I got angry so I turned another somersault, another, a fourth. This time the bump was on my forehead.

4

To-day Tortsov sat in on the dancing class which we have been attending since the beginning of the school season. And then he continued his commentary.

He said, among other things, that this class is not a fundamental part of our body work. Its role, like that of the gymnastics class, is contributory, preparing us for other, more important exercises. This fact does not detract, however, from the great importance Tortsov attributes to dancing as an aid to physical development. It not only serves to make the body more erect but it also opens up motions, broadens them, gives them a definiteness and finish, which is very important, because a sawed-off, choppy gesture is not appropriate for the stage.

"I also place value on dancing," Tortsov explained further, "Because it is an excellent corrective for the position of arms, legs, backs.

"Some people because they are hollow chested and have hunched forward shoulders let their arms dangle in front of them and strike their abdomens or thighs as they walk. Others who are chicken breasted have shoulders thrown way back and a protruding abdomen. They let their arms hang down behind them. Neither one posture nor the other is right. Arms should hang by one's side.

"Frequently arms are held with the elbows turned inward,

towards the body. They must be turned the other way with the elbows on the outside. But this must be done with moderation because exaggeration will distort posture and defeat the purpose.

"The position of the legs is no less important. If it is wrong the whole figure suffers. One is awkward, heavy, lop-sided.

"In the case of most women, the legs from the hips to the knees are turned inward. The same thing is true of the soles of their feet; their heels are often turned out and their toes in.

"Ballet exercises at the bar are a splendid corrective for these defects. They turn the legs at the hips towards the outside and set them at the correct angle. This makes them appear slimmer. The proper position of the legs at the hips has its effect on the feet, the heels. Everything falls into line and the toes point out as they ought to when the legs are held as they should be.

"Incidentally, not only exercises at the bar but many other dancing movements help accomplish this. They are based on various positions and steps which require legs to be turned out at the hips and feet properly planted.

"With this in mind I recommend still another means, rather more home-grown in character, for frequent daily practice. It is extremely simple. Turn the toes of your left foot as far out as you possibly can. Then place your right foot in front of it with its toes turned out as far as possible. As you do it the toes of your right foot should touch the heel of your left foot, and the toes of your left foot should come close to the heel of your right foot. In the beginning you will have to hold on to a chair in order to keep your balance, you will have to flex your knees considerably as well as twist your whole body. But you must try to straighten yourself, your legs and your body as well. This straightening up will force your legs to turn outward at the hips. In the beginning too your feet will not get close together but until they do you will not be able to straighten up. With time, and as your legs begin to turn out, you will achieve the position I have indicated. Once you can do it, do it every day, do it often, whenever you can find the time, the patience and the strength for it. The longer you can stand in that position the more firmly and quickly will your legs turn outward at the hips and at the feet.

"Of equal importance for plasticity and expressiveness of the body is the development of the extremities of the arms and legs, the wrists, fingers, ankles.

"In this work ballet and other dance exercises have much to offer. In dancing feet and toes can be very eloquent and expressive sliding over the floor, executing various steps; they are like a sharp pen carrying out an intricate design on a sheet of paper. When one rises on the toes, flight is suggested. The feet and toes modify jerkiness, give a quality of smoothness, contribute to gracefulness, point up the rhythm and accents of a dance. It is not surprising, therefore, that in ballet training great attention is paid to toes and their development. We must take advantage of methods already worked out by the ballet.

"In the matter of wrists and fingers I am not sure that ballet methods are to be strongly recommended. I am not fond of the ballet dancers' use of wrists. It is mannered, conventional, sentimental; there is more prettiness in it than beauty. Many ballerinas dance with lifeless or muscularly tense wrists.

"There is, however, one more thing in the ballet discipline which is useful for the further development of your physical apparatus for the plastic use of your body, for general posture and carriage.

"Our spinal column, which bends in all directions, is like a spiral spring and needs to be firmly set on its base. It must be, as it were, well screwed in place at the lowest vertebra. If a person feels that this so-called screw is strong, the upper part of his torso has a support, a centre of gravity, stability and straightness. But if, on the contrary, he feels the screw to be undone, his spinal column, and hence his

43

whole torso, loses its stability, its straightness, it shapeliness, and along with these its beauty of motion and plastic fluency.

"This make-believe screw, this central point, which holds up the spinal column, plays a significant part in ballet art. Take advantage of this and from your dancing classes learn to acquire ways of developing, reinforcing and placing your vertebrae.

"For this purpose I also have in addition for you an old-fashioned method, one that you can make use of every day at home, when you are doing corrective exercises for your spine.

"In former times French governesses obliged their round-shouldered charges to lie on a hard table or the floor in such a way as to make the backs of their heads and all their spines touch the flat surface. Children had to lie that way for hours every day, while their patient governesses read aloud to them.

"And here is another way of straightening out round-shouldered children. The governesses made them bend both their flexed elbows back and then slipped a cane between them and their backs. As the child tried to resume his normal posture his arms, naturally, pressed the cane against his back. Under the pressure the child was forced to straighten up. In this position children used to walk around for hours under the strict supervision of a governess, and finally their spinal columns were trained to stay erect.

"Whereas gymnastics develops motions that are clear cut to the point of abruptness, marking the rhythm with a strong, almost military accent, dancing tends to produce fluency, breadth, cadence in gesture. Together they unfold a gesture, give it line, form, direction, airiness.

"Gymnastic motions are in straight lines, in dancing the lines are complex and varied.

"Yet ballet and dancing often lead to an over refinement of form, to an exaggerated grace, to affectation. That is bad. When a ballet dancer has occasion, during some pantomime, to indicate with a gesture of the hand some person who is entering or leaving, or some inanimate object, he will not merely stretch his hand out in the necessary direction, he will first of all lead the object clear across to the other side of the stage in order to enhance the breadth and extent of the gesture. In executing these disproportionately extended and enlarged movements ballet dancers of both sexes try to achieve more beauty, more pomp, than is necessary; this makes for posturing, sentimentality, artificiality, unnatural and often ridiculous exaggeration.

"In order to avoid any repetition of this on the legitimate stage you must remember something I have already said many times. In acting no gesture must be made merely for the gesture's sake. Your movements must always have a purpose and be connected with the content of your part. Purposeful and productive action will automatically exclude affectation, posturing and other such dangerous results."

5

Paul Shustov dragged me to see his uncle to-day and meet an old friend of theirs, a famous actor. Paul insisted that I should take advantage of this chance to have a look at him. He was quite right. I made the acquaintance of a remarkable actor who speaks through his eyes, mouth, ears, the tip of his nose, his fingers with scarcely perceptible movements.

In describing the exterior of a person, the form of an object, the outline of a landscape he had an amazingly vivid way of portraying externally what was in his mind. For example, when he was describing the domestic surroundings of a friend of his who is even stouter than the actor himself, you could see him before your eyes transform himself into a swell-front bureau, a bulging wardrobe or an overstuffed chair. In doing this he did not copy the objects themselves but reproduced the sense of straining at the seams.

When he told about how he and his fat friend toddled around amid this furniture, you had an excellent mental picture of two bears in a den.

To paint this scene he did not even have to leave his chair. Sitting there he swayed slightly from side to side, bending over, or raising his huge abdomen, and that was sufficient to give the illusion of squeezing past an object.

In the course of another of his descriptions, about someone who jumped off a streetcar while it was in full motion and fell against a post, we all exclaimed as one man because he made us see the incident so vividly.

Even more striking was the wordless interplay of this actor with Paul's uncle, who told about how, when young, they had both courted the same girl. Uncle Shustov was very amusing in boasting about his own success and even more amusing in describing the other actor's defeat.

The latter never said a word, but at certain places in the story instead of putting in an objection he merely let his eyes travel around on all the others present as much as to say to us:

"Of all the impudence! He is lying and you fools sit there, listen to him and believe every word!"

At one point the fat man closed his eyes in pretended despair and impatience, remained immobile with his head thrown back and then wiggled his ears. It seemed as though he were using them in place of his hands to wave aside the insistent chatter of his friend.

In the course of Uncle Shustov's other boastful remarks his guest wickedly moved the tip of his nose first to the right and then to the left. Next he raised one eyebrow after the other, did the same thing with his forehead, let a little smile play around his full lips. These tiny, all but unnoticeable, movements did more eloquent damage to his friend's attacks on him than words.

Another comic argument was carried on between the friends without any words at all; they argued with each other only with their fingers but it was perfectly obvious that one was accusing the other of some prank in connection with a love affair.

After dinner, over our coffee, Paul's uncle made his guest do his famous wordless scene from Ostrovski's *The Storm*. His descriptive rendering was pictorially vivid as well as psychologically so, if one may use that term for something portrayed only by facial expressions and the eyes.

5

PLASTICITY OF MOTION

AS A parallel to our rhythmic gymnastics we have now begun a class in plastic movement which Madame Sonova is conducting. To-day Tortsov came to the theatre vestibule where we were working and spoke to us.

"I want you to be fully aware of your approach to this new subject," he began.

"It is generally thought that plastic movement should be taught by a dancing teacher of the routine type, and that ballet and modern dancing with their formalized steps and poses convey the plastic movement that we legitimate actors in the theatre need.

"But is this really so?

"I have already pointed out that there are ballerinas and leading male dancers whose poses become artificial, whose flowing gestures become disproportionate and pompous. They use movement and plasticity for the sake of movement and plasticity. They learn their movements without any relation to inner content; and they create form bereft of meaning.

"Has an actor any need for such purely external, empty motions? Will they give smoothness and grace to his ordinary movements?

"You have seen these dancers when they are off the stage and dressed in ordinary clothes. Do they walk the way we want to when we convey a character from real life? Is their highly specialized grace and exquisiteness applicable to our creative purposes?

48

"Among dramatic actors we know some who use this particular kind of plasticity for the sole purpose of impressing their admirers of the opposite sex. Such actors make up combinations of poses out of the beautiful lines of their bodies; their arms make airy patterns of externally conceived movements. These so-called gestures begin in their shoulders, their hips, their spines; they travel down the surface of their arms, their legs and then return to their starting point without having accomplished anything of creative consequence, without having carried any inner stimulus to action, any urge to achieve a purpose. Such movements travel along like the force in a pneumatic tube carrying letters, indifferent to its content.

"We may admit that these movements are fluent, but they are also vacant and unintelligent. They are like the little hands of a ballerina being fluttered for the sake of their prettiness. We have no use for these practices of the ballet, for stage poses, theatrical gestures which move along an external, superficial line. They can never convey the human spirit of Othello or Hamlet.

"Let us rather try to adapt these stage conventions, these poses and gestures to the carrying out of some vital purpose, the projection of some inner experience. Then the gesture ceases to be just a gesture, it is converted into real action with purpose and content.

"What we need are simple, expressive actions with an inner content. Where are we to find them?

"There are other kinds of dancers and actors than the ones we have discussed. They have worked out for themselves a permanently fixed kind of plasticity and they pay no further attention to that side of their physical actions. Their motion has become for them part of their being, their individual quality, second nature. Ballerinas and actors of this type cannot move except with fluidity.

"If they would lend an attentive ear to their own mechanics, they would sense an energy rising from the deepest wells of their beings, from their very hearts. This is not an empty energy, it is charged with emotions, desires, objectives, which send it pulsing along an inner course for the purpose of arousing this or that action.

"Energy, heated by emotion, charged with will, directed by the intellect, moves with confidence and pride, like an ambassador on an important mission. It manifests itself in conscious action, full of feeling, content and purpose, which cannot be carried out in any slipshod, mechanical way, but must be fulfilled in accordance with its spiritual impulses.

"As it flows down the network of your muscular system, arousing your inner motor centres, it stirs you to external activity.

"It moves not only along your arms, your spine, your neck, but also along your legs. It incites the leg muscles and causes you to walk in a certain way, which is an extremely important factor when you are on the stage.

"Do you ask whether the way you walk on the stage is different from the gait you use on the street?

"Yes it is, and for the reason that in life we walk incorrectly whereas on the stage we are obliged to walk correctly, as nature intended and in accordance with all her laws. Therein lies the greatest difficulty.

"People whom nature has not endowed with a good, normal gait, who are incapable of developing it of themselves, when they go on the stage resort to all kinds of stratagems to conceal this shortcoming. They learn how to walk in some special way, with unnatural form and picturesqueness. Yet that kind of theatrical, stagey walk is not to be confused with a true stage walk based on natural laws.

"Let us speak of this true way of walking, of means for developing it, so that once and for all we can banish from the stage the current stilted gait used by many actors. In other words, let us learn how to walk all over again from the beginning, both on the stage and off it."

The words were scarcely out of Tortsov's mouth when Sonya jumped up and swept by him, showing off her gait, which evidently she looks upon as a model of perfection.

"Ye-e-es," drawled Tortsov with significance, as his eyes studied her little feet with care. "Chinese women use tight shoes to transform human feet into hooves such as cows have. And what of the ladies of our day? Do they differ much from the Chinese in their distortion of a most complex and excellent part of our physical apparatus—the human foot, which plays such an important role? What barbarism they indulge in, especially the women, the actresses! A beautiful walk is one of their most entrancing charms. And it is sacrificed on the altar of fashion and silly heels.

"From now on I shall ask our women students to come to class in footgear with low heels or better yet without any heels at all. Our wardrobe mistress will provide all that you need."

After Sonya our acrobatic Vasya demonstrated his light step. It would be more correct to say, not that he walked but that he floated.

"If Sonya's toes do not fulfil their mission, yours overdo their part," said Tortsov. "There is no harm in that. It is difficult to develop a well-formed foot but it is incomparably easier to reduce its action. I have no worries on your score."

To Leo, who lumbered heavily past him, Tortsov remarked:

"If illness or an accident had left you with a stiff knee you would go from doctor to doctor to find one to restore its flexibility. Why is it that you, who now have two all but atrophied knee joints, are so unconcerned about your disability? Yet in walking the flexing of the knee joint is of enormous importance. One really cannot walk on stiff, unbending legs!"

Grisha's trouble lay in the stiffness of his spine which also plays a large part in a person's walk.

To Paul Tortsov suggested oiling of the hip joints which appeared to be rusty. This prevented him from throwing his leg far enough forward; it shortened his stride and threw it out of proportion to his height.

Anna produced an example of a constant failing among

women. From her hips to her knees her legs were turned in. She will have to do extra exercises at the ballet bar to help get them turned outward.

Maria's toes turn in so far that her feet practically tripped over each other. By contrast Nicholas's toes turn out far too much.

Tortsov found the use of my legs arhythmic.

"You walk the way some people talk; they will drawl their words and then for some reason suddenly rattle them out as though they were dry peas. One group of your steps will be deliberate and then suddenly you dash off as though you wore seven-league boots. You drop steps the way defective hearts drop beats."

As a result of this review we became aware of our own and each other's defects in walking and we found we no longer knew how to walk; like little children we would have to acquire this important and difficult faculty all over again. To help us in this task Tortsov explained the structure of the human leg and foot, and the basis of the proper way to walk.

"You do not have to be so much an actor as an engineer or mechanic to comprehend and fully appreciate the action of our motor apparatus," was his remark by way of introduction.

"The human leg," he continued, "from the pelvis to the foot reminds me of the understructure of a Pullman car. Because of its multiplicity of springs which absorb and moderate shocks in all directions, the upper part of the car, where the passengers sit, remains almost motionless, despite the fact that it is moving at a terrific rate of speed and being buffeted all around. This is what should happen in a person's gait when he is either walking or running. At such times the torso with the thorax, shoulders, neck and head should remain unshaken, serene, entirely free in their own movements, like the passenger riding in a first-class train. This is made possible to a large extent by your backbone.

"Its purpose is to act like a spiral spring bending in any

direction at the slightest movement, in order to maintain the equilibrium of the shoulders and head, which should, in so far as possible, remain tranquil and free from all jerkiness.

"Just as in a railway carriage our springs are situated in the lower part of our bodies, our hips, knees, ankles and all the joints of our toes. Their role is to moderate shocks when we walk or run, and also when we sway our bodies forward, backward, sideways, in any pitching or rolling movement.

"They also have another function to perform, that of moving forward the body they carry. This is accomplished so that this body, again like a railway carriage, will move as smoothly as possible on a horizontal line with few vertical ups and downs.

"In describing to you this manner of walking and running, I am reminded of an incident which greatly impressed me. I was watching some soldiers go by. Their heads, shoulders, chests were visible above the fence that separated me from them. They did not appear to be walking at all but rolling along on skates or skis over an absolutely smooth surface. One had the sense of their gliding, there was no abrupt stepping up and down.

"This effect was brought about because all the corresponding springs in these soldiers' hips, knees, ankles, toes were magnificently fulfilling their functions. Thanks to this the upper parts of their bodies positively floated by behind the fence in a horizontal line.

"To give you a clearer picture of the function of each separate part, comparable to the springs in a carriage, I shall take them up one at a time.

"To begin at the top we have the pelvis and the hip joints. They have a double function. In the first place, like the spinal column, they moderate side shocks and the swaying of the torso from side to side when we walk. Secondly, they thrust the whole leg forward each time we take a step. This motion should be broad and free, in keeping with our height, the length of our legs, the size of our step, the desired speed, tempo and character of our gait.

"The better the leg is swung forward from the hip the more freely and lightly it will swing back, the step made will be larger and more rapid. From now on this swing of the leg from the hips, either forwards or backwards, should not depend on our torso, although it often tries to interfere by bending forward or back to add momentum to our walking motion which should be accomplished only by our legs.

"It requires special exercises to develop our steps, and a free, wide swing from the hips.

"The question is, what kind of exercises? Stand up and lean first with your right and then with your left shoulder and side of your torso against a post or the jamb of a door. This support is necessary to the keeping of a fixed vertical position. It prevents your body from bending in any position whatsoever. Having in this way established the vertical position of your torso now put your weight firmly on the leg next to the post or the door. Raise yourself slightly on to your toes and swing your other leg straight out, without bending it at the knee, first forward and then back. Try, as you do this, to swing it both ways at a right angle. In the beginning you should do this only for a brief time and in slow motion, increasing the length of time so that you exercise all the corresponding muscles. Of course you cannot reach the limit here immediately; this must be done gradually and systematically.

"When you have done this exercise with, let us say your right leg, turn and do the same thing in the same way with your left leg.

"And take care in each case that as you throw your leg out your foot does not remain at right angles to it but is pointed in the same direction as your leg.

"In walking, as I have already pointed out, the hips rise and fall. When the right hip is raised, as you thrust your right leg forward, your left hip falls as your left leg swings back. As this happens you feel a rotary motion in your hip joints.

"The next springs below the pelvis are the knees. They

too have a double function: they help move the body forward and they also absorb the shocks and vertical jolts of the body's weight when it passes from one leg to the other. At this point one leg taking over that weight is slightly bent, just to the extent necessary to maintain the equilibrium of shoulders and head. After the hips have played out their part in moving the torso forward and regulating its balance, it is the turn of the knees to straighten up and thereby push the body they are carrying farther forward.

"A third set of springs, a whole cluster of them, which modify and promote the motions of our body are situated in our ankles, feet, all the joints of our toes. This is a highly complex, quick-witted and important mechanism as related to our walking and I ask you to pay particular attention to it.

"The flexing of the leg at the ankle carries the torso still farther along its way. The foot and the toes participate in this action but they have still another function. They absorb the shocks of motion because of their rotary mechanism.

"There are three ways of using this mechanism in our feet and toes, and they produce three types of walking.

"In the first the heel begins the step.

"In the second the whole sole is planted on the ground at once.

"In the third, known as the Grecian or Isadora Duncan walk the toes are put down first, then all of the sole back to the heel. The weight then returns to the toes in a kind of rolling motion.

"I shall for the present take up the first type, which is most current with people who wear heels on their shoes. When you walk this way your heel is the first part of the foot to take your weight and it is then carried forward to your toes. Yet these do not bend back on themselves; they rather clutch the ground like the claws of an animal.

"As the weight of the body begins to press down along the joints of the toes they straighten out and in this way push themselves away from the ground until the movement has reached the very tip of the big toe. The weight of the body now remains there for a moment, as it does when a ballerina dances on her toes, but it does not impede the forward moving momentum. This lowest group of springs, from the ankle to the big toe, plays a big and important part here. To show you the influence of the toes in increasing the size of one's step and the rapidity of one's gait I shall give you an example from my own experience.

"When I am walking home or to the theatre and the toes of my feet are fulfilling their functions to the utmost I arrive there without increasing my speed five to seven minutes sooner than if I walk along without having my toes and feet do their proper part in expediting my movements. It is important that your toes carry out your steps to their very tips.

"The toes likewise modify shocks and their significance in this role is tremendous. It is especially important at the most difficult instant when you are trying to maintain a smooth gait and when most undesirable vertical jerks may appear in greatest force—the moment when you shift your weight from one foot to the other. This stage of transition is most dangerous to the maintenance of a smooth gait. Here everything depends on your toes (especially the big toe). More than any other of the body's springs they have the power to break the shift of weight through the modifying action of their extremities.

"I have attempted to describe to you the functions of the various component parts of your legs and for that purpose we have examined in detail the action of each of them. But actually they do not operate separately, but simultaneously and interdependently. Take the case of the instant in which the body weight is shifted from one leg to the other, as in the second stage of propelling the body forward, and in the third phase of pushing over, shifting the weight back to the other foot—in some degree all the motor parts of the leg are operating together. It is impossible to write out all their mutual relationships, mutual assistance. You have to discover these things within yourself with the aid of your own sensations while you are in motion. I can only suggest to you the plan of operation of this splendid and complex piece of apparatus which is the human leg."

When Tortsov concluded his explanations all the students began to try out this gait. But they walked noticeably less well than before, neither according to their old habits nor the new precepts. Tortsov noted some progress in me but immediately added:

"Yes, your shoulders and head are free from jerkiness. You glide but only along the earth, you do not fly through the air. Consequently your walk is closer to creeping or crawling. You walk the way waiters do in a restaurant, afraid of spilling the soup. They protect their bodies and arms, and along with them their trays, from being swayed and jolted.

"However, this gliding motion in walking is good only within limits. Beyond them it is exaggerated, the thing we see in restaurant waiters. A certain degree of up and down motion of the body is necessary. Your shoulders, head and torso can float along on air, but let the line be not absolutely straight, let it wave slightly.

"A gait should not be a creeping but a soaring thing."

I begged him to explain the exact difference between the two.

It seems that in a crawling gait when the weight of the body is shifted, let us say, from the right to the left leg the first finishes its function simultaneously with the moment when the second begins its function. In other words the left foot transfers the body weight at the same time that the right one takes it over. As a result, in a creeping or crawling gait there is not that split second when the body seems to be poised in the air, resting solely on the big toe of one foot which is fulfilling to the last fraction its predestined line of motion. In a soaring gait there is a moment when, for a second, a person seems to leave the earth like a dancer rising on her points. After this instant of airy uplift there begins the smooth, imperceptible, unjolted sinking down and the transfer of the body weight from one foot to the other.

According to Tortsov those two moments—the rise into the air and the smooth change over from one foot to the other—are all important because they hold the key to a light, smooth, unbroken step, one that has even an airy floating quality.

It is, however, not such a simple matter as it may seem to float when walking.

In the first place it is difficult to capture that second in which the rise takes place. Fortunately I was lucky enough to sense it. Then Tortsov complained of my hopping up and down in a vertical line.

"But how can I rise without doing that?" I asked.

"You must leave the ground not upwards but forwards in a horizontal line."

Besides, he insisted that there be no break, no slowing down in the motion of the body as a step is taken. The spurt forward must not be interrupted for even a fraction of a second. Poised on the toe of the first foot one must carry the momentum on at the same rate in which the step was initiated. That kind of step skims over the earth, it does not rise abruptly and vertically, but moves horizontally farther and farther ahead, imperceptibly leaving the ground, like an aeroplane at the moment of its take-off, and just as smoothly it sinks again, without any bobbing up and down. This horizontal forward motion produces a slightly curved, wavelike line; hopping up and dropping down in vertical motion makes for a crooked, zigzag, angular line.

Had an outsider dropped into our class to-day he would have believed himself in a hospital ward for paraplegics. All the students were moving around in utter absorption, concentrated on their muscles, and apparently deep in some puzzling problem.

This absorption had the obvious effect of tangling up their motor centres. The things they used to do instinctively, now required the most conscious supervision and revealed how ignorant of anatomy and the system of loco-motor muscles they were. Actually we pulled all the wrong strings and produced the kind of unexpected motions that a puppet gives when its strings are twisted.

The concentration of attention on our movements did have the positive result of teaching us a healthy respect for the refinements and complexity of the mechanism of our legs. Suddenly we realized how interlaced and comple-mentary it all is.

Tortsov asked us to carry each step out to its absolute completion. Under his immediate observation and direc-tion we walked step by step and watched our own sen-sations in the process.

He held a stick in his hand and pointed out exactly where and when the muscles were tensed in my right leg. Simul-taneously Rakhmanov walked along on the other side of me and with his stick pointed out the corresponding muscular tensions in my left leg.

"Watch," said Tortsov, "as my stick moves up along your right leg, which is stretched forward and is taking on the weight of your body, Rakhmanov's stick is moving down along your left leg, which is shifting your body and its weight over to the right leg. And now the reverse move-ment begins, mine starts downward and his goes up. Do you notice that this alternating movement of our sticks from your toes to your hip and from your hip to your toes, moves in opposite directions? Mine goes up when his goes down and vice versa. That is how the pistons work in a steam engine of the vertical type. Be sure to note how the flexing and the relaxing at the joints follow one another in sequence from up to down and down to up.

"If we had a third stick we could point out how a part of this energy goes on up along your spinal column, softening jars and maintaining equilibrium. Having achieved its mission the tension in the spine then moves downward again to the toes from whence it came.

"There is one more detail for you to observe," continued

Tortsov. "When our sticks come up to your hips there is a second's pause while they turn at the point of articulation and then start down again."

"Yes, we notice that," we replied, "but what is the meaning of the stick's turning?"

"Don't you yourselves feel that rotating movement inside your hip joints? Something really seems to revolve before starting down the leg. To me it brings to mind the turntable where the engine, when it reaches the last station, is turned around before starting in the opposite direction. We have just such turn-tables in our hip joints; it is a movement of which I am quite aware.

"One more remark. Do you realize how skillfully our hip joints operate at that instant when they receive the mounting and discharge the descending tension? They are like the balance wheels in a steam engine, they modify the shocks at dangerous moments. This is when our hips move from up to down and from down to up."

2

As I was walking home to-day I dare say the passers-by in the street took me for a drunken or abnormal person.

I was learning how to walk.

But it was very difficult.

The instant when my weight was shifted from one leg to the other seemed especially complicated.

By the time I neared the end of my walk it seemed to me that I had succeeded in getting rid of the jolt when I shifted my body from one foot to the other—let us say from the toes of my right foot to the heel of my left, and then (after the shifting movement had run along the whole plant of my left foot) from the toes of my left to the heel of my right foot. Besides, I came to realize through my own experience that smoothness and an unbroken line of forward motion depend on the correlated action of all the springs of the legs, from the harmonious co-operation of hips, knees, ankles, heels and toes.

I was in the habit of making a stop when I reached the Gogol Monument. As I sat there on a bench I observed the passers-by and their way of walking. And what did I discover? Not one of them took a full step right to the end of his toes nor remained poised even for the fraction of a second on the tip of the last one. It was only in one little girl that I saw a floating gait and not the creeping type of all the others.

Tortsov is indeed right, people do not know how to make use of the marvellous apparatus which is their legs.

So we have to learn. We have to begin from the beginning and learn—to walk, to speak, to see, to act.

Earlier when Tortsov said as much to us I smiled to myself and thought that he expressed all these ideas in order to make a vivid picture. Now I had come to appreciate his words in their literal meaning and as relating to our forth-coming programme of physical development.

This realization is half the battle.

3

Tortsov came to our plastic movement class again. This time he said:

"Movement and action, which take their source in the recesses of the soul and follow an inner pattern, are essential to real artists in drama, ballet and other theatre and plastic arts.

"They are the only kind of movement fit for our use when we are building the physical form of a character.

"How is this to be achieved?" one of the students asked.

"Madame Sonova here will help us solve this problem."

Here Tortsov turned the class over temporarily to Madame Sonova.

"Look at this," she began. "I have here in my hand a

drop of mercury. Now I am going to pour it carefully into my index finger right at the very tip."

As she spoke she acted as if she were injecting the imaginary mercury into her finger, right into the muscles.

"Now you do it and let it course through your whole body," she ordered. "Don't hurry. Do it gradually. First past the joints of your fingers—let them straighten out to let it run along down to your palm, to the wrist joint, then into your forearm, your elbow. Has it reached there yet? Has it rolled by? Did you sense it distinctly? Don't be in a hurry, feel your way. That's splendid. Now, slowly, watch it as it moves along up to your shoulder. That's right. Marvellous! Your whole arm has unfolded, straightened out and been raised up joint by joint. No, no, no! Why let the whole arm drop all at once like a stick of wood! The mercury will roll down and out, there it goes onto the floor! You must let it flow slowly, slowly, first from the shoulder to the elbow. Now bend it, bend your elbow. That's the way. But for the time being do not put the rest of your arm down. Not for anything or you will lose the mercury. That's the way. Now go on. Let it run down to your wrist. Not too fast. Watch it, watch it carefully. Why do you let your wrist drop? Hold it up! Look out for that mercury! Slowly, slowly. That's perfect. Now run it in succession through the joints of your hand and fingers. Like this, let them move down, down. Slowly, that's right. This is the last flection. The hand is empty now, the mercury has flowed out.

"Now I am going to pour the mercury into the crown of your head," she said, addressing Paul Shustov. "You let it run down through your neck, past all the vertebrae in your backbone, through your pelvis, along your right leg, then up again, across your pelvis arch, down your left leg to the big toe in your left foot. Now back up to the pelvis and return the mercury up your spine to your neck and on through your head to your crown."

Then we all did the same, letting the imaginary mercury

roll up and down our limbs, shoulders, chins, noses, then let it run out again.

Did we really feel its passage through our muscular system, or did we imagine that we felt the imaginary mercury coursing through us!

Our teacher did not give us any time for reflection about this, she made us go through our exercises without any dissecting thoughts.

"The Director here will tell you all that you need to learn," said Madame Sonova, "but meantime keep working carefully, carefully and do these exercises over and over and over again! You have to keep at them for a long time before you really acquire the feel of them."

"Come here quickly, Kostya," said Tortsov, "and answer me frankly. Don't you feel that your fellow students have more fluency in their movements than before?"

My eyes turned to fat Leo. I was indeed surprised at the rounded curves of his motions. But I immediately ascribed that to the fact that his rotund figure enhanced the effect.

But I could not think the same of Anna with her angular shoulders, sharp elbows and knees. Where had she found that fluidity of movement? Could it be that the imaginary mercury in its unbroken course through her could produce this result?

The rest of the lesson was conducted by Tortsov.

"Madame Sonova has drawn your physical attention to the movement of energy along a network of muscles. This same kind of attention should be fixed on ferreting out points of pressure in the process of relaxing our muscles—a subject we have already considered in detail. What is muscular pressure or spasm except moving energy that is blocked?

"From your exercises last year in the sending out of certain rays or wordless communications (See *An Actor Prepares* —EDITOR), you know that energy operates not only inside us but outside as well, it wells up from the depths of our beings and is directed to an object outside ourselves.

"Just as in that process we now must fix our attention on the field of plastic motion, where it plays a large part. It is important that your attention move in constant company with the current of energy, because this helps to create an endless, unbroken line which is so essential to our art.

"Incidentally this is also true of other arts. Do you not believe that music must have that same unbroken line of sound? Obviously a violin cannot sing the melody until the bow moves smoothly and steadily over its strings.

"And what will happen if that unbroken line is taken from a painter in his design?" Tortsov probed further. "Can he achieve the simple outline of a drawing without it? Of course he cannot. That line is absolutely necessary to the painter.

"What would you think of a singer who would cough out intermittent sounds instead of pouring forth the unbroken sonorous note?"

"I should suggest he go to a hospital instead of on to the stage," I remarked jokingly.

"Next try to take the long sweep of his line away from a dancer. Can he create his dance without it?" asked Tortsov.

"Of course not," I replied.

"Well, the actor has to have that unbroken line as much as any other artist. Or do you think that we can get along without it?"

We all agreed with Tortsov that we could not.

"Therefore," he concluded, "we can consider it essential to all the arts. But that is not the whole story.

"*Art itself originates in the moment when that unbroken line is established, be it that of sound, voice, drawing or movement. As long as there exist only separate sounds, ejaculations, notes, exclamations instead of music, or separate lines, dots instead of a design, or separate spasmodic jerks instead of co-ordinated movement—there can be no question of music, singing, design or painting, dancing, architecture, sculpture nor, finally, of dramatic art.*

"What I want you to do is to watch how the unbroken line of movement is established.

"Look at me and repeat what I shall do. As you see my arm with the make-believe mercury in my fingers is hanging down by my side. But I want to raise it, so let the metronome be set at its slowest tempo, number ten. Let each beat represent a quarter note. Four beats will constitute a measure of four-four time which I shall take to raise my arm."

Tortsov then set the metronome in motion and gave warning that he was about to begin the session.

"There is the count of one—one quarter note, during which I execute one of the component moves, the raising of the arm and the movement of energy from the shoulder to the elbow.

"That part of the arm which has not yet been raised must be relaxed, free of all tension, and hang limp as a whip lash. Relaxed muscles make the arm flexible and it can then unfurl as it straightens out, like the neck of a swan.

"Note then that in raising or lowering the arm, as in other motions made with it, you should keep it close to the body. An arm held off from the body is like a stick raised at one end. You must put your hand out from yourself and when the movement is accomplished take it back again to yourself. The gesture starts at the shoulder, goes to the extremities of the arm and returns to its starting point in the shoulder.

"Let us continue. Count two. Here is the second quarter of the measure, during which another succeeding movement is made, the imaginary mercury passes from the elbow to the wrist as that part of the arm is raised.

"Next count three. The third quarter is devoted to lifting the wrist and one by one the joints of the fingers.

"Finally at count four, your last quarter note, you lift all your fingers.

"In exactly the same way I now let my arm fall, allowing a quarter note for each of the four flexing actions,

"One, two, three, four . . ."

Tortsov now barked the count abruptly, like a military command:

"One!" Then a pause before the next count. "Two!" Another silence. "Three!" Fresh pause. "Four!" A wait, and so on, over and over.

In view of the very slow tempo the pauses between the words of command were quite extended. The beats, alternating with the silent inaction, interfered with any fluidity of movement. Our arms moved in jerks like a cart lumbering across deep ruts.

"Now let us do the same exercise over at twice as fast a rate. Let each quarter note include two beats—one and one, like a duplet in music, then two and two, three and three, four and four, instead of the simple numbers. As a result we shall preserve the same four quarter notes in each measure, but broken into eight parts, or eighth notes."

We went through the exercise that way.

"As you realized," said Tortsov, "the intervals between the counts were shorter, because there were more of them in the measure and that facilitated a certain fluidity of motion.

"This is strange. Can it be that the mere voicing of the count influences the smoothness of the raising or dropping of an arm? Of course the secret does not lie in the words but in the *attention* fixed on the directing of one's current of energy. The smaller the fractions of each beat, the more of them that are pressed into each measure, filling it up, the more unbroken is the line of attention following each minute move of the flow of energy. As the measure is broken into still smaller fractions, as it grows more compact, the line of attention and the movement of energy become more constant, hence that of the arm as well.

"Now let us put what I have just said to the test."

Whereupon we went through a series of tests during which the quarter note was broken up into three parts, then four, six, twelve, sixteen, twenty-four and even a greater number of fractions in each measure. The movements fused into one another until they became constant and unbroken, like the humming of the beats themselves: one-one-one-one-one-one-one-one-two-two-two-two-two-two-two-two-three-three-three-three-three-three-three-three-four-four-four-four-four-four-four-four. . . .

In the end I could no longer count because it required too rapid diction. My tongue hummed, my tongue wagged, but the words were indistinguishable. At this top speed my arm moved without a break and very slowly because the beat of the metronome was still set at ten.

The result was a marvellous smoothness. My arm really did uncoil and coil up again like the neck of a swan.

Then Tortsov said to us:

"We can make another parallel, this time with an outboard motor. At the outset it makes intermittent explosive noises, then they become constant as does the movement of the propeller.

"The same is true of you. At first you practically spat out the command, and now the calling of the beat has turned into one unbroken sound of humming and slow plastic movement. In this form it is adaptable for the purpose of art because you have achieved a sustained melody and a constancy of movement.

"You will be even more aware of this when you do the exercise to music because instead of the humming of your voice in counting you will have the beautiful, unbroken line of musical sound."

Here Rakhmanov seated himself at the piano and began to play something in slow, languid time. To it we stretched our arms, legs and spines.

"Did you feel," asked Tortsov, "how your energy travelled in stately progress along an unbroken line? *That is the motion which creates fluency, the plasticity of body movement which is so necessary to us.*

"This inner line comes from the deepest recesses of our being, the energy it engenders is saturated with stimuli of emotions, will and intellect.

"When, with the aid of systematic exercise, you grow accustomed to and enjoy basing your actions on an inner rather than an external line, you will come to know what the emotion of movement itself means."

When we had finished the exercises Tortsov went on:

"A solid, uninterrupted line of movement in our art is the raw material out of which we mould the plastic form.

"Just as an unbroken strand of wool or cotton is fashioned as it passes through a spinning machine, our line of action is subject to artistic fabrication. At one point we may make it lighter, at another we may reinforce it, at a third stage we may hasten, slow down, hold it back, break it off, add rhythmic accent, and finally co-ordinate our movement to the emphases of tempo and rhythm.

"What instants in the action produced should coincide with the beat of the measures in our mind?

"These stages are almost imperceptibly minute split seconds during which the current of energy passes the separate points of articulation, the joints of the fingers or the vertebrae of the spinal column.

"It is those split seconds which are noted by our attention. As we roll the imaginary drop of mercury from joint to joint we make a note of the instant in which the energy it symbolizes crosses through the shoulder, the elbow, the bend of the wrists, the finger joints. That is what we did to the accompaniment of music.

"It may be that the coincidence will not have been exact, it may not have occurred when you expected it, it may have come later or earlier. You may not have counted precisely but only approximately the measured beat. The important thing was that the action thus divided did fill you with tempo and rhythm, that you were constantly aware of the measure and your attention pursued and caught up with the increasingly fractionalized count which your tongue could not keep pace with. Even so an unbroken line of attention was created and with it the uninterrupted flow of action which we were seeking."

The thing that turned out to be particularly pleasant was the relating of an inner movement of energy to a melody.

Vanya, hard at work beside me, found that the "music actually smoothed out all our movements so that they slid along like greased lightning."

Sounds and rhythm promote a smooth continuity and lightness of movement which make it seem that an arm flies out from the torso of its own accord.

We did similar exercises with our legs, spines and necks. Here the energy moved along our vertebrae just as it used to do when we were training ourselves in the relaxation of muscular tensions.

When the energy current flowed downwards we felt as though we were sinking into the nether regions. When it rose along our spines we seemed to be lifted right off the earth.

As we did the analogous work on our legs it stimulated the action of our leg and feet muscles in walking.

Whenever we were able to establish a smooth and regular flow of energy we achieved a smooth, measured and elastic step. Whenever the energy came in jerks, became blocked in the points of articulation or other centres of locomotion, then our gait was uneven, choppy.

"Since your gait has its unbroken line of movement," said Tortsov, "it means that tempo and rhythm are inherent in it.

"Any movement there, as in your arms, is divided up into the component fractions of moments when the energy passes along the articulations (in the stretch of the leg, the forward thrust of the body, its repulsion, the shift of the feet, the modifying of the jolts and so on).

"Therefore as you continue your exercises you should co-ordinate the beat of your external tempo and rhythm in your step with the corresponding beat of the internal line of energy movement, in the same way as we did in our work with the arms and spinal column."

How much attention it takes to watch for the regular, rhythmic movement of energy! Let there be the slightest let up and an undesirable jerk appears, the flow and smoothness of the movement is broken, the accent thrown out of gear.

We were also made to cut off the flow of energy. The same was done with tempo and rhythm. The result was a motionless pose. We believed in its truthfulness when it was justified by an inner impulse. That type of pose turned into arrested action, living sculpture. It is very agreeable not only to act out of inner impulse but also to remain inactive in rhythm and tempo.

At the close of the class Tortsov summed up:

"In your earlier work, in your classes of gymnastics and dancing, you were occupied with the external line of movement of your arms, legs, body. To-day you have learned something more, the inner line of movement which is the basis of plasticity.

"It is up to you to decide which of these two lines, the inner or the external, is the more important, which you believe is the more appropriate to the producing of a physical image on the stage of the life of a human being, to the building of a character."

Our unanimous opinion led Tortsov to say:

"Then you realize that at the foundation of plasticity of movement one must establish an inner flow of energy.

"This in turn must be co-ordinated with the measured beat of tempo and rhythm.

"This inner feeling of an energy passing through the body we call the sense of movement."

Now I have understood, through my own feelings, the significance of moving energy in achieving plasticity. I can clearly envisage how it will feel when I am in action on the stage, and it is coursing all through my body. I can sense the inner unbroken line and I realize perfectly clearly that without it there can be no beauty of movement. I now despise in myself all the half-way, sawed off scraps of movements. I do not as yet possess the ability to make that broad gesture which is the externalization of an inner emotion, but realize that I must have it.

Plasticity of Motion

In other words I have not yet achieved plasticity of movement and a sense of movement but I foresee them in myself and I already realize that *external plasticity is based on our inner sense of the movement of energy.*

6

RESTRAINT AND CONTROL

I

TO-DAY there was a large banner across the front of our museum classroom, which by now had been straightened out with the exhibitions effectively arranged. On the banner were the words "Restraint and Finish".

But Tortsov did not refer to them immediately. He asked if we remembered the exercise with the madman (from *An Actor Prepares*—EDITOR), the successful improvisation in which, believing that a man who had escaped from a psychopathic ward was behind the door, I found myself under a table with a heavy ash-tray for self-defence. After detailing the given circumstances of the exercise he set us to repeating it.

We students were all delighted as we were itching to act again and threw ourselves into the improvisation with every ounce of energy. We seemed actually to be in Maria's apartment and to believe that the former tenant, who had become violently insane, had sought refuge there; the problem of how he would try to escape capture became real; and when Vanya, who held the door shut, suddenly jumped away, we fled, the girls screaming with sincere terror. It was some time before we could organize our instinct for self-preservation so as to barricade the door and telephone the hospital.

Tortsov praised us but without enthusiasm. We tried to justify ourselves by maintaining that we had not played the sketch for a long time and had forgotten the details. Yet when we repeated it his manner did not change.

"What is the matter?" we asked. "What are you trying to extract from us?"

As often the Director answered our question with a picturesque illustration. He said:

"Imagine that you have before you a sheet of white paper all criss-crossed with lines and splotched with stains. Imagine further that you are called upon to put a delicate pencil sketch on that same sheet—a landscape or a portrait. In order to do this you must first clean the paper of the superfluous lines and spots which, if they remain on it will blur and ruin your drawing. For its sake you are obliged to have a clean sheet of paper.

"The same thing takes place in our type of work. Extra gestures are the equivalent of trash, dirt, spots.

"An actor's performance which is cluttered up with a multiplicity of gestures will be like that messy sheet of paper. Therefore before he undertakes the external creation of his character, the physical interpretation, the transfer of the inner life of a part to its concrete image, he must rid himself of all superfluous gestures. Only under those conditions can he achieve the necessary sharpness of outline for its physical embodiment. Unrestrained movements, natural though they may be to the actor himself, only blur the design of his part, make his performance unclear, monotonous and uncontrolled.

"Every actor should so harness his gestures that he will always be in control of them and not they of him.

"A person in the midst of experiencing a poignant emotional drama is incapable of speaking of it coherently, for at such a time tears choke him, his voice breaks, the stress of his feelings confuses his thoughts, his pitiful aspect distracts those who see him and prevents their understanding the very cause of his grief. But time, the great healer, tempers a man's inner agitation, makes it possible for him to bear himself calmly in relation to past events. He can speak of them coherently, slowly, intelligibly and as he relates the story he remains relatively calm while those who listen weep.

73

"Our art seeks to achieve this very result and requires that an actor experience the agony of his role, and weep his heart out at home or in rehearsals, that he then calm himself, get rid of every sentiment alien or obstructive to his part. He then comes out on the stage to convey to the audience in clear, pregnant, deeply felt, intelligible and eloquent terms what he has been through. At this point the spectators will be more affected than the actor, and he will conserve all his forces in order to direct them where he needs them most of all: in reproducing the inner life of the character he is portraying.

"It happens only too often that actors on the stage muffle and obscure the action which is right and proper to the roles they are playing by an intrusive, superfluous quantity of gestures. Often an actor who has a superb mastery of facial expression does not give his public the opportunity to appreciate it to the full because he masks it with a lot of finicky gestures with his arms and hands. Such actors are their own worst enemies because they keep others from seeing the splendid qualities they have to offer.

"An excessive use of gesture dilutes a part as water does good wine. Pour a little good red wine in the bottom of a glass and then fill it up with water—you will have a liquid only vaguely tinged with pink. The true line of action in a part becomes just as indistinguishable as that amid a flurry of gestures.

"I maintain that a gesture as such, an independent movement not expressing any action germane to the actor's role, is not necessary except in certain rare instances as, for example, in certain character parts. By the simple use of a gesture one cannot convey either the inner spirit of a part or the main unbroken line of action that flows through its entirety. To accomplish this one must make use of movements which induce physical action. They in turn convey the inner spirit of the part one is playing.

"Gestures per se are the stock in trade of actors concerned with showing off their good looks, with posing, with exhibitionism.

"In addition to gestures actors also make many involuntary movements in an effort to help themselves over difficult spots in their parts. These may evoke external emotional effects or the external physical appearance of emotions which are non-existent in superficial actors. Such movements take the form of convulsive cramps, needless as well as harmful over-tenseness of muscles, supposed to facilitate the wringing out of theatrical emotions. Yet they not only make blotches on a part, they also interfere with restraint and control, and the true, natural state of an actor while he is on the stage.

"Many of you are guilty of this and above all Vanya.

"How agreeable it is to see an artist on the stage when he exercises restraint and does not indulge in all these convulsive, cramped gestures! We see the pattern of his part emerge distinctly because of that restraint. The movements and action of a character being portrayed gain immeasurably in significance and attraction when they are not clouded over with superfluous, irrelevant, purely theatrical gesticulation.

"There is also this to be said against this excess motion. It absorbs a great deal of energy, which could better be used for purposes more closely bound up with the main artery which pulses through a part from start to finish.

"When you will have made the experiment in your own persons of the meaning of this restraint and control of gesture you will sense how much your physical expression will expand, grow fuller, more clean cut, transparent. At the same time the lessening of your gestures will be compensated for by the intonations of your voice, flexibility of your facial expression, all the more exquisitely exact means of communication best calculated to convey the delicate shadings of emotions and the inner life of a part.

"Restraint in gesture is of particular importance in the field of characterization. In order to get away from one's self and not repeat the same externals in every part it is imperative to achieve an elimination of gestures. Every external movement which may be natural to an actor off stage separates him from the character he is playing and keeps reminding him of himself. If an actor cannot get away from himself in his inner concept of a part he must at least cover himself up externally with movements characteristic of that part.

"It often happens that an actor can only find three or four characteristic typical gestures. To be satisfied throughout the whole play with that many gestures requires utmost economy of movement. Restraint is a great help here. But if these three typical gestures get drowned amid a hundred little personal motions related to the actor's own personality and not to his part, the mask he has assumed will slip and reveal his own everyday face. Besides, if this happens in every part he plays it will result in an extremely monotonous effect on the public.

"Nor should an actor forget that the typical gesture helps to bring him closer to the character he is portraying while the intrusion of personal motions separates him from it and pushes him in the direction of his purely personal emotions. This can scarcely serve the purpose either of play or part since what are needed are analogous, not personal emotions.

"Characteristic gestures cannot, of course, be repeated too often or they lose their effect and become boring.

"The more restraint and self-control an actor exercises in this creative process the clearer will be the form and design of his role and the more powerful its effect on the public. His success will be the greater as will that of the author of the play whose works can only reach the wider public through the success of the actors, the directors and the whole collective effort of all who contribute their talents and work to a production.

"One day when Bryulov, a famous painter, was criticizing one of the works of his pupils in an art class he picked up a brush to put just one touch on an unfinished canvas, and the picture instantly came to life. The pupil was astounded at the miracle.

"To this Bryulov explained, 'Art begins with the slightest of touches.'

"And we can apply the same words of that famous painter to our art. We need only the slightest touch or two to make a role come to life, to reach its finished form. Without those slightest of touches it will lack the brilliance of a perfect finish.

"Yet how often we see a role on the stage that is quite lacking in that slight touch. It may be well worked out and one still misses that all-important element. A talented director may come along and drop just a word, the actor will catch fire and his role will glow with all the colours of his soul's prism.

"This brings to mind the conductor of a military band who was well known mainly because he used to walk along the boulevards every day beating out whole concerts with his arms. Leading his band he used the same tempo. In the beginning when your attention was drawn by the sounds, you would listen, but in five minutes you would be only watching the automatic movements of his baton and seeing the white pages of his score, as he methodically turned leaf after leaf with his left hand. Now he was not a poor musician. His band was a good one and was well known throughout the city. Yet his music was uncompelling because the most important element—its inner content—was never revealed and did not reach the listeners. All the component parts of each piece of music were precisely and smoothly performed. They followed one another, however, in such indistinguishable form that the listeners could not tell them apart or understand them. Each part lacked the desired touch which would have given a finish to it and to the work as a whole.

"We have many actors on our stages who beat out their parts in this same way, going through whole plays with the same sweep and paying no attention to the necessary 'touch' that provides 'finish'.

"In contrast to my recollection of this baton-waving conductor I remember Arthur Nikisch, small of stature but a great musician who could say far more with sounds than most people can with words.

"With the tiny tip of his baton he drew an ocean of sound from his orchestra with which he painted broad musical pictures.

"Nor should one forget how Nikisch, before the performance began, looked all his musicians over with meticulous care, then waited until absolute silence fell in the hall before raising his baton and concentrating on its tip the attention of the entire orchestra and audience. At that instant his baton said Attention! Listen, I am about to begin!

"Even in this preparatory moment Nikisch possessed that intangible 'touch' which so beautifully completed his every motion. To Nikisch there was something precious in every whole note, every half note, eighth and sixteenth note, every dot, and the mathematically precise counterpoint, the delicious naturals, the dissonances even and the harmony. All this was performed by him with great relish, without fear of dragging. Nikisch never lost track of a single sound, never failed to give it its full value. With his baton he extracted everything that could be drawn from the instruments and from the very souls of his musicians. Meantime his left hand was working with the expressive colouring of a painter's brush, now smoothing and now slowing the music, now rousing and increasing it. What remarkable restraint he possessed, as well as mathematical precision, which not only did not interfere with but encouraged his inspiration. His tempi were on the same high level. His lento was far from being monotonous, boring, long-drawn out like the drone of a bagpipe, the way the military bandmaster hammered it out with the ticking of a metronome. Nikisch's slow tempo contained within itself the rapid ones. He never hurried the music or held it back. It was only at the end, when all had been said, that Nikisch would hasten or slow the tempo in order either to catch up what had been held back or to return what an earlier intentionally quick tempo had taken away. For this he had prepared a musical phrase in a new tempo. He seemed to say, 'Never hurry! Express everything that is concealed in the music.' Now we come to the very apex of the phrase! Who could foretell how he would set the crown on the whole work? Would it be with a new, great slow movement or, on the contrary, would he give it an unexpectedly bold, quick, emphatic ending?

"Of how many conductors can one say that he knew how to penetrate into, guess at and catch all the fine shadings of a piece of music and to do what Nikisch did with such sensitivity, not only cull them out but also to convey and illume them for the public? Nikisch did it because his work was performed not only with magnificent restraint but also with brilliantly keen finish.

"Sometimes an illustration by opposites is convincing and I shall make use of one here to show you the meaning and value of finish in our field of work. You all know the type of rapid-fire actors, of whom we see so many in farces, vaudeville, musical comedies. They are forever having to be gay, make people laugh, keep stepping at a lively pace. But to be gay, when inside you are feeling sad, is difficult. Therefore they have recourse to an external routine. The easiest way to achieve this is an external tempo and rhythm. Actors of this type rush their lines and dash through the action of the play with exaggerated speed. The entire play is mixed into one chaotic whole which the audience is incapable of disentangling. Here you will find nothing sustained, no restraint, no finish.

"Among the finest qualities of artists in the theatre who have achieved supreme rank are their restraint and finish. As you follow the way they unfold a role before your eyes and watch it grow, you have a sense of being present at some miraculous act of bringing to life a great piece of art.

"The creations of such geniuses of the theatre as Tommaso Salvini—these are enduring monuments. Such great artists shape the beginnings of a character sometimes with disarming quietness in the first act, and proceed in the ensuing ones to add to the role piece by piece, gradually, calmly, surely. When all the component parts are put together and in place we have an immortal monument built on human passions—jealousy, love, horror, vengeance, anger. This would not be possible without control and restraint. A sculptor casts his dream in bronze; an actor takes his dream of a character, realized through his subconscious, his inner creative state, through the subtext and super-objective of the role, and brings it to life by means of his voice, his movements, his emotional power directed by his intelligence."

2

"There is a description of one of Salvini's performances," Tortsov had said, "in *My Life in Art*. You might find it profitable to re-read it."

That evening Paul and I got out a copy of the book and read the following:

"I saw Salvini for the first time at the Bolshoi Theatre where he and his Italian troupe were playing during Lent.

"They were giving *Othello*. I do not know how it happened, whether it was because of absentmindedness or inattentiveness with regard to the arrival of this great genius, or whether I was confused by the arrival of other celebrities, such as Possart who always played the part of Iago rather than the title role, but in any case I concentrated all my attention at first on Iago, thinking it was Salvini.

" 'Well, yes,' I said to myself, 'he has a good voice. He has the elements of a good actor in him, a fine presence, he plays in the usual Italian style but I see nothing exceptional in him. The actor, who plays the Othello is equally good. He also is good material, has a marvellous voice, diction, carriage.' I was rather cool toward the transports of the experts who were ready to swoon after the first speech of Salvini.

"It seemed as though in the beginning of the play the great actor did not wish to draw the attention of the public.

Had he wished to do so he had the opportunity to accomplish his purpose by one brilliant pause. And this is what he did later on in the scene in the Senate. There was nothing new in the handling of the first part of this scene except that I had the possibility of studying Salvini's face, costume, and make-up. I cannot say that there was anything extraordinary to be found in them. In fact I did not like his costume at that point or later. His make-up? I should think that he had none. It was his own face and it may well be that it was useless to attempt to put make-up on it. He wore a large pointed moustache, a wig that was much too obvious. His face was broad, heavy, almost fat. A big oriental dagger dangled from his belt and made him look more fleshy than he really was, especially in his Moorish gown and head-dress. All this was not very typical of Othello, the soldier.

"Yet. . . .

"Salvini moved nearer to the dais of the doges, was wrapped in concentrated thought for a moment and then, without our even noticing it, he took the entire audience of the big Bolshoi opera house into the hollow of his hand. It seemed almost as if he did this with a single gesture; without looking at the public, he stretched out his hand, grasped hold of us as if we had been ants or flies. He clenched his fist—and we felt the breath of doom, he opened his hand —and it was bliss. We were in his power and we would remain there to the end of the play and much longer. Now we knew who and what this great genius was, and what we could expect of him. At first it almost seemed as though his Othello was not Othello at all but Romeo. He had eyes for nothing and no one but Desdemona, he thought only of her, his faith in her was unbounded and we were amazed that Iago was capable of transforming this Romeo into a jealousy-ridden Othello.

"How can I convey to you the powerful impact of the impression made by Salvini? Perhaps by quoting the words of a poet who said, 'Creation is for eternity.' That was how Salvini acted."

7

DICTION AND SINGING

DURING a performance to-night in the theatre to which our school is attached I was operating sound effects, and in the intermission I overheard a conversation between some actors and Tortsov in the wings.

Tortsov had made some comments to an actor on his performance, but unfortunately I missed these and the actor's reply. When I began to listen the Director was relating some personal experiences. As is often his way he was teaching by means of these experiences and what he had concluded from them.

This is more or less the content of what he said:

"When I recited to myself I tried to speak as simply as possible, without false pathos, insincere tonal effects, or exaggerated emphasis in the verse. I tried to keep to the heart of the poem. The impression it produced was due to the fact that the words in a phrase vibrated, sang, and that lent my speech nobility and a musical quality.

"When I carried this way of speaking on to the stage my fellow actors were amazed at the change that took place in my voice, my diction and by my new way of expressing feeling and thoughts. Then it appeared that I had not yet solved all angles to the problem. The actor must not only be pleased himself by the sound of his own speech but he must also make it possible for the public present in the theatre to hear and understand whatever merits its attention. Words and their intonation should reach their ears without effort.

"This demands great skill. When I acquired it I realized what we call the 'feel of words'.

"Speech is music. The text of a part or a play is a melody, an opera, or a symphony. Pronunciation on the stage is as difficult an art as singing, it requires training and a technique bordering on virtuosity. When an actor with a well trained voice and masterly vocal technique speaks the words of his part I am quite carried away by his supreme art. If he is rhythmic I am involuntarily caught up in the rhythm and tone of his speech, I am stirred by it. If he himself pierces to the soul of the words in his part he takes me with him into the secret places of the playwright's composition as well as into those of his own soul. When an actor adds the vivid ornament of sound to that living content of the words, he causes me to glimpse with an inner vision the images he has fashioned out of his own creative imagination.

"When an actor controls his movements and adds to them words and voice it seems to me it becomes an harmonious accompaniment to beautiful singing. A good man's voice entering on the scene with its cue is like a 'cello or an oboe. A pure, high, woman's voice, responding to the cue, makes me think of a violin or flute. The deep chest tones of a dramatic actress remind me of the introduction of a viola. The heavy bass of a noble father resounds like a bassoon, the voice of the villain is a trombone, which rumbles yet gurgles inwardly, as though from rage and accumulated saliva.

"How can actors fail to feel a whole orchestra in just a phrase, even a simple one of seven words such as, 'Come back —I cannot live without you!'

"How many different ways that phrase can be sung, and each time anew! What a variety of meanings can be put into it! How many different moods! Try changing the places of the pauses and accents and you will obtain more and more new meanings. Short stops combined with accents set off the key word sharply and present it distinct from the others. Longer pauses, without sounds, make it possible to impregnate the words with fresh inner content. This is all helped by movements, facial expression and intonation. Such changes produce renewed moods, give new content to a whole phrase.

"Take as an example the first two words, *Come back*, followed by a pause filled with despair because he who has gone will not return. It is the beginning of a pathetic aria.

"*I cannot*—followed by a brief breathing pause which prepares and helps to enhance the key word—*live*—that is the high point. Obviously this is the most important word in the whole phrase. To make it stand out in still greater relief there is another short breathing pause, after which the phrase concludes with the words: *without you*.

"If the word *live*, for the sake of which the whole musical phrase was created, is something alive torn from the quick of a soul, if the woman who has been cast off clings in that word with all her remaining strength to the man to whom she has given herself for all eternity—then it will convey the core, the shattered spirit, of a woman who has been betrayed. But in case of need the pauses and accented words can be distributed quite differently, and this is what we get:

"*Come back*—pause—*I* (breath) *cannot* . . . (breath) . . . *live without you!*

"This time the sharpness of outline is given to the two words: *I cannot*. Through them we feel a despairing woman for whom life has lost its meaning. This colours the whole phrase with an ominous significance and we seem to feel that this cast-off woman has reached the end, that a chasm is opening before her.

"Think how much can be packed into a word or a phrase, how rich language is. It is powerful, not in itself but inasmuch as it conveys the human soul, the human mind. Indeed there is so much spiritual, emotional content in those little words: *Come back. I cannot live without you.* In them lies the tragedy of a whole human life.

"Yet what is one phrase in the larger concept of the playwright, in a whole scene, act, play? Only a tiny speck, a moment, an insignificant part of a great whole.

"Just as atoms go to make up a whole universe, individual sounds convey words, words phrases, phrases thoughts, and out of thoughts there are formed whole scenes, acts and the content of a great play which embraces the tragic life of a human soul—of Hamlet, Othello, Hedda Gabler, Mme. Ranevskaya. These sounds form a whole symphony!"

2

" 'Stym ta'ɔpe nwy dor t'yawn p'ness!' "

These were the unexpected sounds that issued from Tortsov's lips as he came into class to-day. We looked at him and at each other in astonishment.

"Don't you understand it?" he asked after a short wait.

"Not a word of it," we admitted. "What do the scolding words mean?"

" 'It is time to open wide the door to your own happiness.' The actor who pronounced them in a certain play had a good, big voice, audible in all parts of the theatre, nevertheless we could not understand them any better than you could, and we too thought, as you did, that he was scolding us," explained Tortsov.

"The after effects of this slight and ludicrous example were so noteworthy for me that I must expand a little on what happened to me:

"After many years of acting and directing experience I arrived at a full realization, intellectual and emotional, that every actor must be in possession of excellent diction and pronunciation, that he must feel not only phrases and words, but also each syllable, each letter. The fact of the matter is that the simpler the truth the longer it takes to arrive at it.

"We do not feel our own language, the phrases, syllables, letters, and that is why it is so easy for us to distort it; instead of *va* we say *fa*, instead of *ga* we say *kua*. Add to this lisping, gutteral, nasal, and other ugly distortions of good speech!

"Words with substitute parts now look to me the way a man would who has an ear where his mouth should be, an eye in place of an ear, a finger for a nose.

"A word with a telescoped beginning is like a face with a bashed in nose. A word whose end is swallowed makes me think of a man minus a limb.

"The dropping of individual letters or syllables makes as glaring defects for me now as a missing eye or tooth, a cauliflower ear or any other physical deformity.

"When I hear someone, through inertia or slipshod habits, run all his words into an amorphous mass I cannot help thinking of a fly which has fallen into a jar of honey, or autumn weather when sleet and fog and mud blur everything.

"Lack of rhythm in speech, which makes a phrase start off slowly, spurt suddenly in the middle and just as abruptly slide in a gateway, reminds me of the way a drunkard walks, and the rapid fire speech of someone with St. Vitus' dance.

"You have, of course, had occasion to read books or newspapers which were badly printed, with letters missing and various misprints. Doesn't it torture you to have to take the time to guess at and solve the riddles such printing presents?

"And here is another form of torture: reading letters written the way one spreads grease on a surface. Just try to guess who is inviting you to do what, go where and when. Sometimes it is quite impossible. They write: 'You d . . . d. . . .' What they think you are, a dumb-bell or a darling, a friend or a fool—you cannot decipher.

"Difficult as it may be to have to deal with a badly printed book or poor handwriting, you still can reach, if you try hard enough, some understanding of the thought behind the words. The printed or written matter lies before you; you can take the time to go over it again and again and unriddle the incomprehensible.

"But what recourse have you in the theatre when the actors pronounce the text in a fashion comparable to your badly printed book, when they drop out whole letters, words, phrases which are often of cardinal importance to the basic structure of the play? You cannot bring back the spoken word, the play plunges forward towards its denouement, leaving you no time to stop and puzzle out what you do not understand. Poor speech creates one misunderstanding after another. It clutters up, befogs, or even conceals the thought, the essence and even the very plot of the play. The audience will, in the beginning, strain their ears, attention, minds, so as not to miss anything that is going on on the stage; if they cannot follow they begin to fidget, fuss, whisper to each other and finally to cough.

"Do you realize the dire implication for an actor of that word *cough*? An audience of a thousand people which reaches the point of losing its patience and is deprived of contact with what is happening on the stage, can cough the actors, the play, the whole performance, out of the theatre. This spells ruin for the play and the performance. One of the means of guarding against such an eventuality is the use of clear, beautiful, vivid speech.

"One more thing I came to understand: whereas distortion of our conversational speech may be half-way condoned in the surroundings of our home, any such coarse grained way of talking carried on to the stage, and used to pronounce melodious verse on exalted topics, on freedom, ideals, pure love—is offensive and ridiculous. Letters, syllables, words were not invented by man, they were suggested to him by his instincts, impulses, by nature herself, time and place.

"It was only after I had realized that letters are only symbols of sounds, which require the carrying out of their content, that I found myself naturally confronted with the problem of learning these sound forms so that I should be better able to fill out their content.

"I consciously went back to the beginning of the alphabet and began to study each letter separately. I found it easier to make a start with the vowels because they had been well trained, straightened and smoothed out by singing."

3

"Do you realize that an inner feeling is released through the clear sound of the *A*? That sound is bound up with certain deep inner experiences which seek release and easily float out from the recesses of one's bosom.

"But there is another *A* sound. It is dull, muffled, does not float out easily but remains inside to rumble ominously, as if in some cavern or vault. There is also the insidious *A A A* which whirls out to drill its way into the person who hears it. The joyous *A* sound rises from one like a rocket, in contrast to the ponderous *A*, which, like an iron weight sinks in to the bottom of one's wellsprings.

"Do you not sense that particles of you are carried out on these vocal waves? These are not empty vowels; they have a spiritual content.

"That is what I came to realize about the sound forms of vowels and then I went on to the study of consonants.

"These sounds had not been corrected and polished for me by my training in singing so that my work on them proved to be complicated. In his book *The Expressive Word* S. M. Volkonski says, 'If vowels are a river and consonants are the banks, it is necessary to reinforce the latter lest there be floods!'

"In addition to this directing function consonants possess qualities of sonority.

"The most sonorous of them are *M, N, L, R, V, Z, N, G, TH* (voiced); and there are the stop consonants *B, D, G, W*.

"It was with these that I began my research.

"In these sounds you clearly distinguish which tones are almost those of vowels. The difference lies only in that they do not come out unimpeded, but are held in by pressures at various points, which give them their peculiar colouring. When the pressure which has blocked the tonal accumulation breaks, the sound rushes out. An example of this is the letter *B*: the accumulated booming is held in by your closed lips, which give it its character. With the stop removed an explosion occurs and the sound issues forth freely. There is a genuine basis for calling such sounds stop consonants.

"In the pronunciation of a *B* the explosion takes place immediately and abruptly, the accumulated breath and voice comes out instantly and rapidly. In pronouncing the consonants *M*, *N*, and *L* the same process occurs in modified, more delicate form, with a slight delay when the lips are opened (for the *M*) or the tongue touches the gums of the upper teeth (for the *N* and *L*).

"There are other consonants which do not have tone but are drawn out. This group includes the surds, the sounds of *F* and *S*.

"In addition there are, as you know, the explosive consonants *P*, *T*, *K*. They drop abruptly, like the blows of a hammer. But they also push out the vowel sounds that are behind them.

"When these sounds are combined to create syllables, words and phrases, their vocal form, naturally, becomes more capacious so that we can pack more content into it. Pronounce, for instance, the first two letters of the alphabet *A* and *B* together but in reverse."

Good heavens, I thought to myself, do we have to begin all over again to learn the alphabet? We must be going through our second childhood, the artistic one this time.

BaBaBa . . . we all started off in a chorus like a herd of sheep.

"See here," said Tortsov cutting us off short. "I must have a different sound, open, distinct, broad—Ba-a-a—one that will convey surprise, joy, buoyant greeting, something to make my heart beat with greater strength and gaiety. Listen: Ba. You feel how way down inside me a booming *B* has come to life, how my lips can hardly stem the force of the sound, how the obstacle is broken through and from my opened lips, as from outstretched arms or the doors of an hospitable home, there emerges to meet you, like a host greeting a dear guest, a broad, generous *A*, exuding welcoming spirit. If you were to reproduce my exclamation on paper you would put down something like this: g-m-B-A-a. Don't you get from this exclamation a piece of me which has flown out towards you along with the joyous sound?

"And now here is the same *B A* syllable, but in an entirely different character."

Tortsov pronounced the sounds in a gloomy, dull, depressed way. This time the boom of the *B* was like an underground rumble presaging an earthquake. His lips did not open like a welcome; they parted slowly, almost as if in perplexity. Even the *A* sound was not joyous, as it was the first time; it came out dully, without resonance, almost as if it had fallen back without achieving liberation. In its stead there issued from his lips a slightly rustling breath, like a vapour from a large open vessel.

"There is a host of variations you can invent for this syllable of the two letters *B A* and in each of them there will be manifest a small bit drawn from a human soul. Sounds and syllables like this have life on the stage, but those which produce a wilted, inanimate, mechanical pronunciation are like corpses, they suggest not life but the grave.

"Now try developing the syllable to include three letters: bar, ban, bat, bag. With each additional letter the mood changes, each new consonant attracts new little bits of our being from out of this or that recess of our inner selves. If the number of letters is now increased to make two syllables the capacity for emotional expression is again enlarged: Baba, babu, bana, banu, balu, bali, barbar, banyan, batman, bagrag. . . ."

4

We went over the sounds with which we ended the last class with Tortsov and then began to invent our own. It was probably the first time in my life that I really listened to the sounds of letters. I grasped how imperfect they were in our mouths and how full they were in Tortsov's. He was like a phonetics gourmet, enjoying the aroma of each syllable and sound.

The whole room was filled with a variety of noises, wrestling with each other, upsetting each other, but we did not achieve any resonance for all our ardent zeal. In contrast to our dull croaking of vowels and barking of consonants, Tortsov's singing vowels and resounding consonants seemed so bright, sonorous, vibrating through all parts of the room.

How simple and yet how difficult this problem is, I thought to myself. The simpler and more natural it is, the harder it seems.

I watched Tortsov's face. It was beaming like the face of a man who finds sounds delectable and enjoys their beauty. Then I looked at my fellow students and I all but laughed out loud to see their gloomy, unbending facial expressions, bordering on ridiculous grimaces.

The sounds which Tortsov produced gave pleasure both to him and to us, who heard him. Whereas the harsh and grating noises which we forced out of ourselves caused nothing but great distress to us and our listeners.

Tortsov was now happily in the saddle and riding a pet hobby, he revelled in syllables which he joined into words with which we were familiar, or which he made up. Out of these words he made up phrases, he spoke a kind of monologue, then he went back to individual sounds and syllables building them once more into words.

While he was relishing the sounds I kept my eyes on his lips. They made me think of the carefully adjusted valves of a brass wind instrument; as they opened or closed no air was lost in any cracks. Thanks to this mathematically precise structure the sounds he produced were exceptionally clear cut and pure. With an instrument of speech as perfect as the one Tortsov had worked out for himself, the articulation of the lips operates with incredible lightness, speed and accuracy.

This is not true of my own. My lips, like the valves in a cheaply and badly made instrument, do not close with sufficient firmness. They let air escape, they are poorly adjusted. As a consequence my consonants do not have the requisite clarity and purity.

The articulation of my lips is so poorly developed and so far from any standard of virtuosity, that it does not even admit of rapid speech. Syllables and words run into, tumble and sprawl over one another, like the eroding bank of a stream. This results in the constant overflow of vowels and the tangling up of the tongue.

"The famous singer and teacher, Pauline Viardot," Tortsov said, "used to tell her pupils that they must sing with the front of the lips.

"Therefore work hard at the development of your articulation of lips, tongue and all the parts which contribute to the production of well cut and shaped consonants.

"I shall not enter here into the details of this work. You will have your drill for this."

5

To-day Tortsov came into class with a lady on his arm, Madame Zarembo. They stood side by side in the middle of the room, with a bright smile on their faces.

"Congratulate us," announced Tortsov, "we have formed . . . an alliance."

The students naturally thought he was speaking of marriage. Then he went on:

"From now on Madame Zarembo is going to help place your voices with relation to vowels and consonants. And I, or someone in my stead, will simultaneously correct your pronunciation.

"Vowels will not require my interference because singing will naturally set them right. But consonants must be worked on both in singing and speech.

"Unfortunately there are those vocalists who have little interest in words in general and consonants in particular. And there are also teachers of diction who do not always have a very clear grasp of tone production. Consequently singers' voices are often properly placed for vowels and improperly for consonants, whereas in the products of diction teachers the contrary may be true with the consonants over pronounced and the vowels slighted.

"Under such circumstances lessons in singing and enunciation can simultaneously do both good and harm. Such a situation is not normal and the blame for it can often be laid to regrettable prejudice. The fact is that the work of voice placing consists primarily in the development of breathing and the vibration of the sustained notes. It is often held that only vowels can be sustained. But do not some consonants also possess this quality? Why should they not be developed to be as vibrant as the vowels?

"How good it would be if the teachers of singing simultaneously taught diction, and teachers of diction taught singing! But since this is impossible let us have specialists in the two fields working with each other.

"So Madame Zarembo and I decided to try an experiment.

"I am unwilling to countenance the usual theatrical declamatory intoning. That can be left to those whose voices do not of their own accord sing.

"To make them resounding these persons are obliged to resort to vocal twists and tricks, to theatrical, declamatory pyrotechnics. For example, to make an impression of solemnity they drop their voice down and down in intervals of seconds. Or, to relieve monotony they screech individual notes out an octave higher, but the rest of the time, because they possess such a narrow diapason, they pound along in a semi-monotone.

"If these actors would let the sounds sing for themselves would they need to resort to such devious methods?

"Yet good voices in conversational speech are rare. If one does meet them they often lack power and range. Without range a voice cannot possibly project the full life of a human being.

"When Tommaso Salvini, the great Italian actor, was

asked what one must have to be a tragedian he replied: 'Voice, voice, and more voice!' For the time being I cannot explain and you cannot yet grasp in full measure the implications of that point made by Salvini and many others. You will only comprehend with your feelings as well as your mind the essential meaning of these words in your own practice, your own experience. When you sense the possibilities opened up to you by a well-placed voice, capable of exercising its naturally predestined functions, the saying of Salvini will reveal to you its deep significance."

6

"To be 'in good voice' is a blessing not only to a prima donna but also to the dramatic artist. To have the feeling that you have the power to direct your sounds, command their obedience, know that they will forcibly convey the minutest details, modulations, shadings of your creativeness!

" 'Not in good voice'—what a torture that is for singer and actor! To feel that you do not control your sounds, that they will not reach the hall packed with listeners! Not to be able to express what your inner creative being dictates to you so vividly and so profoundly. Only the artist himself knows these tortures. Only he can tell what has been finally forged in the furnace of his inner being, and how it must be conveyed by voice and word. If his voice cracks the actor is shamed because what he has created inside himself is mutilated in its external form.

"There are actors whose normal state is not 'in voice'. As a result they speak hoarsely, thereby deforming what they are conveying. Yet their souls are meanwhile full of beautiful music. Imagine a mute conveying his tender, poetic feelings to a beloved woman. Instead of a voice he has a repulsive, rasping bark. He deforms the thing that is beautiful and dear within him. This deforming puts him into a state of despair. The same is true of an actor capable of fine feelings but possessing a poor vocal apparatus.

"It also happens frequently that an actor may be endowed by nature with a voice of lovely timbre, flexible in powers of expression yet insignificant in volume so that it cannot be heard beyond the fifth row in the orchestra. Those in the very front row can manage to enjoy the enchanting timbre of his sounds, his expressive diction and beautifully developed speech. But what of those in the rows farther back? That part of the audience is doomed to boredom. They begin to cough, no one can hear anything and the actor can scarcely continue. He is obliged to force his beautiful voice and this violence does harm not only to his sounds, his pronunciation, his diction, but also to emotional experience in his part.

"Consider too those with voices which are easily audible throughout the theatre in the highest or lowest registers but absolutely non-existent in the middle register. Some of these are tempted to rise until they are strained and squeak, the others sink until they rumble around in the depths. Any forcing ruins the timbre of a voice and a range of five notes restricts all expressiveness.

"Another distressing thing is an actor's voice excellent in all other respects, with volume, flexibility, expressiveness, capable of conveying all the shadings and intricacies of the inner pattern of a role, yet still suffering from one vital shortcoming: the timbre is disagreeable. If the ears and hearts of the public are closed to him, of what avail is the volume, flexibility and expressiveness of his voice?

"It can happen that these deficiencies are not subject to remedy, because of some inherent idiosyncrasy, or because of some vocal defect due to illness. Most frequently, however, the shortcomings I have mentioned can be corrected by the proper placing of sounds, the getting rid of pressures, tensions, forcing, wrong breathing and articulation of the lips or, finally they can be cured if they have been caused by illness.

"The conclusion to be reached is that even a good natural voice should be developed not only for singing but also for speech.

"What is the work to be? Is it the same as that required for the opera, or does the théatre make quite different demands?

"Some assert that they are quite different. For conversational purposes one must have open sounds but, and here I speak from experience, such broadness of voice tends to become vulgar, colourless, diffuse and above all it frequently mounts in tone—all of which is detrimental to speech on the stage.

"What nonsense, protest others. In conversation sounds should be condensed and closed.

"Yet my experience has been that this leads to a constrained, muffled voice with a small range. It sounds as though it were in a barrel, instead of flying out the sounds drop to the ground at the very feet of the speaker.

"What then should we do?

"Instead of answering this I shall tell you about my own work on sounds and diction in the course of my acting career.

"When I was young I prepared myself to be an opera singer," Tortsov began his story.

"Thanks to this I have a certain knowledge of the usual methods of placing the breath and sound for purposes of singing. I do not need it for singing itself but to help me search out the best methods for evolving a natural, beautiful, pregnant speech. Its function is to convey through words either the exalted feelings in the tragic style or the simple, intimate, gracious speech of drama and comedy. My research has been forwarded by the circumstance of my having worked a great deal these last years in the field of opera. Coming into contact with singers, I have talked with them on the subject of vocal art, I have listened to the sounds of well-placed voices, I have met with the most varied assortment of timbres, learned to distinguish between throat, nose, head, chest, occipital, laryngeal and other shadings of tone. All this has registered on my aural memory. But the main thing is that I came to understand the advantage of voices placed 'in the mask', where the hard palate, nasal cavities, antrims and other chambers of resonance are situated.

"The singers said to me: 'A sound which is laid against the teeth or is driven against the bone, that is, the skull, acquires a ring and power,' sounds which, by contrast, fall against the soft parts of the palate or the glottis, vibrate as though muffled with cotton.

"Another singer said to me: 'I place my sounds when I sing exactly the way a sick or sleeping person does when he sighs, with a closed mouth. By thus directing the sound to the front of my face, into the nasal cavity, I open my mouth and continue to make the moo-ing sound as before. But now the previous sigh turns into a sound, freely emitted and resonant as it detonates against the nasal cavities and other sounding boards of the facial mask.'

"I have tried out all these methods in my own experience so that I might discover the character of the sound of which I have been dreaming."

7

"Accidental occurrences also helped guide me along the way. One example of this was my acquaintance while abroad with a famous Italian singer. One day he was under the impression that his voice was not properly vibrant and that he would be unable to sing in his concert that evening. The poor fellow begged me to go along with him and show him how to act in case things went wrong. His hands were icy, his face was pale, he was distraught as he stepped on to the concert platform and began to sing magnificently. After the first number he came into the wings and executed an entrechat for sheer joy, singing under his breath:

" 'It arrived, it arrived, it arrived!'

" 'What was it that arrived?' I asked in astonishment.

" 'It—the note!' he repeated as he picked up the music for his next number.

" 'Where did it arrive?' I was still mystified.

" 'It arrived here,' said the singer, pointing to the forefront of his face, his nose, his lips.

"On another occasion I chanced to be present at a concert given by the pupils of a well-known singing teacher, and to sit next to her. This gave me the opportunity to witness at close range her excitement over her charges. The old lady kept clutching my arm, or nervously nudging me with her elbow or knee, whenever one of them did something amiss. Meantime she kept repeating with anguish the words:

" 'It's gone, gone,' or else joyously whispering: 'It's come, it's come!'

" 'What has gone where?' I asked in bewilderment.
" 'The note has gone into the back of his head,' she said in a frightened voice in my ear, or else she repeated happily:

" 'It's come, it's come back to his mouth' (she meant the front of his face, the mask).

"I remembered these two incidents and the words 'it's come, it's gone . . . into the mask, into the back of his head,' and tried to find out why it was so terrifying to singers when the note disappears into the back of their heads, or why such cause for rejoicing when it comes forward into the facial mask.

"To ferret this out, I had to work on singing. But as I feared to disturb the other people living in my home I practiced in a low voice and with my mouth closed. This tact on my part bore abundant fruit. It turned out that at first when one is placing a sound it is best to hum softly until one finds the right support for the voice.

"In the beginning I held only one, two, or three notes in the middle register, basing them on the various resonant parts of my facial mask which I could feel out inside it. At times it seemed as though the sound had reached the very spot it should reach, and at others I realized that it had 'gone'.

"Finally after a long period of exercises I established a way of placing two or three notes where they seemed to me to sound quite differently—they were full, compact, ringing, all qualities I had noticed in myself before. But I did not stop there. I decided to bring the sound out into the open in such a way that the very end of my nose would quiver with the vibrations from it.

"I was able to do this except that then my voice became quite nasal. This obliged me to undertake a whole new series of exercises in order to rid it of the nasal effect. I worked on it for a long time, although in the end the secret of the trouble turned out to be very simple. All that had to be done was to remove a small, scarcely perceptible tension in the inner part of the nasal cavity where I was able to sense a slight pressure.

"At last I was able to free myself of that pressure. The notes would come out and be even more powerful than before, but the voice was not as agreeable in timbre as I wished. It still bore traces of an undesirable preliminary sound of which I could not rid myself. Stubbornly I refused to put the tone back and down in my throat, in the hope that in time I should conquer this fresh obstacle.

"In the next stage of my search I attempted to increase the range I had fixed for my exercises. To my astonishment the middle notes, as well as those in the higher and lower registers sounded beautiful of their own accord and equalled in character the first ones I had worked out.

"So, gradually, I checked over and smoothed out the discrepancies among the naturally open notes of my range. The next task was to work on the most difficult of all, the borderline, highest notes, which, as everyone knows, require an artificially placed, closed tone.

" 'If you are looking for something, don't go sit on the seashore and expect it to come and find you; you must search, search, search with all the stubbornness in you!' That is why I used every free moment at home to 'moo', feeling out new resonances, new points of support, constantly adapting myself to them.

"During the period of searching I accidentally noticed that whenever I was trying to bring the sounds forward into my facial mask I tipped my head forward and dropped my chin. This position facilitated the emission of the sound as far forward as possible. Many singers recognize this method and approve of it.

"In this way I worked out a whole scale of high top notes. At first this was accomplished only with my mouth closed, by mooing them and not with real voice and an open mouth.

"Spring came. My family moved to the country and I remained alone in the apartment. This made it possible for me to do my mooing exercises now with an open as well as a closed mouth. The first day after the family left I came home to dinner, as usual stretched myself out on a divan and began, as had been my habit, to 'moo'. For the first time, after an interval of a whole year, I risked opening my mouth on a note well-placed with it shut.

"What was my astonishment when suddenly, most unexpectedly, out of my nose and mouth there floated a long-since matured tone, one I had never known before yet had always dreamed of, a tone I had heard in singers and had long been seeking to produce myself.

"When I increased my voice it was stronger and more substantial. I had never known myself to be capable of such a tone. It seemed as though some miracle had taken place in me. I was so carried away I sang all evening and my voice not only did not tire, it sounded better all the time.

"It used to be, before I did these systematic exercises, that I would get hoarse from singing loud and long. Now, by contrast, this seemed to have a beneficial, cleansing effect on my throat.

"There was still another pleasant surprise in store for me: I was able to produce notes which up to now had not been within my range. New colouring appeared in my voice, a different timbre which seemed to me to be better, finer, more velvety than before.

"How had all this come about of its own accord? It was clear that with the help of the low mooing sounds it had been possible not only to develop a tone but also to equalize all vowel sounds. This is so important.

"With this newly placed voice I had developed, the open sounds of the vowels were all directed to the same spot, in the upper hard palate at the very roots of the teeth and they reverberated from there into the nasal cavities in the forefront of the facial mask.

"Later tests showed that the higher the voice went, moving into the artificially closed note range, the farther forward the points of support moved up into the nasal cavities.

"Besides this I noticed that at the same time as my naturally open notes supported themselves against my hard palate and reverberated in the nasal cavities, the closed notes, supported in the nasal cavities reverberated against my hard palate.

"For evenings on end I sang away in my deserted apartment, enchanted with my new voice. But it was not long before my self-satisfaction was punctured. At an opera rehearsal I heard a well-known conductor criticize a singer because he pushed his tones too far forward and produced, as a result, a kind of gypsy twang.

"This incident destroyed the position I had thought so solid under my feet. It was true that I used to notice that unpleasant nasal quality in my own voice when it was placed in the forefront of my facial mask.

"So a fresh search had to be undertaken.

"Without abandoning my discoveries I began to explore my head for new reverberant surfaces at every point of my hard palate, soft palate, the top and even the back of my head, which I had been taught to be so afraid of, and everywhere I found new sounding boards. Each one contributed in some degree or other and added new colourings to enhance the tone. And incidentally I learned to control the 'gypsy twang'.

"These tests convinced me that the technique of singing is far more complex and subtle than I had thought, and that the secret of the art is not contained only in the mask.

"There was one other secret I was fortunate enough to uncover. In the singing classes I attended I was struck by the teacher's frequent exhortations to the pupils working on high notes: 'Yawn!' he would say.

"It appeared that in order to release tension on a high note the throat and jaw must be put in exactly the same position as when one yawns. When this occurs the throat naturally spreads and the undesirable tension disappears. Thanks to this new secret my upper notes filled out, the pressure was relieved and they acquired a ring to their tone. This made me very happy."

8

At our very next lesson Tortsov continued the story of his research:

"As a result of the various attempts I have described I succeeded in achieving a voice which was correctly placed for vowels. I could do my vocalizing on them and my voice sounded even, strong and full in all registers.

"From that I started on songs but, to my surprise, they all turned into vocalizing exercises because I was singing only the vowels.

"The consonants were not only left without sound, they also impeded my singing with their dry clatter. It was then that I remembered S. M. Volkonski's aphorism to the effect that 'Vowels are rivers, consonants their banks'. That was why my singing with its shaky consonants was like a river without banks overflowing into marshy depths that sucked in and drowned the words.

"After that my attention was centred only on consonants. I watched the handling of them in myself and in others, I listened to singers in operas and concerts. What did I learn? It appeared that even the best of them experienced what had happened to me. Their arias and songs could turn into sheer vocalizing because of the limpness of consonants, not fully or else carelessly produced.

"I realized even more forcibly than ever what my problem was after I heard that the voice of a certain famous Italian baritone sounded weak when he did his vocalizations on vowels, and it was only when he added consonants that the volume increased tenfold. I tried to prove this by my own experience, but for a long time the desired results were not forthcoming.

"More than that, the attempt convinced me that my consonants, whether separately or in combination with vowels, had no tone in them. It cost me a tremendous amount of work to sound absolutely every letter.

"I spent my evenings practising various sounds or singing them. Nor did I have a successful time with all of them. I was particularly unsuccessful with the sibilant and 'roaring' sounds. Evidently there was an innate defect in me to which I was obliged to adapt myself.

"The first thing to be learned was the proper position of mouth, lips and tongue for the correct creation of consonant sounds.

"For this purpose I enlisted the help of one of my students who possessed an excellent natural diction.

"He proved to be a very patient fellow. This fact enabled me to watch his mouth for hours on end, making a note of what he did with his lips, his tongue, when he pronounced vowels that I had recognized as incorrect.

"I realized, of course, that there could never be any question of two people speaking in an identical manner. Each one is bound to adapt his speech in one way or another to his peculiar gifts.

"Nevertheless I did try to carry over to my own enunciation what I had noted in that of my patient student. But there is a limit to all endurance, and he made various excuses for not coming to me any more. This forced me to turn to an experienced diction teacher for instruction, with whom I made new advances.

"I did not have time to enjoy this success before I was again disappointed. What happened was that the opera students with whom I had been working became the target for the harshest kind of criticism on the part of other singers and musicians, who claimed that in their emphasis on consonants they produced not one but several each time. They were right. As a result the sounding of the consonants detracted from the vowels, and the whole enunciation became absurd.

"I had been so absorbed in singing that I forgot the principal object of my search, speech on the stage and methods of declaiming.

"Recalling what I was looking for I tried to speak the way I had learned to sing. To my surprise the sounds slipped into the back of my head and I was utterly unable to drag them forward to my mask. When finally I did learn to use the mask in speaking my speech became quite unnatural.

"What could this mean? I kept asking myself in bewilderment. Evidently one must not speak the way one sings. No wonder professional singers try always to sing differently from the way they speak.

"My questions on this subject brought out the fact that many vocalists do this so as not to wear out the timbre of their singing tone by use in ordinary speech.

"Yet for us actors, I decided, this is a bad precaution since our very purpose in singing is to enable us to speak with timbre in our voices.

"I was hard at work over this question when a famous foreign actor, celebrated for his diction and the emotional impact of his voice said to me, 'Once your voice is properly placed you should speak exactly the way you sing.'

"After that my experiments acquired a definite direction and moved ahead at high speed. Singing alternated with speech; I would sing for fifteen minutes, speak for the same length of time; then sing again and speak again. I continued this practice for a long time, but without the desired results.

"This was not surprising, I concluded, because what could these few hours of proper speech do for me in contrast to the many hours of incorrect speech? Correct speech had to be put into constant use, formed into a habit, introduced into my own life, made second nature.

"Your lessons in singing are given you students not merely as exercises to place voices for that particular hour. During the class you are supposed to learn the things that are to be practiced first under the eye of an experienced coach and then independently, at home and everywhere else you go during the day.

"Until this new method has completely possessed us we cannot consider that we have really assimilated it. We must be constantly on guard to see that we speak correctly and beautifully at all times, in or out of the theatre. That is the only condition under which we can make it second nature, so that we do not have to distract our attention to our diction when we are about to step on the stage.

"If the person who is to play Hamlet is obliged as he enters his scenes to think about his deficiencies in voice and speech, there is little likelihood of his being able to carry out his main creative undertaking. Therefore I advise you to fulfil once and for all the elementary requirements of diction and sound. As for the subtleties of the art of speech, which will enable you to convey with skill and beauty all the intangible shadings of thoughts and feelings—that is something you will have to work on all your life.

"As you have noticed, I was continuing my search long after my student days were over. It was not at all easy for me to accomplish all this, but I did as much as I could for as long as my attention held out.

"There were periods when I watched my voice all of the time. I turned my days into one continuous lesson and in that way was able to shake off incorrect speech habits.

"In the end I did feel that a change came about in my ordinary way of speaking. There were certain individual sounds that came off well, even whole phrases, and I realized just then that I was applying to my conversational speech the things I had learned in singing. I spoke just as I sang.

The disappointing part of it was that this happened only at brief intervals because my sounds tended always to recede to the soft surfaces of my palate and throat.

"Up to the present this state of things still obtains. I am not sure that I shall succeed in keeping my speaking voice as flexible as my singing one. Obviously I shall be obliged to set it aright by means of preliminary exercises just before a rehearsal or a performance.

"Nevertheless there could be no doubt about the general success I had achieved. I learned to carry my voice forward into the mask at will, quickly and easily at any time, not only when I sang but when I spoke.

"The principal result of my work, however, was that in speech I acquired *the same unbroken line of sound as I had evolved in singing and without which there can be no true art of the word.*

"This is what I had been searching for so long, what I had dreamed of. It is what lends a quality of beauty and music not only to common conversational speech but also and especially to elevated poetry.

"I had learned in my own practise that this unbroken line emerges only when the vowels and the consonants ring of their own accord the way they do in singing. If only the vowel sounds are sustained, and the consonants merely bang along after them, all one gets is a chasm, a break, a vacuum; instead of an unbroken line one has sound shreds. I soon realized that not only the stop consonants but the others too —the sibilant, the whistling, the tinkling, the hushing and hawking, the raucous consonants must also participate in and contribute their reverberations and sounds to the creation of the unbroken line.

"Now my conversational speech sings, hums, buzzes, or even roars, as it builds a constant line, and changes the tones and colours of its sounds according to the vowels and the vibrating or sibilant consonants.

"At the end of this period of work which I have described to you at length, I had not yet reached the point of acquiring a sense of words, or a sense of phrase, but there was no doubt that I could distinguish among the sounds of syllables.

"There are specialists in this field who will not hesitate to criticize loud and long the path I pursued in my researches and the results I achieved. Let them do it. My method has been taken from practice, from actual experience and my results are available for investigation.

"This sort of criticism will help stir up the whole question of how to place a voice for the stage and the methods of teaching it, as well as the question of correct diction and the production of sounds, syllables and words.

"After what I told you at our last lesson I believe you can be considered sufficiently prepared to begin responsible work on sound placing, on diction for singing and stage speech.

"It is necessary to make a start on this work now while you are still in school.

"An actor, when he appears on the stage, should be fully armed and his voice is an important item in his creative implementation. Moreover when you become professional actors a false self esteem may prevent you from working like a pupil who is learning his alphabet. So make the most of your youth and your years of schooling. If you do not carry out this training now you will not do so in the future, and at all points in your creative career on the stage the lack of it will act as a brake on your work. Your voice will be a powerful hindrance to you and not of any help. 'My voice—is my fortune,' said one famous actor at a dinner in his honour, as he plunged his pocket thermometer into his soup, his wine and other liquid refreshments. Out of concern for his voice he felt impelled to watch the temperatures of everything he put in his mouth. This shows how much he cared about one of the greatest gifts of a creative nature—a beautiful, vibrant, expressive and powerful voice."

At this point Rakhmanov introduced us to our new diction teacher. After a slight intermission he and Madame Zarembo gave us their first joint lesson.

I have asked myself whether I shall keep a record of these classes and I think not. Everything said and done is common practice in other schools and conservatories. The only difference is that our diction is corrected on the spot and under the double supervision of both teachers. These corrections are immediately carried into our singing exercises under the direction of the singing teacher. And at the same time the singing strictures are immediately carried over into our conversational speech.

8

INTONATIONS AND PAUSES

IN THE auditorium of the school theatre we found, when we came in to-day, a large placard with the words "Speech on the Stage". As is his custom Tortsov congratulated us on reaching a new phase in our work:

"At our last lesson I explained to you that actors must acquire the feel of vowels and consonants of syllables, get inside them.

"To-day we go on, in the same way, to consider whole words and phrases. Do not expect me to read you a lecture on the subject, that is the job of a specialist. All I shall tell you concerns several aspects of the art of speaking on the stage that I have learned about in my own practical experience. It will help you in your approach to your new studies in the 'laws of speech!'

"Many fine books have been written about these laws and about words. Study them carefully. The most appropriate to the needs of Russian actors is the well worked out book of S. M. Volkonski on *The Expressive Word*. I shall be constantly having recourse to it, I shall quote it and draw examples from it in these introductory lessons on stage speech. An actor should know his own tongue in every particular. Of what use will all the subtleties of emotion be if they are expressed in poor speech? A first-class musician should never play on an instrument out of tune. In this field of speech we need science but we must be intelligent and forehanded about acquiring it. There is no point in filling our heads with a lot of new ideas and rushing on the stage to exploit them before we have learned the elementary rules. That kind of a student will lose his head, he will either forget his science or think about it to the exclusion of everything else. Science can help art only when they support and complement each other."

Tortsov reflected for a moment and then went on:

"You have often heard me say that each person who goes on to the stage has to re-train himself from the beginning: to see, walk, move about, hold intercourse with people and, finally, to speak. The vast majority of people make use of poor, vulgar ways of speaking in ordinary life, but they are not aware of this because they are accustomed to these defects in themselves and in others. I do not say that you are an exception to this rule. Therefore, before you begin your regular speech work it is absolutely necessary to be made aware of the deficiencies in your speech so that you can break yourselves permanently of the habit, widespread among actors, of giving their own incorrect everyday speech as an excuse for the slovenly ways of speaking on the stage.

"Words and the way they are spoken show up much more on the stage than in ordinary life. In most theatres actors are required to repeat the text half-way decently. Even this is done in a slipshod, routine way.

"There are many reasons for this and the first of them is that in ordinary life one says what one is obliged to, or what one desires to, for a purpose, to accomplish an end, because of necessity or, actually, for the sake of some real, fruitful, pointed verbal action. It even happens rather frequently that even when one chatters along without paying much attention to the words, one is still using them for a reason: to pass the time quickly, to distract the attention and so on.

"On the stage it is different. There we speak the text of another, the author's, and often it is at variance with our needs and desires.

"Moreover in ordinary life we talk about things we actually see or have in our minds, things that actually exist. On the stage we have to talk about things we do not see, feel, think about for ourselves but in the imaginary persons of our parts.

"In ordinary life we know how to listen, because we are interested in or need to hear something. On the stage, in most cases, all we do is make a pretence of attentive listening. We do not feel any practical necessity to penetrate the thoughts and words of our stage partner. We have to oblige ourselves to do it. And that forcing ends in over-acting, routine, clichés.

"There are other distressing circumstances too, which tend to kill lively human reactions. The lines, repeated so often in rehearsals and numerous performances, are parroted. The inner content of the text evaporates, all that is left is mechanical sound. In order to earn the right to be on the stage the actors have to be doing something. One of the things they do to fill up the blank spaces inside their parts is to engage in automatic repetition of their lines.

"The consequence of this is that actors acquire a habit of mechanical speech on the stage, the thoughtless parrot-like pronunciation of lines learned by heart without any regard for their inner essence. The more rein they give to this habit, the keener their mechanical memory, the more stubborn the habit of such prattle becomes. And gradually we see the development of a specifically stereotyped kind of stage speech.

"In ordinary life we also meet with mechanical expressions such as: 'How do you do?' 'Pretty well, thank you.' Or 'Good-bye. Best of luck!'

"What is a person thinking of while he is saying those automatic words? He is subject neither to the thought nor the feeling essentially contained in them. They just pop out of us while we are absorbed by entirely different interests. We see the same thing in school. While a pupil is reciting something he has learned by rote he is often thinking about his own affairs and the mark the teacher will give him. Actors are prone to the same habits.

"To such actors the feelings and ideas of a part are step-children. In the beginning, when they first read the play the words, both their own lines and those of the others who play opposite them, seem interesting, new; they have some point. But after they have heard them kicked around at rehearsal, the words lose all essential meaning. They do not exist in the hearts or even in the consciousness of the actors, but only in the muscles of their tongues. By then it makes little difference to him what his or anyone else's lines are. The only important thing is to keep going, never to stop in his tracks.

"How senseless it is when an actor on the stage, without even hearing out what is being said to or asked of him, without allowing a thought, even an important one, to be fully expressed to him, hurries to break in on his partner's lines. It also happens that the key word in a cue is so skimped that it does not reach the public, so that the sense of the reply to it is entirely lost, the partner has nothing to reply to. There is no use in his asking to have the question repeated because the first actor has no real comprehension of what he was asking in the first place. All these falsifications add up to conventional, cliché acting which kills all belief in the lines spoken and in their living content.

"The situation is worsened of course when actors consciously give an incorrect turn to their lines. We all know that many of them use their lines as a vehicle to exhibit some vocal attributes, diction, manner of recitation, the technique of their voice production. Such actors have no more relation to art than the salesman of musical instruments who brashly demonstrates his wares by pyrotechnical execution, not for the purpose of conveying the intent of the composer, but merely to sell the instrument.

"Actors do the same when they indulge in calculated cadences and technical effects by emphasizing individual letters of syllables, crooning over or bellowing them without any purpose other than to show off their voices, and to make the eardrums of their hearers tingle with pleasant admiration."

2

Tortsov began with a question to-day: What do we mean by subtext? What is it that lies behind and beneath the actual words of a part?

He expressed his answer this way:

"It is the manifest, the inwardly felt expression of a human being in a part, which flows uninterruptedly beneath the words of the text, giving them life and a basis for existing. The subtext is a web of innumerable, varied inner patterns inside a play and a part, woven from 'magic ifs', given circumstances, all sorts of figments of the imagination, inner movements, objects of attention, smaller and greater truths and a belief in them, adaptations, adjustments and other similar elements. It is the subtext that makes us say the words we do in a play.

"All these intentionally intertwined elements are like the individual threads in a cable, they run all through the play and lead to the ultimate super-objective.

"It is only when our feelings reach down into the subtextual stream that the 'through line of action' of a play or a part comes into being. It is made manifest not only by physical movements but also by speech: it is possible to act not only with the body but also with sound, with words.

"What we call the through line as related to action has its equivalent in the subtext, as related to speech.

"It is superfluous to state that a word taken separately and devoid of inner content is nothing but an external name. The text of a part if it is made up of no more than that will be a series of empty sounds.

"Take as an example the word 'love'. For a foreigner it is only a strange combination of letters. It is an empty sound because it is devoid of all the inner connotations which quicken the heart. But let feelings, thoughts, imagination give life to the empty sound and an entirely different attitude is produced, the word becomes significant. Then the sounds 'I love' acquire the power to fire a man with passion and change the course of his whole life.

"The word 'onward' when inwardly coloured by patriotic emotion is capable of leading regiments to sure death. The simplest words, that convey complex thoughts affect our whole outlook on the world. It is not for nothing that the word has become the most concrete expression of man's thought.

"A word can arouse in him all five senses. One needs to do no more than recall the title of a piece of music, the name of a painter, of a dish, of favourite perfumes and so on and one immediately resurrects the auditory and visual images, tastes, smells or tactile sensations suggested by the word.

"It can bring back painful sensations. In *My Life in Art* a story about a toothache caused a toothache in the person who heard it.

"There should never be any soulless or feelingless words used on the stage. Words should no more be divorced from ideas there than from action. On the stage it is the part of the word to arouse all sorts of feelings, desires, thoughts, inner images, visual, auditory and other sensations in the actor, in those playing opposite him and through them together in the audience.

"This suggests that the spoken word, the text of a play is not valuable in and of itself, but is made so by the inner content of the subtext and what is contained in it. This is something we are prone to forget when we step on to the stage.

"We are also inclined to forget that the printed play is not a finished piece of work until it is played on the stage by actors and brought to life by genuine human emotions; the same can be said of a musical score, it is not really a symphony until it is executed by an orchestra of musicians in a concert. As soon as people, either actors or musicians, breathe the life of their own sentiment into the subtext of a piece of writing to be conveyed to an audience, the spiritual well springs, the inner essence is released—the real things which inspired the writing of the play, the poem, the score of music. The whole point of any such creation is in the underlying subtext. Without it the words have no excuse for being presented on the stage. When they are spoken the words come from the author, the subtext from the actor. If this were not so the public would not make the effort of coming to the theatre, they would sit at home and read the printed play.

"Yet it is only on the stage that a drama can be revealed in all its fullness and significance. Only in a performance can we feel the true spirit which animates a play and its subtext—this is recreated, and conveyed by the actors every time the play is given.

"It is up to the actor to compose the music of his feelings to the text of his part and learn how to sing those feelings in words. When we hear the melody of a living soul we then, and only then, can come to a full appreciation of the worth and beauty of the lines and of all that they hold concealed.

"From your earlier work in this school you are familiar with the inner line of a part with its progressive action leading to the super-objective. You know too how these lines are formed to create an inner state in which you live your part, and how you have recourse to the aids of psycho-technique when this does not occur spontaneously.

"This whole process is equally valid and necessary in the relation to the spoken word."

3

"Cloud. . . . War. . . . Vulture. . . . Lilacs. . . ." There was a long interval between one word and the next as they fell in utterly dispassionate tones from Tortsov's lips.

That was his way of starting us off on our lesson to-day.

"What happens inside of you when you absorb these sounds? Take the word 'cloud'—what do you recall, what do you feel, envision as I pronounce it?

To my mind there came a large smoky blot on a clear summer sky.

"Now make this test. What response do you give to the words in your ears, 'Let's go to the station!'"

I saw myself leaving the house, taking a cab, driving through certain streets, crossing avenues and soon found myself inside the railway station. Leo thought of himself as pacing up and down a platform, whereas Sonya's thoughts had already allowed her to flit off to southern climes and visit several resorts.

After each one of us had described his mental pictures to Tortsov his comment was:

"Evidently the two or three words were scarcely out of my mouth before you mentally carried out the suggestion contained in them! How painstakingly you have told to me all the things my little phrase evoked! With what scrupulous care you used sounds and intonations, chose and matched your colours to draw a visual impression for us, to make us see them with your eyes! How much you really wanted to round out your phrases with complete fullness!

"Also, how concerned you were to convey your picture as a true reproduction of the original of the inner image called forth by an imaginary trip to a railway station.

"If you would always go through that normal process on the stage and pronounce your words with such affection, such penetration into their essential meaning you would soon become great actors."

After a pause Tortsov proceeded to repeat the word 'cloud' in many different ways, asking us what sort of cloud he meant. We were more or less successful in our guessing.

How did he convey the image of the cloud? Was it by intimation, facial expression, personal attitude towards the object drawn, his eyes which searched the ceiling for non-existent forms?

"I did it with all those," said Tortsov. "Ask nature, intuition, what else you will, how they convey their visions to others. I do not care, and I even fear, to be too explicit in a field in which I am not competent. We shall therefore not interfere with the work of our subconscious. Let us rather learn to draw our spiritual, organic natures into our creative work. Let us make the vocal factor in a part both sensitive and responsive so that it will help convey our inmost feelings, thoughts, the images in our mind's eye and so on.

"With the aid of words it is not difficult to convey to others some more or less concrete pictures of a 'vulture', 'lilacs', 'cloud'. It is infinitely more difficult to transmit, by means of words, an abstract conception such as 'justice', 'right'. It would be interesting to investigate just what inner process is set in motion when these words are spoken. . . ."

I began to think about the two words and tried to get inside the feelings they evoked in me. At first I was confused, I could not make up my mind where to fix my point of departure.

My mind tried to reason on the theme suggested by the words, to fix its attention on it and penetrate more deeply into their essential meaning. I had the impression of something large, important, light, noble. But all these epithets also lacked definition. Then I recalled various formula phrases indicated by the words 'justice', 'right'.

But a dry formula neither satisfied nor moved me. Slight emotions flashed through me but immediately evaporated. I reached for but could not grasp them.

It was necessary to search out something more tangible, some form in which to frame the abstraction. At this critical point it was my imagination that responded first and began to paint visual images for me.

Yet how was it possible to represent justice or right? By means of a symbol, an allegory, an emblem? My memory ran over all the hackneyed methods of personifying the ideas of right and justice.

I saw the figure of a woman with scales in her hands, an open book of laws with a finger pointing to a paragraph in it.

Yet neither my mind nor my feelings were satisfied. Next

my imagination hurriedly suggested a fresh visual interpretation: a life based on principles of justice and right. This thought was more easily clothed in physical terms than the abstraction had been. Thoughts about real life are more concrete, accessible, palpable. You can see them, and having seen you can feel them. They are more likely to move you, they naturally lead you to the sense of inner experience.

I remembered an incident in my own life, akin to what my imagination had brought to mind and my feeling of what justice means was somewhat satisfied.

When I related to Tortsov the process of my self-observation he drew from it these conclusions:

"Nature has so arranged matters that when we are in verbal communication with others we first see the word on the retina of the mind's eye and then we speak of what we have thus seen. If we are listening to others we first take in through the ear what they are saying and then we make the mental picture of what we have heard.

"To hear is to see what is spoken of, to speak is to draw visual images.

"To an actor a word is not just a sound, it is the evocation of images. So when you are in verbal intercourse on the stage, speak not so much to the ear as to the eye."

4

Tortsov began by asking Paul to recite something, but as he knew nothing by heart, the Director said:

"In that case, go up on the stage and say some sentence or make up a little story such as: I have just been at Ivan Ivanovich's. He is in an awful state; his wife has left him. I was obliged to go to Peter Petrovich's to tell him what had happened and beg him to help me calm the poor fellow."

Paul said the sentences but he did not make a satisfactory impression with them, so Tortsov explained:

"I did not believe a word you said and I did not feel what

it was you wished to convey to me with these words which were not your own.

"But how could you say them sincerely without the background of imaginary circumstances? You had to know and make a mental picture of them first. But you neither know now nor see what those words I gave you about Ivan Ivanovich and Peter Petrovich suggest. You must imagine some basis for the words as a justification for saying them. You must moreover attempt to make for yourself a clear picture of what your imagination suggests.

"When you have filled in all that then the words of another person become your own, the very ones you need, and you will know just who Ivan Ivanovich, deserted by his wife, and Peter Petrovich are, where and how they live, what the relationship between them is. They will then be real people to you. Do not forget to make a careful mental survey of the apartment, the arrangement of the rooms, the furniture, the small objects around the place. You will also make the trip first to Ivan Ivanovich's and then from his home to Peter Petrovich's, from then on back to the place where you will be called upon to tell your story.

"Meantime you must see the streets, along which you travel, the entrances of the houses you go into. In brief you have to invent a whole film of inner pictures, a running subtext consisting of all kinds of settings and circumstances, against which the domestic tragedy of Ivan Ivanovich, of the words given you to speak, can be played out. These inner images will create a mood and that in turn will stir feelings in you. You know that life does all this for you off the stage, but on it you, the actor, have to prepare the circumstances.

"This is not done for the sake of realism, naturalism, per se, but because it is necessary for our own creative natures, our subconscious. For them we must have truth, if only the truth of imagination, in which they can believe, in which they can live. . . ."

After these necessary facsimiles had been invented Paul repeated the phrases he had been given, it seemed to me, to better effect.

But Tortsov was still not satisfied with him and explained that Paul did not have a focal point to which he wished to convey the images inside his mind, and that without this the sentences could not be pronounced so that the person listening would believe in their actuality and inevitability.

To help Paul, Tortsov sent Maria on the stage to act as a focal point, and he said to him:

"See to it that the object of your attention not only hears and understands the meaning of your words, but that she also sees what you see in her mind's eye while you are speaking to her."

Paul, however, did not feel that he was capable of accomplishing that.

"Don't cudgel your brains about this, don't interfere with your own nature, just do what you are asked to. The result is not the important part. The important thing is that you move toward and try to carry out an objective, how you act on or, to be more exact, how you try to act on Maria, on her inner vision, which is what you are after in this particular instance. The important factor is your own inner activity."

Paul proceeded to describe what he felt when he was making the experiment.

"I shall name the characteristic moments in my feelings," he explained. "First, before I could communicate anything to Maria I had to put some order into the material I wanted to convey to her. I had to probe into the essential meaning of what I would say, recall the facts, the given circumstances I was to reproduce. I had to envisage them all first in my own mind. When this was prepared and I came to the point of putting it into terms of physical expression everything seemed to get into a state of fermentation and movement; my mind, feelings, imagination, adjustments, facial expressions, eyes, hands, body—all set themselves to find the right approach to the set objective. It was like the tuning up of a large orchestra. I began to watch myself carefully."

"Yourself? Not Maria?" interrupted Tortsov. "Evidently it was of no consequence to you whether Maria would understand you, feel what underlay the words you spoke, or see with your eyes all that was going on in the life of Ivan Ivanovich! Does this not mean that while you were communicating the words to her you still lacked the natural impulse to make her see the pictures in your mind?

"All this is evidence of lack of action. Besides, if you were really intent on getting your words over to her you would not have recited them like a soliloquy, without looking at her, without adapting yourself to her, as you have just done, and there would have been moments of waiting to see the effect of your words. These last are essential to the person playing opposite you, so that he can absorb the subtext of your mental pictures. It is impossible to take them in all in one gulp. The process is piecemeal: you convey, you pause, your partner absorbs what you conveyed, you continue, you pause again and so on. Of course, as you do this you must have in mind the whole of what you are to convey. To you as author of the subtext this is automatically clear, but to your partner it is all new, it must be decoded and absorbed. This takes a certain time. You did not allow for this, and consequently all these mistakes resulted not in a conversation with another living being, but a monologue, the kind we hear so often in the theatre."

In the end Tortsov succeeded in getting Paul to do what he had asked, he persuaded him to make Maria hear and feel what he had in his mind. Maria, and indeed all the rest of us, understood and really felt to a certain degree what lay behind his words—his subtext. Paul himself was quite thrilled. He insisted that to-day for the first time he had intellectually and emotionally experienced the practical significance of conveying to others his imaginary subtext.

"Now you know what it is to create that illustrative

stream that flows continually beneath the spoken lines of a play," said Tortsov as he concluded the lesson.

5

All the way home Paul talked to me about what he went through in doing the "Ivan Ivanovich Sketch" to-day. Evidently what struck him most was the fact that in exciting someone else about what was in his own mind, he found that the trite words Tortsov had given him to say had, somehow imperceptibly become the very words he had to have for his own purposes.

"You see, unless you tell the fact of Ivan Ivanovich's wife deserting him there is no story," Paul explained. "If there is no story there is nothing on which to base an illustrative subtext. There is no need for you to make a mental picture of any happenings for yourself, or to convey it to anyone else. And the cardinal fact of the sad occurrence in Ivan Ivanovich's life is something you cannot transmit by sending out rays, by gestures, by facial expression. You must have speech!

"That was when I really appreciated those words that had been foisted on me. I came to love them as if they had been my own. I eagerly took hold of them, rolled them around under my tongue, weighed each sound, doted on their every intonation. Now I no longer needed them to reel off a mechanical report, as a vehicle for my voice or technique, but for the active purpose of making my hearer realize the importance of what I was saying.

"And do you know what was most wonderful of all?" he continued in the same lyric strain. "As soon as the words had turned into mine I felt entirely at home on the stage! Where in the world did that sense of serenity and control suddenly come from?

"It was such a wonderful feeling to be able to govern myself, to have earned the right not to hurry, and calmly to make the others wait!

"I planted one word after the other in the consciousness of my 'object' and along with them I conveyed one illuminating connotation after the other.

"You more than anyone else should appreciate the implications and significance of the calm and control I felt to-day because you well know how afraid we both are when we have to pause on the stage. As a matter of fact they weren't really pauses because even when I was silent I never ceased being active."

Paul quite enthused me with his tale. I stopped at his home and then stayed on to dinner.

During dinner his uncle, who as an old actor takes great interest in his nephew's progress, inquired about the work done in class to-day. Paul told him what he had just been explaining to me. His uncle listened, smiled, nodded his head approvingly and added each time:

"That's right! That's right."

At one point he suddenly jumped up and exclaimed:

"There! You hit the nail squarely on the head: Infect your partner! Infect the person you are concentrating on! Insinuate yourself into his very soul, and you will find yourself the more infected for doing so. And if you are infected everyone else will be even more infected. Then the words you speak will be more inciting than ever.

"*Action—real, productive action with a purpose is the all-important factor in creativeness, and consequently in speech as well!*

"To speak is to act. That action sets an objective for us: to instill into others what we see inside ourselves. It is not so important that the other person will see or not the thing you have in mind. Nature and the subconscious may take care of that. Your job is to desire to instill your inner visions in others, and that desire breeds action.

"It is one thing to appear before a good public, reel off a few tra-ta-tas and walk off. It is quite another to go out on the stage and act!

"The one speech is theatrical, the other is human."

6

"When we consider some phenomenon, picture to ourselves some object, some event, call to mind experiences in real or imaginary life, we not only react to them with our feelings, we also pass them in review before our inner eyes," Tortsov said in opening to-day's class.

"Yet in doing this our inner vision must bear a relationship only to the life of the character being played and not to the actor who does the portraying, because unless his own personal life is analogous to that of his part it will not coincide with it.

"That's why, when we are on the stage, our chief concern should be to reflect at all times in our own inner vision the things akin to those which our character would have in his. This inner stream of images, fed by all sorts of fictional inventions, given circumstances, puts life into a role, it gives a basis for everything the character does, his ambitions, thoughts, feelings, and more than that, it is a great help to the actor in fixing his attention on the inner life of his part. It should be used to bolster wavering attention.

"Last time we worked on a brief monologue concerning Ivan Ivanovich and Peter Petrovich," Tortsov went on. "But now let us suppose that all the lines of all the scenes of a whole play are prepared, as they should be, in the same way as we worked up our few words, illustrated by *ifs* and *given circumstances*. In this case the whole text of the play will be accompanied by a subtextual stream of images, like a moving picture constantly thrown on the screen of our inner vision, to guide us as we speak and act on the stage.

"Watch this carefully and describe with the lines of your part this imaginative illustration each time you act the role. Let what you say convey these images and not just words.

"What is the secret of this method I am proposing that you use? It is very simple and clear. In order to speak the essential meaning of a text one must penetrate deep inside it, and feel it deeply too. Yet this is difficult and not always possible to do because, first of all, one of the prime elements in the subtext is the memory of emotions felt, a most evanescent, capricious, elusive and unstable factor. Secondly, one needs a well disciplined power of attention to be able to concentrate on the meaning behind the words.

"Forget entirely about the feelings and put all your attention on the inner images. Study them as carefully and describe them as fully, as penetratingly and vividly as you can.

"Then when you come to act and the words are spoken not for you, not for the public, but for the person playing opposite you, this method will result in much greater stability and power. This objective of carrying over what is in your mind's eye to that of your partner in a scene requires that your actions be executed to the fullest extent; it will rouse your will, and along with the whole trio of inner motive forces, all the elements of the actor's creative spirit.

"Why should we fail to make use of this fortunate quality of visual memory? Once we have established inside ourselves this easily accessible sequence of images, our task of keeping on the right line of the subtext and through line of action is greatly lightened. Moreover, as we go on describing what we see it is the right way to arouse recurrent sensations which are stored away in the emotion memory, and which we need so much in the course of living our parts.

"Therefore, in keeping these inner images before our minds we think about the subtext of our part and we feel it.

"This method is not new to us. We used similar ones when we were working on movement and action. At that time we turned to the more palpable, steady physical actions for help in arousing our unstable emotion memories, and in order to create the unbroken line of a part.

"Now we have recourse to the same method, and for the same purpose we seek the unbroken line of inner images and convey it with words.

"Earlier it was physical actions that served as lures to our feelings when we were engaged in building action, and now it is the inner images which serve as lures to our feelings when we are dealing with words and speech.

"Let this inner film unroll frequently before your mind's eye and, like a painter or a poet, describe what and how you see during each daily performance. During this review you will at all times be aware of what you have to say when you are on the stage. It may well be that each time you repeat the review and tell about it you will do so with certain variations. That is all to the good, the unexpected and the improvised are always the best impetus to creativeness.

"The establishment of this habit requires long, systematic work. On the days when your attention is insufficiently stable, when the line of the subtext in your part threatens to break down, quickly reach out for the concrete objects in your inner vision as you would to a life-belt.

"And here is another advantage it has to offer. As we all know, the lines of a part soon wear out from frequent repetition. But these visual images on the contrary, become stronger and more extensive the oftener they are repeated.

"Imagination does not rest. It is forever adding new touches, details to fill out and enliven this inner moving picture film. So that only good and not harm can result from the frequent reprojection of these images.

"Now you know not only how to create but how to use the illustrated accompaniment of a subtext. More than that, you hold the secret of this method of psycho-technique."

7

"One function then of the spoken word of the stage is to communicate with your partner in a scene by means of an illustrated subtext to our lines or to pass it in review before ourselves," was Tortsov's opening remark at to-day's lesson.

"Let us see whether this function of speech is properly

g to Vasya. "Go up on the stage and
loose."

g, that . . . Icannotgo onlivingif . . .
tayand . . . chaseawaythedark . . . acloud
. youhavegoneaway . . ." Vasya's words
eir usual spurts and unintelligible stops,
into gibberish and poetry into 'prose

derstood a single word yet," said Tortsov,
n, "and I shan't be able to understand any
on making mincemeat of your phrases. There
serious consideration of any subtext here.
ven any text itself. Something slips off your
rarily, without regard to your will, your
or anything else except your supply of breath.
e, before we proceed further, we must put some
e words of your monologue, arrange them in
ups. Only then shall we be able to distinguish
d is related to what which parts belong together
e or whole thought.

vide speech into measures we have to have stops or
auses.

"As you doubtless know, they have simultaneously a
double and contrasting function: *Logical pauses unite words
into groups (or speech measures) and they divide the groups
from one another.*

"Do you realize that a man's fate, and even his very life
may depend on the position of that pause? Take the words:
'Pardon impossible send to Siberia.' How can we understand
the meaning of this order until we know where the logical
pause is placed? Put them in and the sense of the words will
become clear. Either you say: 'Pardon—impossible send to
Siberia,' or 'Pardon impossible—send to Siberia!'

"In the first it is a case for mercy, in the second, exile.

"Now take your monologue and say it over with the
pauses in, and only then shall we be able to understand it."

With Tortsov's help Vasya divided his phrases into groups

of words and then began to say them over, but after the second measure the Director stopped him.

"Between two logical pauses one should pronounce the text in as unified a way as possible, fused almost into a single word. You must not break it up and spit out the fragments the way you do.

"There are, of course, exceptions which force a pause in the middle of a measure. But there are rules for that which we shall come to in time."

"We already know them," argued Grisha. "We know how to read according to signs of punctuation. If you will pardon my saying so, that is taught in primary school."

"If you learned it why don't you speak correctly?" retorted Tortsov. "Moreover, why don't you carry out the exigencies of correct speech to their utmost limit when you are on the stage?

"I should like to see you take a book and pencil more often, divide up what you read into measures of speech. Pound them into your ears, your eyes, your hands.

"Reading in speech measures contains another element of great practical advantage to you. It is an aid to the process of feeling yourself in your part.

"This division into measures and the reading of a text according to it, oblige us to analyze phrases and get at their essence. If we do not do this we cannot know how to say them. This habit of speaking in measures will make your speech more graceful in form, intelligible and profound in content, because it forces you to keep your mind constantly on the essential meaning of what you are saying when you are on the stage. Until you achieve this there is no use either in your attempting to carry out one of the principal functions of the words, which is to convey the illustrated subtext of your monologue, or even in doing the preparatory work of creating this subtext.

"The first work to be done with speech or with words is always to divide into measures, to place the logical pauses where they belong."

8

I was the first one called on to recite to-day. Given the choice of text I decided to recite a few lines from *Othello:*

> *Like to the Pontic sea*
> *Whose icy current and compulsive course*
> *Ne'er feels retiring ebb, but keeps due on*
> *To the Propontic and the Hellespont;*
> *Even so my bloody thoughts, with violent pace*
> *Shall ne'er look back, ne'er ebb to humble love,*
> *Till that a capable and wide revenge*
> *Swallow them up.*

There is no period in the whole piece, and the phrase is so long that I had to hurry to get to the end of it. It seemed to me that I ought to say it in one gulp, without ever stopping even for breath. But, of course, I could not accomplish that.

It was not surprising that I skimped on some of the measures, was quite out of breath and flushed from tension when I finished.

"To avoid in the future what has just happened to you I suggest that the first thing you do is to enlist the help of the logical pause. Divide up the speech into measures because, as you have found, you cannot deliver it all of a piece," was Tortsov's comment when I had finished.

So this is how I distributed the pause (marked with asterisks):

> *Like to the Pontic sea**
> *Whose icy current and compulsive course**
> *Ne'er feels retiring ebb** but keeps due on*
> *To the Propontic and the Hellespont**
> *Even so my bloody thoughts, with violent pace**
> *Shall ne'er look back, ne'er ebb to humble love,**
> *Till that a capable and wide revenge*
> *Swallow them up.*

"That will do for an exercise," agreed Tortsov, and then he made me say this unusually long sentence over and over again in accordance with the pauses I had fixed.

After I had done this he admitted that the speech was no, easier to listen to and understand.

"The only pity is that we still do not feel it," he added. "The main obstacle to that is you. You are in such a hurry you do not give yourself time to get inside of what you are saying, you cannot get around to examining and feeling what lies behind the words. Until you have done this there is nothing more you can accomplish. That is why you must in the first instance get rid of your haste."

"I'd be glad to, but how shall I do it?" I asked, somewhat puzzled.

"I shall show you one way." He thought for a moment and then said:

"You have learned to recite Othello's speech with its logical pauses and word measures. That's good. Now recite it for me according to the punctuation signs."

"Isn't that the same thing?"

"Yes, but it's only half of it. Punctuation signs require special vocal intonations. The period, the comma, exclamation and question marks, and the rest have their own essential connotations which are characteristic of each one. Without these intonations they do not fulfill their functions. Take away from the period its final rounding out drop of the voice and the listener will not realize that the sentence is ended and that nothing more will follow. Take from the question mark its typical phonetic twist, and the listener will not know that a question has been put to him, and to which he is expected to answer.

"In each of these intonations there is a certain effect produced on the listeners, obligating them to do something: the phonetic symbol of a question calls for an answer; the exclamation sign, for sympathy, approval or protest; a colon demands attentive consideration for what follows, and so on. There is great expressiveness in all these intonations. It is these inherent qualities of punctuation signs which can keep you from being in such a hurry. That is why I have stressed them here.

"Now repeat the Othello speech with all the punctuation signs and their inherent patterns."

When I began to recite the monologue I felt as though I were speaking a foreign language. Before I could pronounce a word I felt an impulse to weigh, guess at, to veil whatever it was that caused me to doubt and—I stopped, unable to go on.

"This only goes to prove that you do not know the nature of your own language and, in particular, the nature of punctuation signs. If this were not the case you could easily have carried out your assignment.

"Remember this incident: It should be one more reason for you to realize the necessity of a painstaking study of the laws of speech.

"It appears that for the present the punctuation signs disturb you when you speak. Let us try to make them help rather than hinder you.

"I cannot undertake to demonstrate all the signs of punctuation," Tortsov said, "so I shall experiment with only one of them. If the demonstration succeeds in convincing you of my point you will want to make your own experiments with the other punctuation marks.

"Let me repeat. My object is not to teach you myself but to convince you that you should study the laws of speech.

"For our experiment I shall take the comma, because that is almost the only punctuation sign that comes into the speech you chose from *Othello*.

"Can you recall what you instinctively wanted to do each time you came to a comma?

"First of all you wanted to pause. But also you had a desire to give an upward twist to the sound of the last syllable of the last word before the comma (not putting an accent on it unless that was logically necessary). After that leave the high note hanging in the air for a bit.

"With that twist the sound is carried from below upwards like some object moved from a lower to a higher shelf. This rising melodic line can take on all kinds of twists and go to all kinds of heights: in intervals of thirds, fifths, octaves, with a short steep rise, or a broad, smooth, small swing and so on.

"The remarkable thing about the nature of a comma is that it possesses a miraculous quality. Its curve, almost like the warning lift of a hand, causes listeners to wait patiently for the end of the unfinished sentence. Do you realize how important this is, especially to such a nervous person as you are, or such a spasmodic creature as Vasya? If you would only believe that after the sound curve of the comma your listeners are bound to wait patiently for you to continue and finish the sentence you have begun, then there would be no reason for all your hurry. This will quiet you and make you really love the comma and all it stands for.

"If you only knew the satisfaction, when you are telling a long story or using a long sentence, like the one you just recited, of lifting your phonetic line before a comma and waiting confidently, because you know surely that no one will interrupt or hurry you.

"This temporary transfer of duties and action to someone else ensures your peace of mind while you wait, because the pauses become a matter of necessity to the person to whom you are talking, the same one who earlier seemed to hurry you. Do you agree with me?"

Tortsov wound up his remarks with the very clear cut vocal twist of a question mark and proceeded to wait for our answer. We tried to think what to say and were all excited because we could not find a reply. But he was perfectly calm because the delay was caused by us, not by him.

During the pause Tortsov began to laugh and then explained the reason for this.

"Not long ago I was explaining to a new housemaid where to hang the key to the front door, and I said to her, 'Last night, when I came in, and seeing the key in the lock, . . .'

Then, after letting my voice rise, I forgot what I wanted to say, stopped speaking, and went to my study. A good five minutes passed. I heard a knock at the door. The maid stuck her head into the room, her eyes were full of curiosity and her face had the question written all over it. ' "And seeing the key in the lock . . ." then what?' she asked.

"So you see the rising inflection in front of a comma had maintained its effect for five whole minutes, and demanded the ultimate descent of the sound to the final period of the completed sentence. This demand brooked no obstacles."

In going over what we had done during to-day's lesson Tortsov ventured to prophesy that I would soon cease to fear pauses, because I had learned the secret of how to make others wait for me. When I reach the point beyond this, of learning to use the breaks to increase the clarity and expression of my speech, to enhance and strengthen my communication with others, then I shall not only cease to fear the pauses but I shall begin, on the contrary, to be so fond of them I shall be inclined to over-use them.

9

Tortsov appeared to be in high spirits when he came into class to-day. Then suddenly, without any reason at all, he announced in a quiet, but extremely firm, voice:

"If you do not devote serious attention to your lessons, I shall refuse to work with you!"

We were entirely taken aback. We looked at each other and were preparing to assure him that we all took the greatest interest in his classes. But before we could say a word Tortsov burst out laughing.

"Do you sense what an excellent humour I am in?" he asked. "I am in the best possible humour because I have just been reading in the newspaper an account of the smashing success one of my favourite pupils has achieved. Yet it was sufficient for me to have my voice follow a pattern of intonation calculated to convey something definite, firm, irrevocable, and I was instantly converted, in your minds, into a severe, choleric, snappish old pedagogue!

"There are certain fixed intonations not only for individual words and punctuation marks, but also for whole phrases and sentences.

"They have definite forms based on nature. They have names. For instance the intonation pattern I just used is called the 'swan neck or double bend period.' There is first the rising inflection to the high point where the comma coincides with the logical pause, then after the turn comes a temporary stop before the voice drops abruptly to the bottom of the pattern. Here is a design of what happens."

Tortsov then drew the following lines for us on a piece of paper.

TO YOUR LESSONS,

IF YOU DO NOT DEVOTE YOUR ATTENTION SERIOUSLY

I SHALL REFUSE TO WORK WITH YOU

"This inflection is compulsory.

"There are many other phonetic patterns for a whole phrase, but I shall not demonstrate them to you as I am not teaching you this subject, but merely telling you a little about it.

"Actors must be familiar with all these phonetic patterns, and here is one purpose, among many others, for which they need them.

"When an actor is on the stage it often happens, whether out of embarrassment or for other reasons, that his vocal range involuntarily shrinks and his phonetic patterns lose their line.

"Actors of Russian nationality, for instance, are inclined to speak in a minor key in contrast to the Latins, who prefer the major. Such a characteristic is magnified when they are on the stage. Where a French actor will give a ringing sharp to the key word in a joyous exclamation, a Russian will distribute his intervals in quite another way and, if possible, drop to a flat.

"Where a Frenchman will lend vividness to an intonation by stretching a phrase to the uttermost limit of his vocal gamut, a Russian will be two or three notes below that.

"Where a French actor will drop his voice way down before a period, a Russian will clip off several notes from the bottom and thereby weaken the ultimate definiteness of the period.

"When this petty larceny of sounds is perpetrated in folk-songs it is not noticeable. But when the Russian actor tries it on Molière or Goldoni he is dragging his minor key into the realm of a fully vibrant major. Unless the subconscious is brought into play here an actor will find that his intonation, quite against his will, can become insufficiently varied.

"How then is this defect to be remedied? People who are not aware of the compulsory patterns, called for in a given phrase, or created by the nature of a given word, find themselves faced with an insoluble problem, whereas those who are familiar with them will find the correct intonation, starting from the external phonetic or graphic line and reaching to the inner bases for the patterns and vocal intervals.

"In such cases you should extend the range of your speech from the outside while basing the increased sound intervals of your intonations on an inner justification. They will help you to arrive closer to the truth which you are seeking. If you are sensitive you will be quick to recognize it. To provide a basis for a wider vocal scale and increased intervals of intonation takes a marked degree of temperament.

"So much the better! It will be forthcoming if your feelings respond in lively fashion to the intonations suggested to them from the outside.

"Consequently, if the intonation lets you down, start with an external sound pattern, find a basis for it and then proceed further to a naturally appropriate feeling."

While Tortsov was still speaking his noisy secretary came in and took him out of our class. He said he would return in a few minutes. So we had a little intermission which Grisha spent in airing some of his regular objections. He was disturbed by forceful methods. He claimed they destroyed creative freedom since they obliged an actor to use certain inflections.

Rakhmanov proved quite rightly that what Grisha was calling force is part of the natural quality of language. And he, Rakhmanov, had the habit of considering the fulfilment of natural obligations as a form of highest freedom. What he considers force are the unnatural inflections of the conventional declamatory style which Grisha so stubbornly defends. To back up this opinion he mentioned a small town actress whose whole charm lay in her erratic speech.

"That's her type, you know," Grisha insisted. "If she were taught the laws of speech she simply wouldn't exist."

"And thank goodness for that," was Rakhmanov's retort. "If your actress has to speak incorrectly for a character part, that's all right, let her do it, and I shall applaud her. But unless it is for that sole purpose it is a detriment, not an asset to an actress. To flirt in poor speech is wicked and in bad taste. You tell her for me that she will be twice as adorable if she goes on doing the same things as before, but with good speech. Then her charms will really carry over to the public. They will be more readily conveyed for the reason that they will not be hampered by uneducated speech."

"First we are told we must not talk the way we do in ordinary life, then we are told we must speak in accordance with some law or other. If you will excuse my saying so, we ought to be told definitely what we need for the stage. Does it mean that we must speak differently from the way we do in ordinary life? We have to speak in some special way, is that it?" asked Grisha.

"Yes, yes, that's just it," Rakhmanov said in picking him up. "Not as in ordinary life, but in a special way. On the stage we may not speak in the uneducated way we do in ordinary life."

Tortsov's fussy secretary interrupted the argument. He came in to say that the Director would not come back to-day.

So instead of the regular class Rakhmanov gave us a session of drill.

10

At to-day's lesson Tortsov had me repeat over and over the speech from *Othello* and give satisfactory twists to my voice at every comma.

At first these rising inflections were purely formal, inert. Then one of them suddenly called to my mind a real, a living inflection and I immediately was flooded with a sense of warmth and familiarity.

Encouraged by this I, little by little, scraped up the courage to give all sorts of successful and unsuccessful phonetic turns to the *Othello* lines: short or broad swings, with small or very large rises. And each time I fell into the right pattern new and various emotion memories were stirred within me.

That is where the true, the spontaneous source of natural speech technique lies. The external word, by means of intonation, affects one's emotion, memory, feelings. This was now fixed in my mind.

So I decided to try holding the pauses after the turn of the angle at the comma. This would give me time not only to probe to the depths of the meaning of what took place inside me but also to experience the sensation to the full.

But then a mishap occurred. I was so absorbed in all my feelings, thoughts, tests, that I forgot the text of the speech right in the middle, I lost my bearings and was obliged to stop. Nevertheless Tortsov was beaming.

"That's the thing!" he exclaimed with delight. "All I had to do was make a prediction and you started right off to explore the possibilities of pauses. In fact you converted many of your logical pauses into *psychological pauses*. Now that is a very good thing to do provided only that the psychological pause does not usurp the functions of the logical pause, but rather enhances it. Moreover, it must always serve to carry out the purpose assigned to it. Otherwise a mishap such as you have been involved in, Kostya, is inevitable.

"You will understand this precautionary advice better after I have explained to you the nature of these two types of pauses: whereas the logical pause mechanically shapes the measures, whole phrases of a text and thereby contributes to their intelligibility, the psychological pause adds life to the thoughts, phrases, measures. It helps convey the subtextual content of the words. If speech without the logical pause is unintelligible, without the psychological pause it is lifeless.

"The logical pause is passive, formal, inert, the psychological one is of necessity brimming with activity and rich inner content.

"The logical pause serves our brain, the psychological, our feelings.

"A great actor once said: Let your speech be restrained

and your silence eloquent. The psychological pause is just that: an eloquent silence. It is an extremely important means of communication between people. You have found out for yourself to-day, Kostya, that you could not refrain from using for your creative purposes that pause which speaks for itself. Words are replaced by eyes, facial expression, the sending out of rays, scarcely perceptible movements that carry a hint—all these and many others conscious and unconscious means of communion.

"They all fill out the words. They often act with greater intensity, finesse, are more irresistible in silence than when used in conjunction with words. Their wordless conversation can be no less interesting, substantial and convincing than one carried on verbally.

"The pause often conveys that portion of the subtext which derives not only from our conscious selves, but also from our subconscious and that does not lend itself readily to concrete expression. All these experiences and their manifestations are, as you know, of precious importance to us in our art.

"Do you realize the exalted position of the psychological pause? It is not subject to any laws, and all laws of speech, without exception, are subject to it.

"The psychological pause will boldly step in at places where a logical or grammatical pause seems impossible. Let us suppose, for example, that our company is going on a foreign tour. We are going to take along all our student actors except two. 'Who are they?' Kostya excitedly asks Paul. 'I and . . .' (Here he makes a psychological pause to soften the impending blow or, on the contrary, to heighten a sense of indignation '. . . and . . . you!' Paul replies.

"Everyone knows that the conjunction 'and' does not allow for any pause after it. But the psychological pause makes no bones about breaking such a rule and introducing an illegal break. Moreover the psychological pause has the right to replace the logical one without destroying it.

"For this latter only a very brief, more or less, definite

period of time is set aside. If that time is extended, the most logical pause must quickly be transformed into an active psychological pause, of which the extent is undetermined. This pause has no concern for time. It lasts for as long as is needed to fulfill the purposes of some action or other. It is aimed at the super-objective and through line of action in a play, so it is bound to hold the interest of the public.

"Sometimes whole scenes are fashioned out of psychological pauses. We sometimes call these star part pauses.

"Nevertheless the psychological pause must be carefully protected from the danger of dragging—a process that sets in the instant it no longer serves action with a purpose. Before this happens it must give way to the spoken word again.

"It is unfortunate when the psychological pause dies away into a simple wait, because then a mishap is bound to occur—the pause for the sake of the pause. That produces a blank hole in the fabric of an artistic creation.

"That is exactly what happened to you to-day, Kostya, and why I hastened to explain your mistake so that you will be forewarned against repeating it in the future. Replace logical with psychological pauses to your hearts' content, but do not drag them out for no good reason.

"There is still one other kind of pause in speech. In singing we use the German expression for it: *Luftpause*, pause for air or breath. It is the briefest of rests, just sufficient for a quick intake of breath. It takes no more time than a snap of the fingers. Often a *luftpause* is not even a real break, but only the slightest lag of a second in the tempo of singing or speech and it leaves the line of sound intact.

"In ordinary speech, and especially in rapid speech or patter, this breathing pause is used to set off certain particular words.

"Now you know all the pauses connected with speech on the stage. You are also aware of the general conditions on which they are to be used. The pause is an important element, a real trump, in our technique of speech."

II

"In our last class we made certain important discoveries about pauses. Earlier we went into another important aspect of our speech—intonations," Tortsov began.

"We spoke of this latter too in connection with the nature of punctuation signs. But we have not yet exhausted the subject. It can be of still greater aid to you in your fundamental problem in speech—*exposition in words of the subtext of your role.*

"Actually then you hold not one trump but two in your verbal communion with others in a play: the intonation and the pause. That is a very great deal! With them you can do a tremendous lot, without even having recourse to the spoken word, just by limiting yourself to sounds."

Here Tortsov settled himself comfortably in an armchair, slipped his hands under him, assumed an immobile pose and began to recite with great warmth, first a prose speech, then verses. He spoke in some strange but vibrant tongue. He pronounced unintelligible words with a tremendous swing and fire, his voice rising to heights in some sort of tirade, then he dropped it as low as possible, until he was silent and let his eyes fill out what he had left unsaid in words. All this was done with great inner force, without any shouting. Some of his outbursts were particularly vibrant, well rounded and fully designed, other phrases were scarcely audible, but deeply impregnated with inwardly experienced feelings. At this point he was almost in tears, he had to make a most expressive pause in order to get control of his emotions. Again a turn took place inside him, his voice was stronger once more and he astonished us with his youthful buoyancy. This outburst was suddenly quelled and he changed back to his mood of silent absorption which quite banished his recent gaiety.

He ended his scene with this magnificently emotional interlude of silence. The verses and the prose, as well as the language in which he conveyed them, were all Tortsov's own invention.

"So you see," he concluded, "I talked in a language incomprehensible to you and yet you listened to me with great attentiveness. I sat perfectly motionless, used no motions of any kind, but you never took your eyes off me. I was silent and you made an effort to penetrate the meaning of my silence. No one supplied me with any subtext but I provided my own conceptions, images, thoughts, and sentiments to put under the sounds—everything that it occurred to me would be germane to them. Of course this bond was only very general and unsubstantial. Obviously the impression produced was of the same nature. All this I achieved on the one hand by the use of sounds, and on the other by intonations and pauses. Isn't this really the equivalent of what happens when we enjoy the readings and recitations of foreign actors? Do not they produce great effects, moods, excite the emotions? And we understand nothing of the words spoken by them on the stage.

"Here is another example: Not long ago a friend of mine was going into raptures over the reading by an actor in a recital.

" 'What did he read?' I asked.

" 'I don't know,' answered my friend, 'I could not make out the words.'

"Evidently that actor was able to make an impression with something other than words.

"In what did his secret consist?

"In the fact that a listener is affected not only by the thoughts, impressions, images, connected with the words, but also by the colour tones of the words, the intonations, the silences, which round out what the words left unexpressed.

"*Intonations and pauses in themselves possess the power to produce a powerful emotional effect on the listener.* As proof I submit my recitation to you in an incomprehensible language."

12

After I had repeated the *Othello* speech to-day Tortsov's comment was:

"Now what you say is not only audible and intelligible but also affecting, although not yet to a powerful enough degree."

In an attempt to expand the emotional effect I stepped on the loud pedal, as it were, and in the old theatrical tradition, played passion for its own sake. This, of course, resulted in tension, haste, the blurring of all rhythmic proportions.

"What on earth have you done?" Tortsov clapped his hands to bring me up sharply. "With one sweep you have destroyed your entire work! You have killed the sense, the logic of your words!"

"I was trying to make it livelier, stronger," I said in embarrassed self-defence.

"Don't you know that the power lies in the logic, the coherence of what you are saying? And you destroy it!

"Have you never heard, either on the stage or off it, quite simple speech, shorn of all special vocal emphasis, without rising or falling, without unduly expanded tonal intervals, or intricate phonetic patterns?

"Despite the lack of all these means to emphasis, stripped speech often makes an irresistible impression, thanks to the convincingly clear exposition of thought, to distinctly grouped words and phrases and controlled delivery.

"So for the very sake of the powerful effect you seek you must learn in the first instance to speak logically, coherently, with proper spacing."

I then went back to reciting the lines in their previous form. They were as clean cut but they were also as dry as before. I seemed to feel I was in a vicious circle and did not know how to extricate myself.

"Perhaps you realize now that it is rather too early for

you to be thinking about the strength of your effect. That will evolve of itself out of the conjunction of many conditions and circumstances. These we shall have to search out."

"Where? How?"

"Different actors have different conceptions of effect through speech. Some of them try to find it in physical tension. They clench their fists, they heave, are rooted to the spot, make themselves shake from head to foot, all for the sake of impressing the public. Under that method the voice is pressed out the way I am doing it now, in a horizontal line.

"In our theatre jargon this pressure on the sound for the sake of volume is what we call 'high-tension acting'. Actually it does not produce volume; it leads only to shouting, to hoarseness with a narrowed vocal range.

"Test it out. Use only several notes, in seconds or thirds and say, with all the force you can muster, this short phrase: 'I cannot tolerate it any longer!' "

I did as Tortsov suggested.

"That's too little, make it louder!" he commanded.

I repeated the phrase, forcing my voice as far as I could.

"Louder, louder!" urged Tortsov. "Don't expand your range!"

I did as he ordered. The physical tenseness produced a spasm. My throat contracted, my range shrank to thirds, and I still made no effect of volume.

Using all the strength I could scrape together I found myself obliged, when Tortsov drove me on, simply to shout.

"There's the end result of your 'high-tension' tactics, that is, of the physical production, under forced pressure, of sound in a horizontal line," said Tortsov.

"Now try another, an opposite type of experiment. Relax all the muscles of your vocal apparatus, remove all tension pressure, forget about playing on passions, do not be too concerned about volume. Now say the same phrase over to me, quietly but with your broadest vocal range, and well based inflections. Think up some imaginary circumstances likely to stir your feelings."

The thing that popped into my mind was: if I were a teacher and had a student, like Grisha, who was a half hour late for class for the third time in a row, what would I do to put a stop to such slipshod ways in the future?

On that basis the phrase was easy to say and my voice range naturally expanded.

"Do you see how much more effective your phrase was this time than when you shouted it? Yet you did not need all the labour pains," explained Tortsov.

"Now say the same words to me with an even wider gamut, not on a fifth, as last time, but a whole well-founded octave."

For this purpose I had to invent a new imaginary basis for the phrase. I supposed that despite my categoric demands, my rebukes, warnings, inveighings, Grisha was again late for class, this time not a half hour but a whole hour late. All my measures were exhausted. I now was obliged to take a last, a supreme step.

"I cannot tolerate it any longer! ! !" the phrase ripped out of me. It was not loud because I held myself in, thinking that my emotions were not at their peak.

"There!" exclaimed Tortsov gleefully. "It came out strong, not loud but without any strain. That is what the movement of sound up and down in a vertical direction can do, and without any high tension voltage, or pushing along a horizontal line the way you did in your first attempt.

"When you need power pattern your voice and your inflection in a varied phonetic line from top to bottom, just the way you use chalk to draw all possible kinds of designs on a blackboard.

"Do not take as your models the actors who think they are showing power when it is only loudness. Loudness is not power, it is only loudness and shouting.

"Loud or not loud is forte or piano. But as you know forte is not forte in itself, forte is only not piano.

"And conversely piano is not piano it is not forte.

"What do I mean by those expressions: forte is not forte in itself, or piano is not piano in itself? It means that there is no such thing as an absolute measure for either of them. They cannot be weighed or their extent marked by rulers.

"Forte is a relative concept.

"Let us suppose that you began the *Othello* speech in a low voice.. If in the next line you continue in a slightly louder voice you will no longer be speaking in the piano of the opening line.

"The next line you read is still louder, it will be even less piano and so on until you reach the forte. By increasing your volume in gradual degrees you will eventually reach the ultimate stage of loudness which cannot be described as anything other than forte fortissimo. It is in that scale of sounds from piano pianissimo to forte fortissimo that we have the whole extent of relative degrees of loudness. But when you use your voice in this way you must make nice calculations and be very sure of your measure, otherwise it would be very easy for you to fall into exaggeration.

"Some undiscriminating singers think it is smart to make abrupt contrasts between loud and soft tones. They will sing the first words of a Tchaikowsky serenade forte fortissimo and the next in an almost inaudible piano pianissimo. Then they will start shouting again forte fortissimo when they come to the words about the 'enticing tone of the guitars' and continue with an abrupt piano pianissimo: 'Come down to me my darling. . . .' Can you imagine any greater triviality and lack of taste than these cataclysmic contrasts?

"The same happens in the theatre. There is shouting and ranting followed by hushed whispers in tragic scenes quite regardless of the essential meaning of the words spoken or of any common sense.

"Yet there is another type of singers and actors, who may have only small voices and meagre temperamental gifts who can use the forte and the piano in a way to increase tenfold the illusion of their natural endowments.

"Many of them even have the reputation of possessing great vocal resources. Yet they know themselves that it is technique and art which have made their names for them.

"As for loudness as such there is scarcely any use for it at all on the stage. In the great majority of cases it serves no purpose except to deafen those who have no understanding of art.

"Therefore when you need real power in your speech, forget about volume and remember your rising and falling inflections, and your pauses.

"It is only at the end of a soliloquy, a scene, a play, after you have used all the methods and means of intonations: step by step development, logical, consecutive gradation, all sorts of phonetic lines and patterns—then you may for a brief moment use a loud voice for the closing lines or words, if the sense of the play calls for it.

"When Tommaso Salvini was asked how he had the strength, at his advanced age, to shout with such vigour in a certain role, he replied: 'I do not shout, you do the shouting for me. All I do is open my mouth. My job is gradually to bring my role up to its high point, and when that is done let the audience do the shouting if they feel they need it.'

"There are, of course, exceptional instances in the theatre when it is necessary to speak with a loud voice. This is notably true of mob scenes, or else when one is speaking to the accompaniment of music, singing, other sounds and sound effects.

"Even here one must never forget that it is still necessarily a question of relative, varied gradation of sound, and that allowing the voice to hang on one of several extreme notes in the vocal gamut is disturbing to the public.

"What then shall we conclude from these various aspects of the volume of sound in speech? It is true that this volume is not to be sought in high tension use of the voice, not in loudness or shouting, but in the raising and lowering of the voice, in intonations. Furthermore, volume is to be sought in the gradual expansion from piano to forte and in their mutual relationship."

9

ACCENTUATION:
THE EXPRESSIVE WORD

I

"SONYA, will you go up and say something for us?" This question with which Tortsov started to-day's lesson sounded more like an order.

She went up on to the stage and began to speak:

"A wonderful individual . . ."

"But you accent all the words equally!" exclaimed Tortsov, "You cannot squander your accents recklessly! A stress misplaced distorts a word or lames a phrase, whereas it should be a help to it.

"The accent is a pointing finger. It singles out the key word in a phrase or measure. In the word thus underscored we shall find the soul, the inner essence, the high point of the subtext.

"You still do not realize the importance of that high point and therefore you do not estimate the accent at its full value.

"Learn to love it the way the others have come to love pauses and intonations, because the accent is the third important element of speech.

"Both in ordinary talk and in your speech on the stage you let your accents ramble all around like a herd of sheep in a meadow. You must put some order into your accentuation. Say the word: individual."

"Indi-vidual," came the crisp reply.

"Better and better!" Tortsov's surprise was well feigned. "Now you have two accents and the word has broken down in the middle. Are you not able to say the word 'individual'" as one unit, not two, and put the accent on the third syllable?"

"Individual," Sonya said with great effort.

"That is not a vocal stress but a blow on the head," was Tortsov's joking comment. "But why do you feel you must cuff your words around? You not only have your voice give a smart blow, but you emphasize it with your chin and butt your head forward. That is a poor habit and, unfortunately, you are not alone among actors in using it. As if the thought in a word could be brought out by a thrust of the head or the jut of the nose! How simple!

"As a matter of fact it is much more complex than that: an accent may indicate affection or malice, respect or scorn, frankness or slyness; it may be ambiguous, sarcastic. It serves up a word on a salver.

"Besides," Tortsov went on, "when you have sliced your word 'individual' into two parts you treat the first half with disdain by almost swallowing it, and you hurl the second half at us to explode like a hand grenade. Let it be one word, one idea, one meaning. Let its composition of sounds, letters, syllables be one melodic line. Then you can raise, lower or twist it.

"Take a length of wire, bend it here, twist it up there, and you will have something which is more or less attractive in form. There will be a high point which, like a lightning rod, will catch the accent, and the rest will make some kind of pattern. That line will have form, definition, wholeness and integration to it. It will be better than a piece of wire broken up into bits, scattered around separate from each other. Now try bending the phonetic line of the word 'individual' into a variety of tones."

The whole class began to hum with a confusion of sounds.

"You are doing it mechanically," interrupted Tortsov. "You are producing dry, formal, inanimate sounds, only externally connected with each other. Put some life into them."

"But how?" we asked in bewilderment.

"First of all, by giving to the word the meaning with which nature endowed it—the thought, feeling, idea, image—and not by reducing it to a simple series of sound waves striking the ear drum.

"Make a painting with the word so that the individual you are drawing, that you have in your mind's eye and are describing to the character playing opposite you, will be clear to him. He will sense whether the human being behind the word is beautiful or deformed, tall or short, agreeable or repulsive, kind or cruel.

"Try to convey what you see and feel with the aid of sound, intonation and all the other means of expression."

Sonya made another try but still could not meet the test.

"Your mistake lies in the fact that you first say the word and only afterwards try to understand what it means. You are not drawing from a live model. Try doing things the other way around: first call to mind someone among your acquaintances, stand him up in front of you, the way a painter would, and then tell us what you see in the retina of your inner eye."

Sonya made a conscientious attempt to do as she was asked. Tortsov encouraged her by saying:

"Although I still do not feel what kind of an individual you are painting it is enough for me that you are trying to acquaint me with him, that your attention is working in the right direction, that the word has made you feel the need of action, of real communication and is no longer just something to say. Now say the phrase for me again."

"Wonderful . . . individual." Her pronunciation was meticulous.

"Again you are telling me about two ideas or people: one is called 'wonderful' and the other plain 'individual'. Yet the two combined add up to only one person.

"After all there is a difference between: 'wonderful . . . individual' and the two words woven together, 'wonderful-individual.'

"Let me mould together the adjective and the substantive into one inseparable whole and you will see that the outcome will be an integrated idea, not of an 'individual' in general but of a 'wonderfulindividual'.

"The adjective characterizes, colours the noun and sets off this particular 'individual' from all others.

"But first of all simplify things by taking the accents off these two words, then later we shall restore them."

This proved to be far more difficult than we might have supposed.

"That's how it should be!" said Tortsov, finally satisfied by our prolonged efforts.

"Now put just one accent, the last one, on the two words 'wonderful individual'. But please do not bang down on it, do it caressingly, with a good taste in your mouth, serve it up carefully, this word set apart with its accent. Softly, softly, not hard hitting," pleaded Tortsov.

"Listen: Here are the two words, stripped of all accent, wonderful individual'. Do you hear how uninteresting they are, a straight stick of sound? And now let us take the same two words moulded into one with a very slight tonal twist of an accent—'wonderful individual'. Do you feel the scarcely perceptible, caressing curl on that one syllable?

"There are innumerable other ways which can help you design a naïve, decisive, gentle, severe cast to a word."

After Sonya and all the other students had experimented with the suggestion Tortsov had made, he stopped us and said:

"There is no use in listening so hard to your own voices. That sort of thing is not far removed from self-admiration, exhibitionism. The point is not so much in how you say a word as it is in how others will hear and absorb it. 'Self listening' is not a proper objective for an actor. It is far more important that he affect others by transmitting to them the things that are in his mind and heart. So do not speak to the ear but to the eye of your partner on the stage. That is the best means of getting away from listening to yourself, a habit which is harmful and distracts an actor from his true path."

2

When Tortsov came into class to-day he said to Sonya with a laugh:

"Well, how is our 'wonderful individual' to-day?"

Sonya answered that the wonderful individual was very well, and as she said it she accented it perfectly.

"Now repeat the same words with the accent on the first word," proposed Tortsov. "Incidentally, before you make this test I must acquaint you with two rules," said Tortsov interrupting himself.

"The first is that an adjective modifying a noun does not take *any* accent. It defines, supplements the noun and combines with it. This rule is implicit in the meaning of the word adjective.

"On the basis of this rule it would seem that you could not do as I proposed and put the accent on the first word, namely the adjective.

"But there is another more powerful law which like the psychological pause transcends all other rules and regulations. This is the law of juxtaposition. On the basis of this we are obliged at all costs to emphasize words in juxtaposition which express thoughts, feelings, notions, concepts, actions, images, etc.

"This is especially true in speech on the stage. At first do this as and how you like. Let one contrasting part be expressed in loud, the second in soft tones; one in high the other in a low voice; one in this or that colour or tempo, the other in a contrasting one. All that is required is that the difference between the two ideas be clear and as vivid as possible. On the basis of this law, if you want to put the stress on the first of your two words, on the adjective, you must have a noun after it which implies a contrast.

"So that the words will say themselves naturally and

spontaneously you should think to yourself before pronouncing them that you have in mind not a 'horrid' but a . . ."

"*Won*derfulindividual," Sonya took the words quite naturally out of his mouth.

"That's it, exactly!" was Tortsov's encouraging remark.

Next he gave one, two, three more words and then four, five, six and more until she had a whole story. "A wonderful individual came here but did not find you at home, so, in a state of distress he went away, saying he would never return."

But as the phrase expanded Sonya redoubled her accents until she was soon so involved in them that she could not keep the phrases apart.

At first Tortsov was much amused by the distress on her face. Then he turned serious.

"Your panic," he said to her, "stemmed from your feeling that you must pile on instead of take off the accents. The fewer there are of them in a phrase the clearer it becomes, that is if the few accents are on the key words. It is just as difficult an art to diminish the accents as it is to put them on. But you must learn both."

As Tortsov was playing in an evening performance he interrupted the class at this point and turned us over to Rakhmanov for a period of drill.

3

"I have come to the conclusion that before you learn to add accents you must find out how to diminish them," Tortsov began.

"Beginners are over zealous in their attempts to speak well. They misapply accentuation. They should learn as a counterweight how to take off the stresses where they are not needed. I have already said that it is an art in itself and a very difficult one. What it does, first of all, is to rid your speech of the incorrect accentuation which bad habits have allowed to become fastened on it. Once this is cleared away it is easier to determine the proper accent. In the second place, this art of excision will be of great practical assistance in certain cases, such as when you are relating involved thoughts or complicated facts. For the sake of clarity actors are often obliged to relate separate episodes, intricate details concerned in their play, but they have to do it in such a way that the attention of the listeners will not stray from the main thread of the story. All commentary must be presented in a form which is clear, clean cut, but not too inflated. Here it is wise to be economical with both inflections and stresses. On other occasions, when you have to handle long, heavy phrases, you should emphasize only a few individual words and let the others come along clearly, but unnoticed. In this way a difficult text is lightened by your speech, a job actors often have to accomplish.

"In these various cases the art of eliminating accents will be of great help to you."

Paul was then assigned the same story, built around the words "wonderful individual", with the problem of accenting only one word in it and finding an imaginary basis for the lack of emphasis on all the rest. It was practically the same assignment which Sonya had failed in before. Nor did Paul succeed in it at first. After several unsuccessful attempts Tortsov said to him:

"Sonya had concentrated only on placing accents and you only on eliminating them. But one must not exaggerate in either direction. All thought contained in the words is equally sacrificed when they are over or when they are under accentuated.

"The reason why Sonya laid the accents on too liberally and you were so miserly with them is the same: neither of you had a sufficiently clear idea of what lay behind your words, the subtext. That is your first concern. You must create that in order to have something to convey to, some basis for communication with, others. Use your imagination now to justify your lack of emphasis in your story."

Not too easy a thing to do, I thought to myself.

Yet Paul, it seemed to me, extricated himself creditably from his dilemma. He not only found a basis for the sparse accentuation but he also was able to throw the one accent allowed him from one word to another, as Tortsov required. His idea consisted of this: we, who were sitting in the auditorium, cross-questioned him about the visit of a "wonderful individual". Our inquiry was supposedly based on our lack of confidence in the reality of the facts submitted to us, on the truth of his assertion concerning the visit. In defending himself Paul was obliged to insist on the correctness, the truth, of every word of his story. That is why he threw into relief one word after another in repeating it, as if to impress the stressed words on our minds.

"A *won*derful individual came, etc." "A wonderful indi*vid*ual came, etc." With a stress meticulously placed in rotation on one word after another, Paul assiduously repeated each phrase in its entirety, with all other accents regularly removed. This was done so as to enhance the meaning and the effect of the stressed word. Because the words taken separately, apart from the context, would naturally lose all inner meaning.

When Paul had finished his assignment Tortsov's comment was:

"You did well as far as putting on and taking off the accents. But why the hurry? Why did you telescope that part of the phrase which you needed only to tone down?

"Haste, nervousness, babbling of words, the spewing out of whole phrases, does not tone them down, it utterly destroys them. And that is alien to our intention. Nervousness on the part of a speaker only annoys his listeners, blurred pronunciation angers them because it forces them to strain and guess at the things they do not understand. All this attracts the attention of the listeners and underscores the very part of the text you intended to tone down. Fidgeting makes speech heavy. Calm and control lighten it. To soft pedal a phrase you need a deliberate, unvarnished inflection, an almost complete lack of accentuation, an exceptional control and assurance.

"This inspires calm in your hearers.

"Set off your key word clearly and then add lightly, precisely, deliberately whatever is necessary for the general intelligibility of the phrase, but which must not be emphasized. It is on this that the art of non-accentuation is based. You will work out this control of speech in your classes in drill."

The next exercise consisted of taking the same incident as before and breaking it up into separate episodes which were to be clearly drawn.

Episode One: The wonderful individual arrives.

Episode Two: He hears the reasons why he cannot see the person on whom he has come to call.

Episode Three: The wonderful individual is distressed and bewildered: should he wait or go away?

Episode Four: He feels offended, decides to leave and never return, and goes away.

This produced four independent statements with four accents, one in each.

To begin with all Tortsov required of us was that we make a clear presentation of each fact. For this purpose we had to have a vivid inner vision of the thing we were talking about, and the expressive, proper spacing of the accents in each sentence. We had to see inwardly the image we were trying to convey to the person to whom we were speaking. In addition Tortsov asked Paul not only to describe but also to make us feel the manner in which the individual in the episode came and then went away; not only what he did but how he did it.

Tortsov probed into the mood of the individual. Was he cheerful, gay, or, on the contrary, sad or worried?

To project this effect Paul had to add to his accentuation the colour of intonation. Furthermore Tortsov insisted on knowing the degree of the individual's state of mind. Was his disappointment strong, deep, violent, mild?

What, moreover, was his mood when he made the decision to go away and never return? Was it one of resignation or threatening violence? Colour had to be lent not only to the key points but also to the entire episode.

Similar experiments in adding and eliminating accents were then made by the other students.

4

As a means of reassuring myself that I had grasped correctly the subjects we had been working on recently I asked Tortsov to hear me do the *Othello* speech again. After listening to it he pointed out various mistakes in my spacing and ways of accentuation.

"Correct accentuation facilitates, but an incorrect stress hampers your work," he remarked in passing.

In order to correct my mistakes he had me transpose the accents in the speech and do it over.

I recited it measure after measure and emphasized in each the one word that deserved to be set above the others.

> *Like to the Pontic sea*
> *Whose icy current . . .*

Then I explained:

"Customarily the accent would be put on the word 'sea'. But now that I think it over I shall change the accent to 'current' since that is the point of this measure."

"You decide," said Tortsov, turning to the other students. "Is this right?"

They all began to call out at once. Some said "sea", others "icy", still others "Pontic". Vanya outdid them all by insisting on "like".

We were bogged down in a mire of accented and unaccented words as I proceeded with the speech. We kept ending up with the accent on every word in a given measure, and Tortsov reminded us that phrases in which all the words are stressed are deprived of their reason, their sense.

So we went through my whole speech without arriving at any clear decision. In fact I was more befuddled than ever because I found that I could put on and take off the accent from each word yet preserve one meaning or another. Which was the more correct? On that I was still confused.

Perhaps the same thing was happening to me as it does when my eyes look at too many things at once. In a store, in a pastry-shop, before an array of hors-d'œuvres I find it difficult to make a choice. In the *Othello* speech there were so many possible stresses that I lost my head.

In the end we could not decide, yet Tortsov refused to say anything: he just watched us with a malicious smile. After a long and rather awkward pause he finally controlled his amusement at our expense.

"None of this would have happened to you if you knew the laws of our language. They would immediately have come to your aid and oriented you by automatically fixing the major part of the necessary and therefore proper accents."

"What should we have done?" we asked.

"First of all, of course, you would have to know the rules of accentuation in Russian and then . . . Well, suppose you have moved into a new apartment and your various pieces of furniture are strewn around the premises," said Tortsov immediately illustrating his remarks with a concrete example.

"Now how would you go about making order?

"First you will gather all the plates in one spot, put the tea-cups together, collect your scattered oddments of one kind or another, then place your large pieces of furniture according to their proper uses and so on.

"After you have done all this it will be easier for you to find your way about.

"You must do a similar piece of work on a text before you can assign the accents to their rightful places. To explain this process to you I shall touch at random on certain rules mentioned by S. M. Volkonski in his book *The Expressive Word*. Remember that I shall not do this in order to teach you the rules themselves. I do it only in order to demonstrate to you the necessity of your knowing them and how you will in time learn to make use of them. Once you have come to a realization of the value of its ultimate goal it will be easier for you to undertake a consciously careful study of the subject.

(Here the fictional Director-Teacher Tortsov cites certain accentuation rules which do not apply with equal strength in English. Since it was not Stanislavski's intention to teach the details of stress here, it was thought best to delete them in the English translation. It should be noted, however, that although good English follows fewer generally applicable rules for the placing of accents, idiomatic usage dictates many places where the accent will fall under given circumstances. This usage must be learned and applied by the actor—EDITOR.)

"See how many words and accents fall into place merely by the application of the rules of the language," Tortsov continued. "You should not have trouble now in making your choice among the remaining words still unsorted and unaccented. The subtext, with its warp of innumerable threads, the through line of action and the super-objective will also help guide you.

"After that there remains only co-ordination among the accents you decide on: some will receive a heavy and others a lighter stress.

"This is a difficult and important aspect of our work and we shall discuss it in detail in our next lesson."

5

As he had promised Tortsov took up to-day the question of co-ordinating many accents in separate phrases and in a whole series of them.

"A clause with one accented word is the most comprehensible and simple of all," he explained. "Take as an example: 'A person familiar to you came here.' Accent any word you like and the sense will vary each time.

"Try putting two accents in that same clause, say, on 'familiar' and 'here'. It will be immediately more difficult both to provide a basis for this and to pronounce the phrase. Why? Because you are injecting a new significance into it. First it is not just any person who has come but someone with whom you are familiar, and secondly he did not come somewhere in general, but here.

"Put a third accent on 'came' and the phrase grows more complex in underlying meaning and in its transmission, because in addition to the other factors a fresh one suggests that he did not ride or drive here, but came on foot.

"Imagine a very long sentence all accented and without an underlying basis for the stresses. The only way you could describe it would be: A sentence full of accented words of no significance. Yet there are occasions when you must provide subtextual reasons for accenting all the words and the fresh connotations they add. It is easier to break them up than to express them as one unit."

Here Tortsov took a slip of paper from his pocket and said: "Here is a speech from Shakespeare's *Antony and Cleopatra:*

> *Hearts, tongues, figures, scribes,*
> *bards, poets, cannot*
> *Think, speak, cast, write, sing,*
> *number,—ho!*
> *His love to Antony. . . .*

"The celebrated scholar W. S. Jevons," Tortsov continued, "said that Shakespeare had joined in this one phrase six subjects and six predicates, so that, strictly speaking we have six times six, or thirty-six propositions.

"Who among you will undertake to read those lines so that each one of the thirty-six propositions will stand out?" he asked.

We all remained silent.

"You are quite right. I should not dream of taking on the task either. I should not possess the speech technique necessary to accomplish it. But we are not now concerned with that. What interests us is the technical method of singling out, of co-ordinating many accents in one proposition.

"How are we to single out, in a long speech, the key word and a series of words which are of minor importance but necessary to the comprehension of the whole? They cannot all be equally important; naturally some will require more and others less emphasis, a third group will be even less essential, they must be deliberately toned down and relegated to the background.

"As for the unimportant, unstressed, secondary words, which are needed for the general sense of the sentence, they too must be moved into the background and toned down.

"This calls for a complex scale of accentuation: heavy, medium, light.

"As in painting, where there are strong and light tones, half tones, quarter tones, in colours or chiaroscuro, there is in speech a corresponding gamut of varying degrees of force and accentuation.

"These must be computed, combined, co-ordinated, yet in a way calculated to use the weaker stresses for the purpose of enhancing the strongly stressed key word. They must not compete with each other, but rather fuse into a whole line facilitating the transmittal of a difficult phrase. There must be perspective in the separate parts as well as in the entire structure of a speech.

"You know how the third dimension is used to produce depth in a picture. It does not exist in reality—the canvas is a flat surface stretched on a frame and on it the artist paints his work. Yet painting produces the illusion of many planes. They seem to go deeper and deeper into the canvas itself and the foreground comes out of the frame to meet the onlooker.

"With us we have as many planes of speech which create perspective in a phrase. The most important word stands out most vividly defined in the very foreground of the sound plane. Less important words create a series of deeper planes.

"In this work the essential point is not so much the volume as the quality of the accent.

"This is what is important: Is the accent coming down from above or is it, on the contrary, moving up from below? Is it bearing down heavily or skimming lightly upwards with a keen thrust? Is the blow heavy or gentle, rough or barely palpable, does it fall suddenly and vanish instantly, or linger for comparatively long? Besides, there exists what might be called masculine and feminine accents.

"The one (the masculine stress) is definite and harsh, like the blow of a hammer on an anvil. Such an accent is brief, cut short. The other (the feminine stress) is no less definite in character but it does not end at once, it lasts a little while. As an illustration let us suppose that, for whatever reasons, after you have brought the hammer sharply down on the anvil you immediately draw it back towards yourself along the anvil, perhaps to make it easier to lift it again. That long drawn out action would be a feminine stress.

"Here is another example drawn from speech and action: If an irate host is putting an unwelcome guest out of his house he will use strong language, accompanied by appropriate gestures energetically pointing to the door. In his words and gestures he will be using masculine stress.

"If a more refined person does the same thing his words of dismissal are the same, they will be definite and firm but then his voice will drop, his actions will slow and the harshness of the initial moment will be modified. That kind of a sharp blow with a lingering aftermath corresponds to a feminine stress.

"Another factor in singling out accents and co-ordinating words is intonation. The designs and patterns it gives to a word add great expressiveness and effect. *Accent can be combined with intonation.* In this case the latter will colour a word with varied shades of feeling: caressing, malicious, ironical, a touch of scorn, respect and so on.

"In addition to intonation we have a variety of other means of throwing a word into relief. We can, for example, place it between two pauses. For further reinforcement one of them or both may be psychological pauses. We can also mark the key word by eliminating accents on all minor words. By contrast the one word which stands alone will be stronger.

"Among all these stressed and unstressed words it is necessary to establish the inter-relationship, the degree of emphasis; the quality of the accentuation; one must create a tonal plan with the necessary perspective to lend movement and life to a phrase.

"When we speak of co-ordination what we have in mind is this harmonious integration, inter-relationship of degrees of accentuation volume for the purpose of setting forth certain words.

"This is how we produce a harmonious form, a phrase possessed of architectural beauty."

6

"All that we have said concerning accentuation and the co-ordination of stressed words in a clause can be applied equally to the process of underscoring separate clauses in a whole story or soliloquy. The important clause can be more heavily accented in comparison with others of minor importance, whereas the key word in the key clause will also carry a heavier stress than those in the unstressed clauses.

"The key clause may be set off by placing it between two pauses. This is attained by heightening or lowering the phonetic tonality of the stressed phrase or by introducing a more vivid pattern of inflection, giving it some fresh colour.

"Another method of emphasis for a key phrase is to change the tempo and rhythm in comparison with that of all the other subordinate parts of a soliloquy or story. Finally one may leave the stressed clause in its customary force and colour, but tone down all the rest of the lines, and scale down all the accented points in them.

"It is not my job to go into all the possibilities that exist for achieving subtle shadings of accents in words and sentences. I can only assure you that these possibilities as well as the ways to exploit them, are numerous. With their aid you will be able to work out the most complex plans for the co-ordination of various accents for individual words and whole sentences.

"If they are meshed in with the super-objective of a play along the line of the subtext and the through line of action, these accents will lend the words you speak an exceptional importance, because they will help you achieve the great goal of our art: *To create the life of a human spirit in a role or a play*.

"Your ability to make the most of your speech possibilities will depend on your experience, knowledge, taste, sensitiveness and talent. The actors who have a real feeling for words, for their native tongues, will raise their methods of co-ordination, of creating planes and perspectives in their speech to a point of virtuosity.

"Those who are less talented will have to be more conscientious in acquiring great knowledge, studying their own language; they will have to work harder to achieve experience, practice and art.

"The greater the means and the possibilities at the disposal of an actor the more lively, powerful, expressive and irresistible will be his speech."

7

To-day I recited the speech from *Othello* once more.

"Your work has not been in vain," was Tortsov's encouraging comment.

"In detail what you do is all good. In places it is even

powerful. But as a whole the speech has spots where it treads water, does not move forward. You go ahead for two measures, and then step back for two more, and you do this right along.

"By repeating the same phonetic effects they grow insistent, rather like the monotony of showy designs in wall-paper.

"You must handle your means of expression differently on the stage, not simply, but with a certain calculated purpose.

"Instead of going into further explanation I had better say the speech myself, not to show off my own skill but to make clear to you step by step the secrets of speech technique, as well as the various calculations, considerations in an actor's mind concerning the dramatic effect on him and on his partner in the scene.

"I shall begin by clarifying the problem with which I am faced." Here Tortsov turned towards Paul.

"It is to make you, who play the role of Iago, feel and believe in the elemental impulse of the Moor in the direction of terrible revenge. For this purpose, and in accordance with Shakespeare's requirements, I shall make the juxtaposition of the vivid picture of the Pontic tides surging on and on with that of the spiritual storm within a man consumed with jealousy. To accomplish my end the best thing would be to arouse your feelings by making you conscious of what I see inside myself. This is a difficult task but capable of achievement, especially since I have all prepared, sufficiently vivid and exciting visual and other material."

After a brief moment of preparation Tortsov fixed Paul with a look he might have bent on the faithless Desdemona herself.

" 'Like to the Pontic sea, . . .' he spoke the lines softly, with comparative calm, and then he added laconically:

"I shall not show all that is inside me! I am giving less than I might.

"I must save, build up my emotion.

"The phrase is not intelligible by itself.

"So that I finish it out to myself:

"*Like to the Pontic sea*, (whose icy current and compulsive course keeps due on to the Propontic and the Hellespont . . .)

"I must take care not to hurry. After 'sea' I shall make a tone rest.

"It will last for two, at most three notes.

"When I come to the next rests (there will be many of them) I shall begin to raise my voice more.

"I shan't take the highest note yet.

"I must move vertically.

"From now on no more horizontal line!

"No high tension voltage!

"Not too flat, put some design in!

"I must climb, but not all at once, gradually.

"See that the second measure is stronger than the first, the third stronger than the second, the fourth than the third. But no shouting!

"Noise is not power.

"Power lies in heightening.

"*Whose icy current and compulsive course* . . . (keeps due on to the Propontic and the Hellespont).

"If I raise each measure by a third, then the fifty-two words of the sentence will require a range of over three octaves. I do not have any such range!

"Therefore after a rise I shall make a light downward dip.

"Five notes up, two down again.

"Total rise: three tones.

"But the effect will be of five!

"Then again four notes up and slip down two.

"Total: only two tones higher. But the impression is of four. So I shall keep on going.

"By making these economies in my vocal range it will last me for the fifty-two words.

"Not only in emotions, but also in my voice register!

"Later, if I don't have enough notes left in the register

to raise my voice further I must increase stress and elaborate the rests!

"I must roll them under my tongue!

"That also makes the impression of increased power.

"But now this pause is over.

"You are waiting, don't be in a hurry!

"Nothing prevents my putting in a psychological pause. In addition to the logical one.

"A rest sharpens curiosity.

"A psychological pause does the same for one's natural reactions, intuition . . . imagination . . . and subconscious . . .

"A rest gives me time to check over my mental pictures . . . to act them out by means of movements, facial miming, the sending out of rays. . . .

"This will not relax the dramatic tension.

"On the contrary, a dynamic pause will excite me and you!

"But I must not go off into sheer technique.

"I should keep my mind on my immediate job: At all costs I must make you *see* the images in my mind

"I will be active! I will act to a purpose

"But . . . I must not let the pause drag

"I'll go on . . .

"*Ne'er feels retiring ebb* . . . (but keeps due on to the Propontic and the Hellespont)

"Why are my eyes opening wider?

"Are they sending out rays with greater energy?

"And why are my arms stretching slowly, majestically upwards?

"And my whole body and my whole self as well?

"Is it the rhythm of the heavily surging waves?

"Do you think this is calculated?

"A theatrical effect?

"No! I assure you . . .

"It happens by itself!

"I only realized it after it happened while I was acting!

"After it was all over!

"What does it?

"Intuition?

"My subconscious?

"Creative nature?

"Perhaps

"All I know is that the psychological pause precipitated it!

"It induced the mood!

"It prods emotion!

"It lures it and puts it to work!

"It also helps the subconscious!

"If I had done this consciously, calculating the theatrical effect you would have thought I put it on!

"But it was nature itself that did it . . . and then you have to believe in everything!

"Because it is natural!

"Because it is the truth!

"*But keeps due on*

"*To the Propontic and the Hellespont;* . . .

"Again I realized post factum that something malign had taken hold inside of me!

"I myself do not know why or how!

"But I am glad! I like it!

"I shall hold the psychological pause!

"I have not expressed everything yet!

"How the delay provokes and fires me!

"It has grown more active too!

"I shall give nature another prod!

"I shall put my subconscious to work!

"I have all sorts of means to get at it!

"I come to the high note: Hellespont!

"I shall say it and then I let the sound drop! Before I take the next, the final dash

"*Even so my bloody thoughts, with violent pace,*

"*Shall ne'er look back, ne'er ebb to humble love,* . . .

"I underscore the turn here. This is the supreme point of the speech

"*Ne'er ebb to humble love.* . . .

"I am afraid of lapsing into false pathos here.

"I must cling more securely to my objectives!

"My inner images must be more firmly rooted!

"Intuition, subconscious, nature!

"Do what you will!

"You have free rein! But I hold myself in, I tease you with my waits.

"The more one holds himself in, the greater the provocation this produces.

"The moment has come to pull out all the stops!

"To mobilize all means of expressiveness!

"Everything to the rescue!

"Tempo and rhythm!

"And . . . I am afraid to say it . . .

"Even loudness!

"Not a shout!

"Just on the last two words of the next phrase.

". . . *ne'er ebb to humble love* . . .

"And on the crowning end!

"*Till that a capable and wide revenge*

"*Swallow them up*

"I hold back the tempo!

"To drive in the meaning!

"Then I add the period!

"Do you realize what this means?

"The period of a tragic speech?

"It is the end!

"It is death!

"Do you want to feel what I am talking about?

"Climb to the top of the highest peak!

"Overhanging a bottomless chasm

"Take a heavy stone and . . .

"Cast it . . .

"Down to the very bottom

"You will hear, you feel, the stone crash to pieces, if you can hear it at all. . . .

"Little pieces . . .

"There must be just such a fall!

"In one's voice!

"From the highest note to the very bottom of one's register!

"The nature of the period demands it."

At this an inner revolt welled up inside me. In moments like these can actors be moved by such technical and professional considerations? Where then is inspiration? I was offended and crushed.

8

Having scraped together my courage I started to tell Tortsov what I had been going through in the days since the last lesson.

"It is too late for that," he stopped me short and, turning to the other students, announced:

"My mission with regard to your speech is now ended. I have taught you nothing because that was not my intention in the first place. But I have introduced you to the conscious study of a new and highly important subject.

"By means of our small experiments you have come to an understanding of how many technical voice means—tonal colouring, inflections, every sort of phonetic design, all kinds and aspects of accentuation, logical and psychological pauses etc., etc.—actors must have at their disposal to meet the demands our art makes on us with respect to words and speech.

"I have said all I could. The rest will be told you by Mr. Sechenov, your new teacher in accentuation."

He came forward and Tortsov made a few pleasant remarks of introduction. He was on the point of leaving us to him for our first lesson, but before he could get out of the auditorium I stopped him:

"Don't go away! I beg you not to leave without having told us the most important thing of all!"

Paul backed me up in this.

Tortsov was embarrassed, he flushed and then he led us

both aside to rebuke us for our lack of tact towards the new instructor. Finally he asked:

"What's the matter? What has happened?"

"It's terrible! I can't speak any more!" I choked on my words as I tried to pour out my feelings to him. "I have tried so hard to put what I have learned from you to use in speaking or reciting, but in the end I get all mixed up and I cannot hold two words together. I place an accent but, as if to spite me, it does not stay where the rules say it should, it bounces off. I struggle to get the intonation necessary to go with certain signs of punctuation and my voice does such phonetic somersaults that I am utterly bewildered. I try to express a thought but I lose it because I find myself floundering amid rules of speech and my mind wanders up and down the phrase, trying to decide how to apply them. In the end this work puts me into a state of brain concussion and vertigo."

"This all stems from impatience," said Tortsov. "You must not be in such a hurry! We must stick to the curriculum. In order to pacify you I should have to upset our consecutive programme and go ahead of it. This would confuse all the other students who are not complaining and not in such a hurry as you two."

After thinking the matter over for a moment Tortsov asked us to come to call on him that evening at 9 o'clock. He left and we went back to our class with the new speech teacher.

10

PERSPECTIVE IN CHARACTER BUILDING

IT WAS exactly 9 o'clock when Paul and I reached Tortsov's home.

I explained to him how crushed I had been to find that inspiration had been replaced by theatrical calculation.

"Yes . . . by that too," admitted Tortsov. "One half of an actor's soul is absorbed by his super-objective, by the through line of action, the subtext, his inner images, the elements which go to make up his inner creative state. But the other half of it continues to operate on a psycho-technique more or less in the way I demonstrated it to you.

"An actor is split into two parts when he is acting. You recall how Tommaso Salvini put it: 'An actor lives, weeps, laughs on the stage, but as he weeps and laughs he observes his own tears and mirth. It is this double existence, this balance between life and acting that makes for art.'

"As you see, this division does no harm to inspiration. On the contrary the one encourages the other. Moreover we lead a double existence in our actual lives. But this does not prevent our living and having strong emotions.

"Do you remember what I told you back in the beginning, when we were working on objectives and the through line of action, about the two parallel lines of perspective?

"The one is the perspective of the role.

"The other is the perspective of the actor, his life on the stage, his psycho-technique while he is acting.

"The stream of *psycho-technique* which I illustrated for you with the *Othello* speech is the line of the *perspective of the actor.* It is close to the *perspective of the role* because it runs parallel with it, the way a foot-path may stretch along beside a highway. But at certain moments they may move farther apart when, for one reason or another, an actor is drawn away from the main course of his part by something extraneous and irrelevant to it. Then he loses the perspective of his role. Fortunately our psycho-technique exists for the very purpose of giving ways constantly to attract us back to the true path, just as the foot-path will always lead the pedestrian back to the highway."

Paul and I asked Tortsov to go into more detail on the subject of the two types of perspective. He was rather reluctant to upset our whole plan of study and repeated that this was part of our future work. But we finally succeeded in drawing him out and soon he was so carried away by his subject that he did not notice how far ahead he went in his explanations.

"I went to the theatre recently to see a five-act play," he began. 'After the first act I was delighted with the production as well as the acting. The actors gave vivid characterizations, showed much fire and temperament, acted in a special manner which interested me very much. I was curious to see how the play and the acting would develop.

"But after the second act I found they had shown the same thing as in the first. Because of this fact the interest of the audience, as well as my own, suffered a definite decline. After the third act the same thing was repeated to an even more marked degree because the actors plumbed no new depths, their characters were transfixed, there was still the same fiery spirit to which the public was by now accustomed. The same manner of acting by this time had become so routine that it was boring, dull, and at times annoying. By the middle of the fifth act I was unable to take in any more. My eyes were no longer on the stage, my ears were deaf to the lines, my mind was preoccupied with the thought: How can I get out of here unnoticed?

"What is the explanation of this descending scale of

impressions gathered from a good play, well acted and produced?

"Monotony," I ventured.

"A week ago I went to a concert," Tortsov went on. "The same 'monotony' was evident in the music. A good orchestra performed a good symphony. They ended it as they began it, they scarcely altered the tempo or the volume of the sound, there was no shading. It was most boring for the listeners.

"Why did they have no success, this well acted play and this good symphony performed by a good orchestra? Was it not because in both cases they were playing without perspective?

"Let us agree that the word 'perspective' means: the calculated, harmonious inter-relationship and distribution of the parts in a whole play or role.

"This means further that there can be no acting, no movement, no gestures, thoughts, speech, no word, feeling, etc., etc., without its appropriate perspective. The simplest entrance or exit on the stage, any action taken to carry out a scene, to pronounce a phrase, words, soliloquy and so on, must have a perspective and an ultimate purpose (the super-objective). Without those an actor may not so much as say 'yes' or 'no'. Even a tiny phrase taken by itself, has its own brief perspective. A whole thought expressed in a number of clauses is even less able to do without it. A single speech, a scene, an act, a play all need perspective.

"It is customary, in referring to speech, to have in mind the so-called logical perspective. But our practice in the theatre leads us to a broader terminology. We use the descriptions:

1. The perspective of the thought conveyed. This that same logical perspective.

2. The perspective in conveying complex feelings.

3. Artistic perspective, used to add colour, vivid illustration to a story or a speech.

"In the first, the perspective used in conveying a thought,

logic and coherence play an important part in the unfolding of the thought and the establishing of the relation of the various parts to the whole expression.

"This perspective is achieved with the aid of a long series of key words and their accents which give sense to the phrase.

"Just as we underline this or that syllable of a word, this or that word in a phrase, we have to throw into relief the most important phrase carrying a whole thought, and do the same in a long story, a dialogue, a soliloquy. We follow the same principle of choosing the significant component parts in one large scene, a whole act and so on, the important episodes. Out of it all we evolve a chain of outstanding points which vary among themselves as to their volume and fullness.

"The lines of perspective which are used to convey complex feelings move on the subtextual, inner plane of a role. These are the lines of inner objectives, desires, ambitions, efforts, actions which are grouped, inserted, separated, combined, accented, toned down. Some represent important fundamental objectives and appear in the foreground. Others of medium or minimum value are grouped on a secondary plane, or sink quite into the background, according to the peculiar factors causing the development of the emotions throughout the play.

"These objectives, which go to make up the lines of an inner perspective, are to a large and important degree expressed in words.

"When we come to the laying on of colour along the lines of artistic perspectives we again are obliged to adhere to qualities of consecutiveness, tone and harmony. As in paintings, artistic colouring does a very great deal to make it possible to distinguish planes of speech.

"The important parts, which must be filled out most, are most highly coloured, whereas those relegated to the background are less vivid in tonal shades.

"It is only when we study a play as a whole and can

appreciate its overall perspective that we are able to fit the various planes correctly together, make a beautiful arrangement of the component parts, mould them into harmonious and well rounded forms in terms of words.

"Only after an actor has thought through, analyzed and felt himself to be a living person inside his whole part there opens up to him the long, beautiful, beckoning perspective. His speech becomes, as it were, far-sighted, no longer the myopic vision it was at the start. Against this depth of background he can play out whole actions, speak whole thoughts, rather than be held to limited objectives, separate phrases and words.

"When we read an unfamiliar book aloud for the first time we lack perspective. Moment by moment we have only the immediate action, words, phrases in mind. Can such a reading be artistic and true? Of course not.

"Broad physical actions, the conveying of great thoughts, the experience of wide emotions and passions are made up of a multiplicity of component parts, and in the end a scene, an act, a play cannot escape the necessity of a perspective and an ultimate aim.

"Actors who play a role they have not studied well and thoroughly analyzed are like readers of a complicated, unfamiliar text.

"Such actors have only a dim perspective of the play. They do not understand where they must lead the characters they portray. Often when they play a scene they are familiar with they either do not distinguish or they do not know what lies still unrevealed in the obscure depths of the rest of the play. This obliges them to keep their minds constantly fixed on only the nearest action, the immediate thought expressed, utterly without regard for the whole perspective of the play.

"Take as an illustration of this the fact that some actors who play the part of Luka in Gorki's *The Lower Depths* do not even read the last act because they do not appear in it. As a result they cannot possibly have a true perspective and are unable to play their role correctly. The end hinges on the beginning. The last act is the outcome of the old man's preaching. Therefore one must have one's eyes always trained on the climax and lead all the characters whom Luka affects towards that end.

"In a different way the tragedian who plays the title role of *Othello* knowing the end but without a careful study of the whole play begins to roll his eyes and gnash his teeth in the first act, gloating over the prospect of the murder.

"But Tommaso Salvini was much more calculating than that in working out the plan for his roles. Take *Othello* again. He was always aware of the whole perspective of the play from the moment of his fiery outburst of young passionate love in his first entrance to his supreme hatred as a jealous killer at the end of the tragedy. With mathematical precision and unrelenting consistency, from point to point, he plotted out the evolution of the emotions as they matured in his soul.

"To express this in more understandable terms let me give you another example.

"Let us suppose you are playing *Hamlet*, the most complex role of all in its spiritual colouring. It contains a son's bewilderment over his mother's suddenly transferred love— 'or ere those shoes were old' she had already forgotten her beloved husband. In it, too, is the mystic experience of a man who has been afforded a brief glimpse into the world beyond where his father languishes. After Hamlet learns the secret of that other life this one loses its former meaning for him. The role embraces the agonizing recognition of man's existence and the realization of a mission above his strength, on which depends the liberation of his father from his sufferings beyond the grave. For the part you must have the feelings resultant from filial devotion to your mother, love for a young girl, renunciation of that love, her death, the emotions of revenge, horror over your mother's death, of murder, and the expectation of your death after you have fulfilled your duty. Try jumbling up all these emotions on one dish and you can imagine what a hash will result.

"But if you apportion all these experiences along the perspective of the part in logical, systematic and consecutive order, as required by the psychology of such a complex character, and the life of his spirit which unfolds and develops throughout the whole course of the play, you will have a well-built structure, a harmonious line, in which the inter-relation of its component elements is an important factor in the gradually growing and deepening tragedy of a great soul.

"Can one project any single part of such a role without bearing in mind the perspective of the whole? If, for example, you do not convey in the beginning of the play Hamlet's deep pain and consternation caused by his mother's frivolity, the famous scene with her later will not be properly prepared.

"If you do not feel the whole impact of the shock Hamlet receives from what the ghost tells him of life beyond the grave, there will be no understanding his doubts, his painful efforts to uncover the meaning of life, his break with his beloved, and all the strange conduct which makes him appear abnormal in the eyes of others.

"Does all this not suggest to you that it is the more incumbent on the actor who plays Hamlet to take care how he plays his first scenes, because so much will be required of him in expanded passion as his part unrolls?

"The result of that kind of preparation is what we call 'acting with perspective'.

"As a part moves along we have, as you might say, two perspectives in mind. The one is related to the character portrayed, the other to the actor. Actually Hamlet, as a figure in a play, has no idea of perspective, he knows nothing of what the future has in store for him, whereas the actor who plays the part must bear this constantly in mind, he is obliged to keep in perspective."

"How is it possible to forget about what is coming when you play a part for the hundredth time?" I asked.

"You cannot and need not do it," explained Tortsov. "Although the character being played should not know what lies ahead, still perspective is necessary for the part so that he can appreciate more fully each present moment and more fully give himself up to it.

"The future in a part is its super-objective. Let the character keep moving towards it. It will do no harm if the actor meanwhile remembers for a second the whole line of his role. This will only reinforce the meaning of each segment as he lives it and it will pull his attention with increased power.

"Let us suppose that you and Paul are playing a scene between Othello and Iago. Is it not important that you should remember that you, the Moor, only yesterday arrived in Cyprus, were forever united with Desdemona, that you are experiencing the best days of your life—your honeymoon?

"Where else would you get the joyousness necessary to the opening of the scene? It is all the more important because there are so few gay colours in the play. Moreover is it any less important for you to recall for a brief moment that from this scene forward the lucky star of your life will begin to set and that this decline must only gradually become apparent and distinct? There must be a powerful contrast between the present and the future. The brighter the first the darker the second.

"You need that rapid glance into the past and the future in order to make a proper estimate of the present action, and the better you sense its relationship to the whole play the easier it will be for you to focus the full extent of your attention on it.

"Now you have the necessary basis for the perspective of a part," concluded Tortsov.

But I was not satisfied and pressed him further with the question:

"Why does the actor himself have to have that other perspective?"

"His own perspective, as the person playing the role, is necessary to him so that at every given moment while he is on the stage he will be in a position to assess his inner creative powers and ability to express them in external terms, to apportion them and make reasonable use of the material he has amassed for his part. Take that same scene between Othello and Iago. Doubt steals into the former's jealous soul and gradually grows. The actor who plays Othello must remember that he will have to play many more scenes of mounting passion between that point and the end of the play. It would be dangerous for him to break loose in this first scene, to show all his temperament without holding it in reserve for the gradual reinforcement of his unfolding jealousy. To squander his inner powers here would throw the whole role out of proportion. He must be prudent, calculating and always have his eyes on the final, culminating point of the play. 'Artistic emotion is weighed not in pounds but in ounces.'

"We must not forget one extremely important quality inherent in perspective. It lends a breadth, a sweep, a momentum to our inner experiences and external actions, all of which is of extreme value to our creative achievement.

"Imagine yourself running a race for a prize, but instead of pressing on over a long distance you stopped every twenty paces. If you did this you would never get into your stride or acquire any momentum, and that is enormously important in a race.

"We actors face the same problem. If we stop short at the end of every bit in a role and then start over again with the next we never get up momentum in our efforts, our desires, our actions. Yet we must have it because it prods, stirs, inflames our feelings, our will, thoughts, imagination and so on. You should never spend yourself on a short sprint. You must have the depth, the perspective, the far away beckoning goal in mind.

"What I have said here is equally applicable to the sound of the voice, to speech, gestures, movements, actions, facial expression, temperament and tempo-rhythm. In all these fields it is dangerous to break loose, to squander your all.

You must be economical and make a just estimate of your physical powers and means of transposing the character you play into terms of flesh and blood.

"To regulate them you will need not only your inner powers but also the perspective of a dramatic artist.

"Now that you have made the acquaintance of perspective in a play and in a part, think it over and tell me if it does not bear a close resemblance to your old friend the through line of action?

"Of course they are not identical, but there is a kinship between them. The one is the other's closest aid. Perspective is the path through the entire extent of a play, along which the through line of action constantly progresses.

"*Everything happens for the sake of these two elements, perspective and the through line of action. They contain the principal significance of creativeness, of art, of our approach to acting.*"

II

TEMPO-RHYTHM IN MOVEMENT

TO-DAY we found a placard hung on the wall of the school auditorium. It bore the words: "Tempo-Rhythm".

This means that we have reached a new stage in our work.

"I should have spoken to you much earlier about inner tempo-rhythm, at the time when you were studying the process of establishing an inner creative state on the stage (*An Actor Prepares*, Chapter XIV), because the inner tempo-rhythm is one of the important elements in it," explained the Director.

"The reason why I postponed talking about it is that I wished to make your work easier.

"It is much more convenient, and above all more demonstrable to speak of inner tempo-rhythm at the same time as the outer tempo-rhythm—when it becomes manifest in physical actions. At this point it becomes visible and not merely a sense perception as it is in our inner experiences beyond the reach of the eye. As long as it was inaccessible to your sight I said nothing and mention it now, much later on, when we have come to external tempo-rhythm visible to the eye.

"Tempo is the speed or slowness of beat of any agreed upon units of equal length in any fixed measure.

"Rhythm is the quantitative relationship of units—of movement, of sound—to the unit lengths agreed upon in a given tempo and measure.

"A measure is a recurrent (or presumably recurrent) group of beats of equal lengths, agreed upon as a unit, and marked by the stress of one of the beats"—this Tortsov read from a prepared statement handed to him by Rakhmanov.

"Did you understand that?" he asked when he had finished reading.

We admitted with embarrassment that we had not understood anything he had read.

"Without criticizing too adversely any scientific formulas," Tortsov went on, "I imagine that at present, when you have not yet experienced in your own persons the effect of tempo-rhythm, these formulas will be of little practical value to you.

"On the contrary, an intellectual approach might easily keep you from easy, carefree enjoyment of tempo-rhythm on the stage, from playing with it like a toy. Yet that is just what you should do with it, especially in the early phases. It will be bad if you begin to squeeze rhythm out of yourselves, or if you knit your brows to solve the intricacies of its complex variations as though it were a brain teasing mathematical problem.

"So let us put aside the scientific formulas and for the time being devote ourselves to playing with rhythm.

"Look, here come the toys with which you are to play. I resign my place to Rakhmanov. This is his field!"

Tortsov and his secretary withdrew to the other end of the auditorium as Rakhmanov set up a series of metronomes as watchmen on the stage. The largest one he set on a round table in the centre, and beside it, on small tables, he put three others of smaller dimensions. The largest one was set in motion and ticked loud and clear at No. 10 speed.

"Listen, my friends!" said Rakhmanov. "This big metronome will now tick with slow beats. See how slowly it works: One . . . one . . . andante . . . one-(and)-andantissimo!

"The number ten is really remarkable.

"Now if I press the weight down on the indicator we have a simple andante. This is a shade faster than the one-and-andantissimo.

"Listen: One . . . one . . . one. . . .

"Let the weight slip still farther down. How it works now: One-one-one. Faster; a real allegro!

"And now this is presto!

"And this is presto prestissimo!

"These are all rates of speed. There are as many of them as there are notches on the metronome pendulum. What an intelligent thing it is!"

Next Rakhmanov began to strike a hand bell, marking every two, then every three, then every four, five, six ticks of the metronome again set at No. 10 speed.

"One . . . two. Ring. One . . . two. Ring." Rakhmanov demonstrated the two beat count.

"Now: One . . . two . . . three. Ring. One . . . two . . . three. Ring. That is the three beat count.

"And now: One . . . two . . . three . . . four. Ring. So it goes on, the four beat count," Rakhmanov spoke with excited interest.

After that he started one of the small metronomes and set it to tick at twice the speed of the big one. As the one beat the whole notes this one beat the half notes.

The second small metronome beat the quarter notes and the third beat eight times as fast as the first. They ticked four and eight times to the one beat of the large one.

"It's too bad we don't have a fourth and a fifth little metronome! I should set them for sixteenth and thirty-second notes. That really would be fun!" sighed Rakhmanov.

He was soon consoled because Tortsov came to his aid and he and Paul tapped out the rhythm of the sixteenth and thirty-second notes with their keys on a table.

The beats of all the small metronomes fell together with that of the large one only when it marked the beginning of each measure. The rest of the time all the beats went their own ways and seemed to be all scattered and out of order, only to come together in orderly fashion for that one second.

The effect was of a whole orchestra—full of sounds. It was difficult to distinguish the various beats amid the clatter of dizzying sounds. Yet there was always that one second of perfect order when they combined into the one beat.

The confusion was compounded by the mixing in of uneven beats, the two, four and eight beat with the three, six and nine beats. This combination produced even greater fractional sounds and confusing effect. It was an unimaginable chaos of sounds that delighted Tortsov.

"Listen to it, it's a labyrinth of sounds and yet what order, what harmony there is in this organized chaos!" he exclaimed. "It is created for us by a miracle-working tempo-rhythm. Let us analyze this amazing phenomenon, its individual and its component parts.

"Take the tempo, the time." Here Tortsov pointed to the large metronome. "This is a question of mechanical, pedantic measurement.

"The tempo is the slowness or the fastness. It hastens or draws out the action, hastens or slows up speech.

"The execution of action, the speaking of words takes time.

"If the tempo is stepped up, there is less time available for action, for speech, so that one has to act and speak more rapidly.

"If the tempo is slowed, more time is freed for action and speech, there is more opportunity to carry out the action, to say fully whatever is important.

"Now this is the beat." Here Tortsov pointed to the bell Rakhmanov had been striking. "It does its work in complete accord with the big metronome and also works with mechanical precision.

"The beat is a measurement of time. But there are various beats. Their extent hinges on the tempo, the speed. If that is so then it means that our measures of time vary.

"The beat is a conventional, relative concept. It is not the same as measure which marks the size of a material surface.

"That measure or bar is always the same. You cannot alter it. But the beat, as a measurement of time, is constantly changing.

"What do all the other, the small metronomes, and the beats Paul and I added by hand in supplement to them, represent? That is what makes for *rhythm*.

"With the aid of the small metronome we break up the intervals of time which fill a measure and we produce fractional parts of varying sizes.

"Out of them we make innumerable combinations to form an infinite number of every sort of rhythm within the framework of the one constant factor of a given measure.

"The same thing occurs in acting. Our actions, our speech proceed in terms of time. In the process of action we must fill in the passing time with a great variety of movements, alternating with pauses of inactivity, and in the process of speech the passing time is filled with moments of pronunciation of sounds of varying lengths with pauses between them.

"Here is one of the simplest formulas or combinations which makes up a measure: 1/4 plus 2/8 plus 4/16 plus 8/32 equals 1 measure of 4/4 time. Another set of combinations would be: 4/16 plus 1/4 plus 2/8 equals 1 measure in 3/4 time.

"This rhythm is made up of individual moments of every conceivable length, dividing up the time of a measure into varying parts. Countless permutations, combinations, groupings are possible. If you listen carefully to the chaos of these rhythms as ticked off by the metronomes, you will surely be able to search out among them everything you need to make your own rhythmic combinations and groupings to express the most varied and complex formulas.

"In collective action and speech on the stage you will have to find out and extract from the general chaos of tempo-rhythms those you need and then regroup them so that you can shape your own independent, individual lines of speed or measures of speech, movements, emotional experience in the roles being played by you.

"You must get accustomed to disentangling and searching out your own rhythm from the general, organized chaos of speed and slowness going on around you on the stage."

2

"To-day we are going to play at tempo-rhythm," announced Tortsov as he came into class. "We will clap our
hands as little children do. You will see that it is fun for
grown ups too."

With that he began to clap his hands to the very slow
tick of a metronome.

"*One* . . . two . . . three . . . four, and repeat:

"*One* . . . two . . . three . . . four, and once more:

"*One* . . . two . . . three . . . four, and so on ad
infinitum."

For a minute or two we went on clapping the first beat.
In unison we beat each "one" with a loud clap of our palms
together.

But it turned out to be not much fun. In fact it was
more conducive to drowsiness. It created a mood of boredom, monotony, laziness. At first our clapping was energetic
and loud, but as we sensed the generally flat atmosphere
they grew weaker and weaker, and our faces looked more
bored.

"*One* . . . two . . . three . . . four, and repeat:

"*One* . . . two . . . three . . . four, and again:

"*One* . . . two . . . three . . . four."

How sleepy it made one!

"I don't see that you are getting any fun out of this at
all! Next thing I know you will all be snoring!" remarked
Tortsov, and hastened to introduce a change in our game.
"In order to wake you up I am going to put in two accents
in each measure while keeping the same slow time," he
declared. "Clap all together not only on the 'one' but on
the 'three'. Like this:

"*One* . . . two . . . *three* . . . four, and repeat:

"*One* . . . two . . . *three* . . . four, and again:

"*One* . . . two . . . *three* . . . four, and so on ad infinitum."

This made it a little more lively, but it was still far from fun.

"If that does not help then accent all four beats still at the same slow time," suggested Tortsov.

This roused us somewhat and although we were not excited by it we put more life into our clapping.

"Now," said Tortsov, "give me two eighth notes in the place of each quarter note, with the accent on each first eighth note, like this:

"*One*, and . . . *two*, and . . . *three*, and . . . *four*, and."

This made everyone sit up, our beats were more distinct, louder.

We continued in this fashion for several minutes.

When Tortsov pushed us up to doing sixteenth and thirty-second notes with the same accent on the first note in each quarter of the measure our energy was in full swing.

But Tortsov did not stop there. He gradually increased the time of the metronome. We were finally unable to keep up with it and found ourselves lagging way behind. This disturbed us. We really wanted to keep up in tempo and rhythm with the count. Perspiration broke out on some of us, our faces flushed, we beat our palms sore, we used our feet, our bodies, our mouths; we groaned.

"Well, have you learned how to play? Are you having fun now?" asked Tortsov laughing. "See what a magician I am—I control not only your muscles but your emotions, your moods. According to my wish I can put you to sleep, or I can raise you to the highest pitch of excitement, put you into a fine lather.

"I am not a magician, but tempo-rhythm does possess the magic power to affect your inner mood."

"I consider that the conclusion arrived at from this experiment is the result of a misunderstanding," objected Grisha. "If you don't mind my saying so we all come to life not so much because of the tempo-rhythm as of the quicker movements requiring ten times as much energy. A night-watchman in cold weather, who stamps his feet and thumps his arms against his sides, is not warming himself with tempo-rhythm, you know, but simply with extra movements."

Instead of arguing Tortsov suggested our making another experiment. He said:

"I shall give you a 4/4 measure in which there is one half note, equal to 2 quarter notes, then one quarter rest and finally one quarter note to fill out the bar. Clap this for me with the accent on the first half note:

"*One*—two, hm, *four*.

"*One*—two, hm, *four*.

"*One*—two, hm, *four*.

"By the sound of 'hm' I convey the quarter note rest. The final quarter note is accented slowly, in a sustained way."

We clapped this for a time and then admitted that it had the effect on us of a stately, rather quiet mood, which was an inner response.

Then Tortsov repeated the experiment, except that this time he changed the final quarter note to an eighth note. So the measure ran:

One—two (a half note), hm (quarter note rest), hm (eighth note rest), and one eighth note, or:

One—two, hm, hm, 1/8. One—two, hm, hm, 1/8.

"Do you feel that the last note seems to be behind time and almost spills over into the next measure? Its spasmodic action almost disconcerts the following staid and respectable half note, which shrinks each time like a nervous lady."

Even Grisha did not argue, but this time admitted that the rather solemn mood of the foregoing experiment was replaced, not so much by a sense of disturbance as just the implication of it. This fact sank right into us. Then the half note was replaced by two quarter notes, and later these two quarter notes were replaced by eighth notes with rests, then sixteenth notes, all of which caused the serenity of the earlier mood to be more and more dissipated and to be replaced by a sense of disturbance.

This was repeated with syncopation, which increased the disturbance.

Next we combined some beats, like duples, triplets, quadruplets. These heightened the tremulousness still further. The experiments were repeated at ever faster tempos. This in turn created constantly new moods and corresponding emotional reactions.

We varied the ways of doing these things, the strength and kind of accent; we used the rich, thick accent, then the dry, staccato, or the light, the heavy, the loud, the soft.

These variations were executed at all kinds of tempi and rhythms and produced the most contrasting moods: andante maestoso, andante largo, allegro vivo, allegretto, allegro vivace.

I lost track of the many experiments we tried, which in the end obliged us to recognize that with the aid of rhythm one can be put into a state of genuine excitement and get from it an emotional impact.

When all these experiments had been concluded Tortsov turned to Grisha and said to him:

"I trust that now you will no longer compare us to your night-watchman, warming himself up in the freezing weather, and that you will admit that it is not what we do but the tempo-rhythm itself which can have this direct, immediate effect."

Grisha had nothing to say but the rest of us were unanimously in accord with the Director.

"You are to be congratulated on having made the great and highly important discovery of a truth which we all know about, but which actors are prone to forget: The right measure of syllables, words, speech, movements in actions, together with their clear cut rhythm is of profound significance to an actor. Yet we must never overlook the fact that tempo-rhythm is a two-edged blade. It can be as harmful as it is helpful. If we use it correctly it helps induce the right feelings in a natural unforced way. But there are incorrect rhythms as well which arouse the wrong feelings of which it is impossible to rid one's self without the use of the appropriate ones."

3

A new game with tempo-rhythm was invented for us to-day by Tortsov.

"Have you had any military training?" the Director suddenly asked Paul.

"Yes, I have," he replied.

"Did you go through the drills in the manual?"

"Of course."

"Do you still have the feel of them inside you?"

"Probably."

"Try to bring it back to your consciousness."

"There has to be some approach to that."

Tortsov was seated so he began to tap out with his feet a measure in imitation of marching. Leo followed his example. Vanya, Maria and all the students joined in and soon the entire room was throbbing to the measured beat of a military march.

It seemed as though a regiment was passing through it. To enhance the illusion Tortsov began to tap out a rhythm reminiscent of the ruffle of drums.

We added other touches until we sounded like an entire drum corps. The clean cut dry beats of hands and feet made us straighten ourselves up and feel as though we were going through a military drill.

In this way Tortsov was instantly able to achieve the result he sought with the aid of tempo-rhythm.

After a slight pause he went on further:
"Now I shall rap out quite a different motif—Listen!

"Rap-*rap*, rap-rap, rap-rap-rap, *rap*-rap-rap, *rap*-rap.

"I know, I know, I guessed it!" cried Vanya. "It's a game.
One raps out the rhythm and the other is supposed to guess
what it is. If he misses he has to pay a forfeit."
We guessed what Tortsov had rapped out, not the motif
itself but only the general mood of it. The first thing he had
rapped was a military march, the second motif had a stately,
solemn quality. It turned out that it was the Pilgrim's
Chorus in *Tannhäuser*. After that Tortsov went on to
another experiment.
This time we were unable to define what he was rapping.
It was something agitated, confused, full of effort. Actually
he was beating the rhythm of a passenger train. Each one
in turn rapped out a rhythm for the others to guess. Next
to me Vanya was beating a sentimental rhythm to Maria
and then a stormy one.
"What am I beating?" Vanya said to her. "Listen to this:

"Tra-ta*ta*, tra*ta*ta-*ta*-ta!"

"I don't know, I don't understand at all. You're not
beating anything really."
"But I know what it is, honest I do!" insisted Vanya. "I'm
beating love and jealousy! Tra-ta-*taaa*. Pay your forfeit!"
Meanwhile I was tapping out a mood of mine on reaching
home. I could see myself come into my room, wash my hands,
take off my jacket, lie down on the sofa and begin to think
about tempo-rhythm. And then the cat would jump up to
lie down cosily beside me. Quiet, rest!
It seemed to me that I was conveying this domestic idyll
in terms of tempo and rhythm. But no one else had any
conception of what I was doing. Leo thought it was eternal
rest. Paul sensed boredom. Vanya had the peculiar notion
of connecting it with a silly nursery rhyme with a repetitious
refrain.

It was impossible to record all the different things we beat out. Among them were a storm at sea, one in the mountains, with wind, hail, thunder and lightning. There were evening bells, alarms, quacking ducks, dripping taps, gnawing mice, headaches, throbbing tooth-aches, grief, ecstasy. We rapped and tapped and pounded as though we were making mince-meat for a pie. Had any outsider happened in on this scene he would have thought we were all either drunk or insane.

Several of the students had clapped their palms and fingers so sore that they had to convey their emotions by waving their hands like an orchestra conductor. This last method was the best and soon we all adopted it.

Nevertheless it must be stated that no one ever guessed exactly what the beats meant. Obviously this new experiment had ended in a fiasco.

"Well, are you convinced now of the powerful effect tempo-rhythm can have?" asked Tortsov with a triumphant look.

This question quite dumbfounded us because we were all prepared to ask him the very contrary question: "What about your much vaunted tempo-rhythm? Here we have been beating away and no one has understood anything."

Actually we stated this in gentler terms, but still express-ing our bewilderment, and this was his reply:

"Do you mean to say you were beating rhythms for others and not for yourselves? I gave you these exercises not for the ones who listened but for you who were doing the beating. My first object was to have you infected with tempo-rhythms, and through the beating of them to facilitate the awakening of your emotion memory. Nevertheless your listeners did receive a general impression from the rhythm and that in itself is significant.

"As you notice, even Grisha has no objection to offer to the effect of tempo-rhythm on feelings."

Here Grisha protested:

"But it wasn't the tempo-rhythm, you know, it was the proposed circumstances that affected us to-day," he argued.

"And what suggested them?"

"Tempo-rhythm!" chorused all the other students in opposition to Grisha.

"It is not important here whether the others understood you or not," said Tortsov in emphasizing his objective. "It is far more essential that the rhythms you were conducting spurred your own imaginations to work, suggesting to you certain surrounding circumstances and corresponding emotions."

4

There is no end to Tortsov's resourcefulness. To-day he thought up a new game.

"Quickly, without reflecting, take this baton and beat out the tempo-rhythm of a traveller setting out on a long journey by train."

For my part I saw in my mind's eye a corner of a station, the ticket window, the long line of prospective passengers. The ticket window was still closed. Then it was opened. The ticket buyers pushed ahead slowly, boringly, step by step, until the ticket was purchased, the change counted. Next I went through the emotional fuss of arranging for my hand luggage. In between I had the mental picture of looking over the newspapers and magazines on the stands. Finally I dropped into the station restaurant for a bite of food before hunting up my train, my car, my berth. After getting settled and casting a glance around at my fellow travellers, I opened a paper, began to read, and so on. As the train had supposedly not started yet I introduced another ·suggested incident: I lost one of my pieces of baggage. This necessitated a call on the station master.

Tortsov remained silent as it occurred to me to introduce the buying of cigarettes, dispatch of a telegram, the hunting up of friends aboard the same train, etc. Thus I created an unbroken line of all kinds of objectives which I achieved in a quiet and leisurely fashion because there was still plenty of time left before my train was scheduled to start.

"Now repeat exactly the same thing except for the condition that you have reached the station only a short time before the train time," ordered Tortsov. "At first you had a quarter of an hour, now you have much less, yet you must attend to just as many things, necessary to be done before you start off on a long journey and all you have is five minutes in which to do them. At the ticket window, worse luck, there is a long line. Now conduct for me the tempo-rhythm of your departure."

That was enough to make my heart thump, especially as I am always nervous when I travel.

This was, of course, reflected in the tempo and rhythm, whose previous measured beat was now replaced by one full of agitation and hurry.

"Now here is a new variation for you," announced Tortsov after a short pause. "You reach the station just at train time!"

To excite us still further he made the sound of the engine hooting impatiently.

Every superfluous act must be eliminated; only think about the absolutely essential things. Terrific excitement! Difficult to sit still! One hardly had hands agile enough to beat out the tempo-rhythm of one's nervous agitation.

When the test was over Tortsov explained to us that the point of this exercise lay in proving that tempo-rhythm cannot be clearly recalled and felt unless there are inner images present to correspond to it, unless certain circumstances are suggested to affect the emotions concerning objectives and actions to be achieved. These are all so solidly inter-related, each giving rise to the other—given circumstances stimulating tempo-rhythm, and tempo-rhythm challenging one's thoughts about the given circumstances.

"Yes," agreed Paul, as he looked back on the exercise just finished, "it really obliged me to think and see what happens and how, when one is starting off on a long journey. It was only after this that I arrived at a realization of what tempo-rhythm is.

"Consequently tempo-rhythm excites not only your emotion memory," Tortsov said, "as you felt so convincingly when we were beating time at the previous lessons, but it also brings your visual memory and its images to life. That is why it is wrong to take tempo-rhythm to mean only a measure and speed.

"We need it in combination with the given circumstances which create a mood, we need it for the sake of its own inner substance. A military march, a stroll, a funeral procession may all be measured in the same tempo-rhythm, yet what a world of difference there is between them as to their inner content, moods, intangible characteristic peculiarities!

"In a word tempo-rhythm carries with itself not only external qualities which directly affect our natures, but also our inner content which nourishes our feelings. In this guise tempo-rhythm remains in our memories and may be used for creative purposes."

5

"At our previous lessons I entertained you with games, but to-day you shall entertain yourselves. Now you have grasped what tempo-rhythm is and it no longer worries you. There is nothing to prevent your playing with it.

"Go on to the stage now and do whatever you choose.

"The only thing to be made quite clear in advance is how you will mark the important points in your actions by means of rhythmic accents."

"By moving our arms, legs, fingers, whole body, by turning our heads, necks, waists, by facial miming, sounds of letters, syllables, words," the students shouted, their words tumbling over each other.

"Yes. Those are all actions capable of marking any tempo-rhythm," agreed Tortsov. "We walk, run, ride on a bicycle, speak, do all kinds of jobs in one tempo-rhythm or another. But what of the times when we do not move, when we sit quietly and silently, lie down, rest, wait, do nothing, are they left without any rhythm or tempo?" asked Tortsov searchingly.

"No, there is tempo-rhythm in all that, too," the students stated.

"But it is not external and visible, only internal and felt by the emotions," I added.

"True," agreed Tortsov. "We also think, dream, grieve about things to ourselves in a special tempo-rhythm because each moment is manifest in our lives. Wherever there is life there is action; wherever action, movement; where movement, tempo; and where there is tempo there is rhythm.

"What about the sending and receiving of wordless messages, are they without movement? If not then it means that when a person looks, conveys, accepts impressions, communes with another person, convinces him of something or other, he does it all in a certain tempo-rhythm.

"We often speak of flights of thought and imagination. That means they are subject to movement and consequently there must be tempo and rhythm in them.

"Listen to how your emotions tremble, throb, race, are stirred inside you. In these invisible movements lie hidden all manner of rapid and slow beats, hence tempi and rhythms.

"Every human passion, every state of being, every experience has its tempo-rhythms. Every characteristic inner or external image has its own tempo-rhythm.

"Every fact, every event takes place inevitably in its corresponding tempo-rhythm. For example, a declaration of war, a solemn gathering, the reception of a deputation— each requires its own tempo and rhythm.

"If they do not correspond to what is going on an absurd impression is easily produced. Imagine that instead of the usual stately progress we see the Imperial couple drive to their coronation at a hectic gallop.

"In brief there is some kind of tempo-rhythm inherent in every minute of our inward and outward existence.

"Now you know how to convey this when you are on the

stage," concluded Tortsov. "Let us only agree still on how you will mark the moments of rhythmic coincidence.

"You know that in music the melody is shaped in measures, these measures contain notes of varying values and strength. It is they which produce the rhythm. As for the tempo, that is invisible, the musicians reckon it to themselves or the conductor beats it out for them.

"The same thing is true of us artists of the stage. Our acts are made up of larger or smaller component movements of varying lengths and measurements, and our speech is composed of short or long, accented or unaccented letters, syllables, words. They mark the rhythm.

"Our acts are carried out, the text of our parts is spoken to the mental count, the tempo of our individual interior metronomes.

"So let your accented syllables and movements consciously or unconsciously *create an unbroken line of moments when they coincide with your inner count.*

"If an actor is untuitively right in sensing what is being said and done on the stage the correct tempo-rhythm will be created of its own accord; it will apportion the stressed and unstressed words and the points of coincidence. If this does not happen you will have no other recourse except to establish tempo-rhythm by technical means, in the ordinary way of working from the outside in. For that purpose beat out for yourself the rhythm you need. You realize now that you cannot do this without inner images, without imaginative invention, without suggested circumstances, all of which taken together act to stimulate feelings. Let us make one more test of this tie between tempo-rhythm and feelings.

"Let us begin by examining the tempo-rhythm of action, and then we shall come to the study of tempo-rhythm in speech."

Rakhmanov wound up the big metronome and set it going at a very slow pace. Tortsov picked up a stiff portfolio that chanced to be lying on the table and began to set things on it as though it were a tray: an ash-receiver, a box of matches, a paper weight and so on. To the deliberate beat of the metronome he had Leo carry the objects away and then to the count of 4/4 time he was to bring them back, take them from the tray and distribute them to those present. Leo proved to be quite without rhythm and was not at all successful. He had to be prodded and made to do all sorts of exercises to help him along. Other students joined in. This is what we had to do: we were supposed to fill in the long interval between the beats of the metronome with just one act or movement.

"That is the way in music one whole note fills up an entire measure," explained Tortsov.

How was one to justify such slow motion, such paucity of action?

I undertook to justify it by the great concentration of attention required by the examination of an indistinct point at a great distance. I found one on the wall at the far end of the auditorium. A sidelight on the stage prevented my seeing it clearly. To shade my eyes from the lights I had to hold the palm of my hand to my temple. That was the only action I allowed myself for the first period. Thereafter, with each measure, I adapted myself in some fresh way to the same object. This gave me an excuse to move the position of my arms and of my body, even of my legs, as I leaned forward or back in an effort better to see the faraway point. All these movements helped me to fill in new measures.

After this one of the small metronomes was set going beside the big one. It ticked first two, then four, eight, sixteen beats to the measure, the equivalents of half, quarter, eighth and sixteenth notes in music.

Consecutively we had to fill the measures with two, four, eight, sixteen movements.

These rhythmic actions were based on slow and increasingly hurried searchings in our pockets for an important slip of paper which had been mislaid.

When we reached the quickest tempo-rhythm of movements I pictured to myself that I was beating off a swarming hive of bees.

Little by little we grew accustomed to this tempo-rhythm of action and then we began to play with it. When an action coincided with the beat of the metronome it gave us an agreeable sensation, made us believe everything that was happening on the stage.

When that instant passed and the mathematically precise count was resumed we went back to work in earnest.

6

The next lesson began with the tray exercise again. Leo was still unable to do anything with it so I was given the tray.

Because of the extremely slow tempo of the metronome, with only one whole note to the measure and consequently only one motion, it was necessary to extend it to fill the entire space between the beats. This, naturally, induced a smooth, flowing, serious mood, with inner repercussions which in turn evoked corresponding actions.

I had the notion that I was the president of some sort of sporting club, that I was distributing ribbons and prizes.

The ceremony ended I was required first to leave the room and then to return and in the same grave rhythm take back the ribbons and prizes I had given out.

I executed the requirement without reflecting on what might warrant this new action. But the action itself, the ceremonious atmosphere, created by the tempo-rhythm, suggested new surrounding circumstances to me.

It seemed to me that I was a judge unfairly ousted by the recipients of the prizes. Intuitively I reacted with unpleasant feelings towards the objects of my attention.

When I was obliged to repeat the exercise in another tempo-rhythm, in quarter notes, I felt that I was a butler subserviently handing around glasses of champagne on some formal occasion. The same action speeded up to eighth notes converted me into a plain waiter in a railroad station buffet with a trainful of passengers in for a short stop. I dashed furiously around with plates of food for everyone.

"Now try doing it in the same 4/4 time but divide the second and fourth quarter notes into eighth notes," ordered Tortsov.

All sense of ceremony vanished at once. The teetering eighth notes, sandwiched in between the quarter notes, created an atmosphere of distraction, awkwardness, lack of confidence. I felt like Epikhodov in *The Cherry Orchard*, with the "twenty-two misfortunes" he was always stumbling on. When I had to replace the eighth with sixteenth notes my sense of diffidence was sharply increased. Everything seemed to fall from out of my hands. I kept trying to catch the dishes as they slipped from my fingers.

Can it be that I am drunk? The thought flashed through my mind.

After this we were made to do analogous exercises in syncopated time. This heightened the feeling of agitation, nervousness, uncertainty, hesitation. This state suggested the most idiotic imaginings as a basis for our actions; nevertheless I quite believed them. For example it occurred to me that the champagne was poisoned; the thought caused me to be uncertain in my movements.

Vanya was more successful than I in these exercises. He produced real tempo shadings—a "largo lento" followed by a "staccato", was the way Tortsov defined it. He scored a real triumph.

I must confess that to-day's lesson convinced me that *tempo-rhythm of movement can not only intuitively, directly, immediately suggest appropriate feelings and arouse the sense of experiencing what one is doing but also it helps stir one's creative faculty.*

This influence on emotion memory and imagination is felt keenly when the rhythmic action is carried out to music. Of course then we meet the combination of sheer tempo-rhythm, as ticked off by the metronome, with sound, harmony, melody, all of which move us with considerable force.

Tortsov asked Rakhmanov to play something on the piano and then told us each to act to the music. Our motions were supposed to convey, in the corresponding tempo-rhythm, whatever the music suggested to our imaginations. This is an extremely interesting experiment and all of us were carried away with it.

Each one of us interpreted the tempo-rhythm and the music in his own way, quite differently, even in direct contradiction to others, irrespective of what Rakhmanov himself was trying to convey by the sounds. Yet for each one of us his own interpretation was convincing.

In accompaniment to some of the agitated rhythms, I thought of someone galloping. A Circassian! I must be in the mountains! I may be captured! I plunged past chairs and various pieces of furniture which to me represented boulders. I crouched behind them, believing the man on horseback could not reach me there.

Then the melody grew tender, sentimental, suggesting new rhythms, fresh action. My thoughts turned to love. Instead of a mounted bandit, could it be my sweetheart, hurrying to meet me?

Now I am ashamed of my cowardly behaviour! How happy I am and touched by her urgent haste. But how the music has turned baleful, snatching her away from me. She was only pulling the wool over my eyes.

Apparently tempo-rhythm has the power to suggest not only images but also whole scenes!

7

To-day Tortsov called all students on to the stage and ordered them to set three metronomes going, each at a different rate, and then he proposed that we act as we chose.

We broke up into groups, set our objectives, proposed circumstances and went into action: some on whole notes, some on quarter notes, a third group on eighth notes and so on.

But Sonya was upset by the tempo-rhythms of the others. She wanted the same to be set for all.

"What do you want such regimentation for?" asked Tortsov with a puzzled expression. "In ordinary life, as here on the stage, each person has his own tempo-rhythm. One rhythm for all, if it ever occurs, is only a coincidence. Suppose you are in the actors' dressing-room in the inter-mission preceding the last act of a play. The first group, acting on the beats of the first metronome, have already finished their performance and are slowly taking off their make-up so they can go home. The second group, which will be acting at the faster rate of the smaller metronome, will be changing costumes and doing over their make-up for their performance still to come in the last act. You, Sonya, find yourself in this second group. You have ten minutes in which to do your hair and put on a stunning ball dress."

Our pretty sister student barricaded herself with chairs and began to engage in her favourite occupation of beauti-fying herself, quite oblivious to the tempo-rhythms of anyone else.

Suddenly Tortsov started the third metronome off at a breakneck speed and at the same time Rakhmanov began to play something with an erratic and furious rhythm. The third group of students had to make their change of costumes in unusual haste, as they were to play in the first scene of this last act. Besides, the various parts of their costumes were scattered around the room and it was necessary to search them out in a confused pile of clothing.

This new tempo-rhythm, contrasting sharply as it did with the first two, made the scene more complex, vivid and tense. Sonya, however, completely disregarded the clash of rhythms and went calmly on preparing her coiffure.

"Why did no one interfere with you this time?" Tortsov asked her when the exercise was ended.

"I really can't tell you," she replied. "I was too busy."

"That was just it," Tortsov said, seizing on her explanation. "At first you were just doing rhythms for the sake of it, but this time you were acting fully and with a purpose, in rhythm, and that is why you had no time to be bothered by what others around you were doing."

Tortsov went on to speak concerning general, collective rhythm:

"When a number of people live and act together on the stage in one and the same rhythm, like soldiers in a formation, or dancers of a corps de ballet in an ensemble, a stylized tempo-rhythm is created. Its power lies in the mass performance, in general mechanical training.

"Aside from the rare cases when a whole crowd is seized with one general urge, this kind of tempo-rhythm designed for everyone is not appropriate to our realistic art which requires that we reproduce all the varying shades of life.

"We dread the conventional! It leads us toward routine, stereotyped make-believe acting. We do use tempo-rhythm, but not the same for all participating in a scene. We mix in the greatest variety of tempi and rhythms which in their sum total create the nuances of real, true pulsing life. This union of various rhythms is necessary, for instance, in building mob scenes.

"I can illustrate the difference between a general, elementary and a more detailed approach to rhythm in the following way:

"When children paint pictures they use basic colours, green for grass and leaves, brown for tree trunks, black for earth, light blue for sky. This is elementary and conventional. An artist mixes the shades he needs from these basic colours. Dark blue is combined with yellow to produce various shades of green, red is mixed with blue to make shadings of violet and so on. In this way he gets on to this canvas a varied scale of colours which includes all tones and shadings.

"We deal with tempo-rhythm the same way a painter

does with colours: we make combinations of all sorts of different speeds and measures."

Later Tortsov explained to us that different rhythms and tempi are to be found in simultaneous action not only among the various actors performing in the same scene at the same time, but also inside one of them. At the point when the hero of the play or some particular person has to take a definite and strong stand there are no contradictions and doubts—one all-embracing tempo-rhythm is not only appropriate, it is even necessary.

But when, as in Hamlet's soul, resolution wrestles with doubt, various rhythms in simultaneous conjunction are necessary. In such cases several different tempo-rhythms provoke an internal struggle of contradictory origins. This heightens the actor's experience of his part, reinforces inner activity and excites feelings.

I wanted to try this out on myself and fixed on two contrasting tempo-rhythms. One was very quick and the other very slow. In what way and by what means could I justify this? Here is the foolish notion that popped into my mind:

I am a drunken pharmacist. I stamp around the place without being aware of what I am doing. I shake medicine up in vials. This fiction made it possible for me to use most unexpected rhythms. My drunken gait on my unsteady feet justified the slow tempo and the shaking up of the vials called for a quick, mixed rhythm.

First I worked out a manner of walking. To slow myself up more I had to emphasize the drunkenness. I felt the rightness of what I was doing and this gave me an agreeable sensation.

Then I elaborated the movements of my arms in shaking up the medicines. To justify the rapid rhythm I wanted to make the most idiotic, erratic motions which would correspond properly with my imaginary state.

Thus the two contradictory rhythms came together and merged of their own volition. By now I was amused by playing a drunkard and the applause of the auditorium egged me on.

The next exercise had us combining in one person three absolutely different tempi, ticked by three metronomes.

To justify this the following was proposed:

Say I am an actor, getting ready for a performance, I am reciting verses and pronouncing them deliberately, with pauses, in the tempo of the first metronome. As I do this I am so nervous that I tramp up and down my dressing-room at the tempo of the second metronome, and at the same time I am hastily dressing myself, tying my necktie and the rest at the most rapid tempo of the third metronome.

To organize these varying tempo-rhythms and actions I set out as I had done in the previous exercise to combine two sets of actions and tempo-rhythms: the dressing and the walking. After I had accustomed myself to them and practiced them to the point of their becoming automatic, I introduced the third action at the new tempo-rhythm with the reciting of the verses.

The next exercise proved even more difficult.

"Let us suppose you are playing the role of Esmeralda, who is being led to her execution," Tortsov explained to Sonya. "The procession moves along slowly to the ominous sound of drum beats. Inside the condemned woman her heart races and beats wildly, sensing that these are her last minutes on earth. Simultaneously the hapless woman recites, at a third tempo-rhythm, the words of a prayer for the preservation of her life, while her hands smooth the region of her heart in a new, fourth tempo-rhythm."

The difficulty of this assignment made Sonya hold her head in her hands. Tortsov hastened to reassure her:

"The time will come when at such times you will take hold, not of your head, but of the rhythm itself as a life-line. For the time being, however, perhaps we had better try something easier."

8

To-day Tortsov had us repeat all the exercises in tempi and rhythms that we did at our last lesson, except that this time we were obliged to do them without impetus lent by the metronome, with only a mental count.

Each one of us was supposed to choose any rate of speed he preferred, any measure, and then stick to it and act in accordance with it, seeing to it that the big moments of the action coincided with the beat of the imaginary inner metronome.

The question arises: what line should one pursue in searching out the high moments of the rhythm, the inner or the external line? The line of the inner images and imaginary circumstances? Or the line of wordless communion with others? How can one grasp and fix the stresses? It is not easy to take hold of them during an interval of inner activity and complete external inactivity. I began to work along the line of thoughts, desires, inner promptings, but I could not make anything of them.

Then I took to listening to my pulse. Yet that did not define anything for me. Where could my imaginary inner metronome possibly be, and in what part of my organism should the beat of the tempo-rhythm take place!

At times it seemed to me it was going on in my head, at others in my fingers. Fearing that they were moving too obviously I switched to my toes. But their twitching also might attract attention, so I stopped their moving. Thereupon my supposed metronome moved of its own accord to some muscles at the root of my tongue, but that interfered with my speech.

Here my tempo-rhythm was flitting around from one spot to another inside me and manifesting itself first with one physical means and then another. I told Tortsov about this. He wrinkled his brow, shrugged his shoulders and remarked:

"Physical twitching is more palpable, more tangible, for that reason actors like to have recourse to it. When one's intuition is sluggish and has to be prodded, a physical beat may be used. If it works, use it, but only when you need it to stimulate and support uncertainty of rhythm. You accept this necessity grudgingly but you should not approve of such means as a steady and correct procedure.

"Therefore as soon as you have established your physical beat of rhythm use your imagination and invent appropriate circumstances on which to base it.

"Then let *them*, and not your arm or your leg, support the right rate and measure of rhythm in you. Then again, at times when you seem to feel that your inner tempo-rhythm is hesitant, help yourself, as a measure of necessity, by having recourse to external, physical means. But allow yourself to do this only for the briefest moment.

"In time, when your sense of tempo-rhythm will be more firmly established, you will of your own accord give up this less subtle way of achieving your end and replace it by a more delicate mental beat."

The great importance of what Tortsov was saying made me feel that I must get to the very bottom of what he was proposing we learn to do. In reply to a question from me he suggested that I do the following problem: To a very fast, agitated, uneven inner tempo-rhythm I was to appear outwardly not only quite calm, but even apathetic.

First I fixed both the external and internal rates of speed and measure and reinforced them by imperceptible tensing of my fingers and toes.

Having thus established the speed and the measure I quickly sought an imaginary basis for them by asking myself what circumstances would provoke such a quick, excited tempo-rhythm in me.

After casting around in my mind for a long time I concluded that this might occur after I had committed some dreadful crime which would have the effect on me of remorse, consternation, fear. I imagined I had murdered

Maria, apparently in a fit of insane jealousy. Her lifeless body lay before me on the floor, her face was pale, a huge red spot of blood stained her light coloured dress. This imaginary apparition so upset me that I seemed to feel my inner rhythm was well founded.

When I came to producing an external tempo-rhythm of lazy calm I again took the preliminary step of fixing the beat in my clenched fingers and then quickly looking for a basis for the rhythm in some new figment of given circumstances. The question I now asked myself was what would I do now, here in class among my fellow students, in the presence of Tortsov and Rakhmanov, if the horrible fact I had imagined were really true. I should be forced to appear not only calm but even carefree, nonchalant. I was not able to find at once the adjustment necessary in myself, nor could I find the answers to the questions put to me. I seemed to feel the need of avoiding the eyes of the others, and of not looking at anyone myself. This, however, spurred the rhythm. The greater my effort to appear calm, the more agitated I grew inside. Once I had come to believe my invention I felt that I had something to hide, and having begun to hide it I became more and more agitated.

Then I began to think of all the given circumstances. What was I to say to my comrades after class, to Tortsov? Are they aware of what has happened? How shall I answer them? Where shall I look when they begin to ask me about the tragedy? At her? Look at my victim in her coffin?

The more I saw in detail the situation that derived from the catastrophe, the more violent were my own emotions, the more I gave myself away, the more I forced myself to appear unconcerned.

In this way the two rhythms created themselves: an inner one which was rapid, and an outer one of enforced calm. The combination of the two extremes affected me even more strongly.

Now that I had discovered a line of convincing and justifiable circumstances, of continuing action underneath the plot, I no longer needed to think about time and rhythm, I naturally went on living the story in the rhythm I had established. I was confirmed in this by the fact that Tortsov sensed what was going on inside of me, although I made every effort to conceal it.

Tortsov realized that I avoided showing my eyes, fearing they would give me away. I was using all sorts of excuses to fix them on one object after another, examining each one carefully, as though I were particularly interested in it.

"Your restless calm more than anything else revealed your inner turmoil," he said. "You yourself were not aware of the fact that involuntarily the movements of your eyes, the turn of your head, your neck, were made on the tempo-rhythm of your inner agitation. When you pulled out your handkerchief, when you raised yourself up and then sat down again as if to find a more comfortable position, I realized clearly that you were doing this to mask your state of mind. But you gave yourself away by making these motions, not in calm, casual·manner, but in the quick, nervous rhythm which you were forcing yourself to hide from us. Yet you immediately caught yourself, were alarmed and looked around to see whether anyone had noticed anything untoward. After that you proceeded to move again with your artificially imposed calm. It was that seeming imperturbability, constantly broken by your inner disturbance that betrayed you.

"That is what happens all the time in life when we conceal great inner emotions. Then too a person will sit motionless, plunged in thought, absorbed by his feelings which he is obliged, for one reason or another, to conceal. Catch him suddenly off guard and you will see how for a second or two he will start, jump up and run towards you, in the rapid rhythm of what was going on inside him. Then he will immediately regain control of himself, slow his movements, his steps, and pretend outwardly to be serene. If there is no impelling reason for him to hide his agitated state he will continue to move and walk in the quick tempo-rhythm of his disturbed condition.

"Sometimes whole plays, whole roles are predicated on the combination of several contrasting tempo-rhythms. Many of the Chekhov plays are based on this: *The Three Sisters, Uncle Vanya* (the parts of Astrov and Sonya for instance) and others. The characters are almost always outwardly calm while inwardly throbbing with emotional turmoil."

Once I had sensed that my slow movements were best suited to convey the rapid rhythm of my inner agitation I began to misuse them, but Tortsov was quick to put an end to that.

"We spectators judge the state of mind of another person, in the first instance, by what we see. Naturally when physical movements are uncontrolled they attract our attention. If they are quiet, slow, we get the impression that the person is in a contented state. But if we look closer into, let us say, his eyes, we come to feel with his emotions and we sense the inner import of what he is keeping from us. This means that in the instances given one has to know how to show one's eyes to an audience of thousands of people. This is not a simple matter. It requires knowledge of how to do it, and control. It is not easy for the audience to see the two small points of an actor's eyes. It requires the prolonged immobility of the person they are looking at. Therefore, although it is quite proper for you to turn and move about, you must do so in moderation when your play is centred on your face and your eyes. You must act so that your eyes will be visible to us."

After my turn Grisha and Sonya played a scene they had invented about a jealous husband cross-questioning his wife. Before he could state his accusation he had to trap her. In such a situation he had to make a show of calm, shrewdly veil his inner state, and not let her see his eyes.

Tortsov's comment to Grisha was:

"You are entirely calm and are not making any effort to hide inner agitation, because there isn't any there to hide. Kostya was deeply disturbed so he had something to conceal.

Two tempo-rhythms were contained simultaneously in him, one outer and one inner. He just sat there and did nothing but it excited us. You sat there but we were not affected because in the complex, split state of mind you imagined yourself to be in you still had only the one tempo-rhythm, a calm one which gave to your conversation the wrong tone, that of a peaceful, friendly, family chat.

"Let me repeat that in complicated and contradictory inner patterns and trends of emotions you cannot get along with just one tempo-rhythm. You must combine several of them."

9

"Up to now we have been talking about the tempo-rhythm of individual groups, persons, moments, scenes. But whole plays, whole performances have their tempo-rhythms," explained Tortsov.

"Does this mean that once initiated a rate of space and measure should be sustained without further consideration for an entire evening? Of course not. The tempo-rhythm of a play or a performance is not one thing, it is a series of large and small conjunctions of varied and variegated rates of speed and measures, harmoniously composed into one large whole. All of these tempi and rhythms in their totality create an imposing and stately, or a gay atmosphere!

"The meaning of a tempo-rhythm is very great for any performance. Often a fine play, which has been beautifully designed and acted, fails to meet with success because it is performed with undue slowness or inappropriate briskness. Just imagine the result if you tried playing a tragedy in tempi suited to vaudeville!

"Quite as often we see a mediocre piece, produced and played in a mediocre fashion, yet rendered in strong, buoyant tempi, meet with success because it makes a cheerful impression.

"Surely there is no need to prove to you that methods of

psycho-technique would be of immense assistance to us in the complicated and elusive process of determining the right tempo-rhythms for a whole play, or for a role.

"But we do not possess any exact psycho-technical means in this field, so this is what happens in actual practice:

"The overall tempo-rhythm of a dramatic production usually creates itself accidentally, of its own accord. If an actor, for whatever reason, has the right sense of the play and his part, if he is in good form, if the public is responsive, then he will live his part in the right way and the proper tempo-rhythm will be established all by itself. When this does not occur we appear to be helpless. If we had an appropriate kind of psycho-technique we could enlist its aid to fix the basis, first for an external and then an internal tempo-rhythm. Through them the feelings themselves would be evoked.

"The lucky ones are the musicians, the singers, the dancers! They have metronomes, conductors, choir masters. They have their problems of tempo-rhythm all worked out, they are aware of its prime importance in their creative work. The accuracy of their musical performance is to a certain extent guaranteed, that is to say it is established, from the point of view of correct time and measure. These things are entered on their musical scores and are always regulated by conductors.

"With us actors the story is by no means the same. It is only in the verse form that measure is carefully studied. But for the rest we have no laws, no metronomes, no notes, no printed scores, no conductor. That is why the selfsame play may be performed on different occasions in such different tempi and rhythms.

"We actors have no recourse to any help in this matter of tempo-rhythm, and yet we stand in sore need of some help.

"Let us suppose that an actor, just before his performance, receives some disturbing news, with the result that his own tempo-rhythm on this particular evening is upset. He

comes on to the scene in this heightened, speeded up condition. On some other day this same actor may have been
robbed and the poor fellow may be in a state of despair.
His tempo-rhythm will drop, on the stage and in real life.

"Consequently the performance is directly dependent on
the passing incidents of life and not on any psycho-technique
of our art.

"Let us suppose further that an actor has, to the best of
his ability, calmed himself or keyed himself up before
coming on the stage and that he has augmented his ordinary,
daily life rhythm from No. 50 (on the metronome) to a
greater degree of intensity, perhaps No. 100. The actor is
satisfied and believes he has accomplished all that was
required. Yet in reality he is still far from coming up to the
right rhythm of the play which calls, say, for No. 200. This
discrepancy reflects on the proposed circumstances, on his
creative objective and its achievement. But the most serious
thing is that it reflects on his own emotional reactions and
experience in the part.

"We constantly see this lack of co-ordination between the
human being and actor on one side and his part on the other.

"Remember your own state of being when you made your
appearance at your first test performance (in *An Actor
Prepares*—EDITOR), standing in front of the big black hole
of the proscenium arch and facing an auditorium you
believed was filled with a huge crowd.

"Now try to be a conductor and beat out for me your
tempo-rhythm at that time!"

We did as we were told, but for my part my arms were
scarcely agile enough to convey all the needed thirty-second
notes with their dots, their triplets and syncopations to
reproduce that memorable occasion. Tortsov fixed No. 200
as the speed of the tempo I was "conducting".

After that he asked us to recall the quietest, dullest times
of our lives and to "conduct" them in their tempo-rhythms.
I thought back to my old life in Nizhni Novgorod and waved
my arms in accordance with my feelings. Tortsov rated the

speed of my tempo-rhythm at No. 20 on the metronome.

"Now imagine that you are playing the part of a phlegmatic character like Podkolesin in *Marriage* by Gogol. For this you need the tempo of No. 20. Yet you as an actor are in a state of excitement over opening night just before the curtain is going up and your own tempo is No. 200. How are you going to combine the state of the human being with the exigencies of the actor? Let us suppose that you can succeed in calming yourself somewhat and reducing your inner tempo to No. 100. It seems to you that you have accomplished a great deal, but actually it is far from sufficient because the role of Podkolesin calls for a tempo of No. 20. How can this discrepancy be reconciled? How can it be made good in the absence of any metronome?

"The best way out of such a situation is to learn to feel tempo-rhythm the way good conductors do. Name any degree of speed on the metronome to them and they can conduct it. If only there were a group of actors with such an absolute sense of tempo-rhythm! Just think what one could get from them!" exclaimed Tortsov with a sigh.

"Exactly what could one get?" we asked.

"I'll tell you," he explained. "Not long ago I had occasion to direct an opera and in it there was a big crowd, a choral scene. The participants included not only the principal singers and chorus but also ordinary members of the cast and some more or less experienced supernumeraries. They were all more or less trained in tempo-rhythm. If one compared them with the members of our groups, not one of them could stand out as an actor.

"Nevertheless I must confess that in this particular scene the opera actors outclassed us more competent dramatic artists, despite the fact that they had far fewer rehearsals than we have in our theatre.

"This operatic crowd scene proved to be something we have never yet achieved in our theatre with its incomparably superior opportunities for more careful rehearsing.

"What was the secret of this?

"Tempo-rhythm gave colour, smoothness, shapeliness, suppleness to an otherwise ragged scene.

"Tempo-rhythm lent to the singers a quality of magnificent clarity, fluency, finish, plasticity and harmony.

"Tempo-rhythm helped the artists, who were not yet far advanced in psycho-technique, to a true feeling for and possession of the inner aspects of their parts."

We suggested to Tortsov that his dream of an acting company with an almost absolute sense of tempo-rhythm was scarcely one that could be realized.

"I agree, and I am ready to make some concessions," he replied. "If I cannot count on everyone in the group let me at least see some of you develop a sense of tempo-rhythm. In the wings just before a play begins one often hears the remark: No need to worry about to-day's performance because so-and-so is acting. What is meant by this? It means that even one or two actors can draw all the others and the whole play along with them. That is the way, at least, that things used to be.

"Tradition has it that our great predecessors Shchepkin, Sadovski, Shumski, Samarin always arrived in the wings well ahead of their entrances so that they could have ample time to catch the tempo of the performance under way. That is one reason why, when they came on they brought with them a certain liveliness, truthfulness and struck the right note for the play and their parts in it.

"There can be no doubt that they were able to achieve this not only because they were great artists who had carefully prepared their entrances but also because they were consciously or intuitively *sensitive to tempo-rhythm* and used it in their own way. Evidently they retained in their memories a conception of the rapid or slow pace, the measured beat of the action of each scene and of the play as a whole.

"Or it is also possible that each time they made a fresh start in finding the tempo-rhythm of a performance by sitting for a long time in the wings before their entrances, and by following closely what was going on on the stage. Thus they attuned themselves, consciously or unconsciously, to the tempo-rhythm. They may have had special ways of doing this about which we, unfortunately, have no information.

"You too should try to be that kind of artist able to infect the whole cast with the proper tempo-rhythm."

"What is the basis of the psycho-technique for the establishing of the tempo-rhythm of a play or a part? What does one build on?" I asked.

"*The tempo-rhythm of a whole play is the tempo-rhythm of the through line of action and the subtextual content of the play.* You already know that the through line of action calls for two angles of perspective: that of the actor and that of the part. Just as the painter distributes the colours over his picture and seeks to establish the true balance of relationship among them, so the actor seeks the rightly balanced distribution of tempo-rhythm along the whole through line of action in a play."

"We shall never in the wide world be able to do that without a conductor," mused Vanya.

"Then Rakhmanov here will invent something to take the place of a conductor for you," said Tortsov laughingly as he left the class.

10

To-day as every day I reached class well ahead of time. The stage was lighted, the curtain drawn, and there stood Rakhmanov in his shirt sleeves hastily arranging something or other with an electrician.

I offered my services. This caused Rakhmanov to take me into his confidence before he had intended to reveal his secret preparations.

It appeared that he had invented some kind of an "electrical conductor for plays". His invention was still in a very rough stage, but this was what he had in mind: In the prompter's box, hidden from the public but visible to the actors there would be a small contraption with two noiselessly blinking electric lights which would take the place of the indicator and the tick of a metronome. When necessary the prompter would set it in motion according to the indications in his prompt book of the tempi agreed upon in rehearsal for each important segment of the play. Thus he could remind the actors of the proper pace for them.

Tortsov took an interest in Rakhmanov's invention and the two men proceeded to act out various scenes while the electrician switched on a tempo at random. Whereupon these two actors with their magnificent control of tempo-rhythm, their marvellously fluent imaginations, proceeded to find a justification for expressing any and every rhythm set for them. Beyond all doubt they demonstrated by their own example the effective purpose of the electrical conductor.

After them Paul and I and others had our turns to make a series of tests. It was only accidentally that we hit the pace squarely. The rest of the time we wobbled.

"The conclusion to be drawn from this would seem to be obvious," Tortsov said. "The electrical conductor is an excellent aid to actors and can be used as a regulator for a performance. It is a possible and useful adjunct in practice but only where all or at least some of the actors possess a well trained sense of tempo-rhythm. Unfortunately there are, with rare exceptions, very few of them in our branch of art.

"Worse than that," Tortsov continued in a depressed tone, "there is little or no awareness of the importance of tempo and rhythm in drama. Therefore it is all the more necessary that you give your special attention to your future exercises in tempo-rhythm."

The class wound up in general conversation. A number of students offered their own ideas about how to replace a conductor for plays.

Tortsov made one remark here that was noteworthy.

In his opinion actors should get together before performances and during the intermissions to do exercises with
music calculated to set them going on the right pulsations
of tempo-rhythm. This would be in the nature of setting
up exercises.

"What would the exercises consist of?" came the question
from various quarters.

"Don't be in such a hurry!" warned Tortsov. "Before
you come to them you will have to do a whole series of
elementary exercises."

"What kind of exercises?" the students again demanded.

"I shall tell you about that in our next class," replied
Tortsov and left the stage.

II

"Good day and good tempo-rhythm to you," was Tortsov's greeting to us as he came into class to-day. Then
noting our puzzled faces he added: "Are you surprised by
my wishing you good tempo or good rhythm instead of,
shall we say, good health? Your health can be good or bad
but if your tempo-rhythm is good it is the best evidence of
your well-being. That is why to-day I wish you good
tempo-rhythm as the equivalent of good health.

"But seriously, tell me what state of tempo-rhythm are
you in?"

"I really don't know," said Paul.

"What about you?" Tortsov asked, turning to Leo.

"No idea," was the muttered reply.

"And you?" Tortsov put the question to me and the
others in turn.

No one had a clear answer to give.

"So that's the kind of a company gathered here!" Tortsov
exclaimed with elaborately feigned astonishment. "It's the
first time in my life that I have ever met people like that!
Not one of you is aware of the rhythm, the tempo of his own
life. And yet one would really think that any human being

must sense the rate of speed or some other measure of his movements, actions, feelings, thinking and breathing, of the pulsing of his blood, his heart beat, his general condition, in other words.

"But we do, of course, feel all that. What we don't understand is at what point do we make our measurements? Is it when I think of the pleasure in store for me this evening thereby evoking a cheerful tempo-rhythm, or is it at some other moments when I may be in doubt about the agreeable prospects for the day and this causes my tempo-rhythm to slacken?

"If you beat both of those speeds out for me," said Tortsov, "you would produce an alternating rhythm. That is what you are living on at present. You may make mistakes, but there is no harm in that. The important thing is that in searching out the tempo-rhythm inside you you discover your own feelings.

"What was your tempo-rhythm when you woke up this morning?" was Tortsov's next question.

The students knit their brows and took a very serious view of how to make their replies.

"Don't tell me you have to make such a great effort to answer my question!" said Tortsov, surprised. "Our sense of tempo-rhythm is always right there, on tap. We always have some notion, if only an approximate one, of every moment we have lived through."

I tried to make a mental picture of the circumstances when I woke up this morning and I recalled a sense of concern. I was afraid of being late for my first class, I had to shave, stop by at the post office to cash a money order, which I should have done several days before. Hence a worried, rapid tempo-rhythm which I beat out and which I re-lived as I did it.

After a bit Tortsov invented a new game. He beat out for us a rather quick, uneven rhythm. We repeated it a number of times so that we could familiarize ourselves with it and get the swing of it.

"Now," said Tortsov, "you decide in what imaginary circumstances and from what emotional experiences could such a rhythm emerge?"

To fulfill the objective it was necessary to invent an appropriate fiction. In turn I had to rouse my imagination by asking myself a series of questions: where, when, for what purpose, why am I here? Who are these people around me? It appeared that I was in a surgeon's ante-room in a hospital and I was on the verge of hearing a decision regarding my health: either I am seriously ill, faced with an operation, perhaps death, or I am quite healthy and shall go out of here as I came in. This fiction had its effect on me, in fact I was much more excited by it than I needed to be for the purpose of the tempo-rhythm given us.

So it was necessary to dilute the plot somewhat. I was not waiting to see an imaginary surgeon, but a dentist who would pull one of my teeth. But even that proved too strong an incitement for the tempo-rhythm under consideration. I was obliged mentally to transfer to a throat doctor who would inflate my ear-drums. That was the most appropriate invention for the purposes of Tortsov's tempo-rhythm. One after the other we explained our imaginary given circumstances.

"So you see," Tortsov said, "for the first half of the lesson you concentrated on your own inner experiences and you expressed them externally in terms of a tempo-rhythm you conducted. Now you have just taken another person's tempo-rhythm and brought it to life by your imaginative inventions and remembered emotions. You went from feelings to tempo-rhythm and back again from tempo-rhythm to feelings.

"An actor should be in technical control of both these approaches.

"At the end of our last lesson you were curious about exercises to develop tempo-rhythm.

"To-day I have pointed out to you the *two main avenues to follow as guides in making a choice of exercises.*"

"But where shall we find the exercises themselves?" I asked.

"Remember the experiments we made earlier. For all of them tempo and rhythm are needed. They contain sufficient materials for training and drill. This is the answer I promised to the question you put to me last time," said Tortsov in ending the class.

SPEECH TEMPO-RHYTHM

I

"OUR study of this thing we call 'tempo-rhythm' has progressed considerably," Tortsov remarked. "First of all we tried to discover what it was in its most obvious manifestations. Like kindergarten children we clapped in time to the metronomes. Then we progressed to more complicated tempi; we even tried to send messages by beating out the rhythm of a series of actions seen by our inner eyes. And we discovered that the beats conveyed a feeling however nebulous to our hearers but which had an even stronger effect on ourselves. It actually aided in the process of our inner creation.

"We went on to subtler evidences of tempo-rhythm, found that our tempo-rhythm could be in seeming conflict with that of others on the stage, in life; we discovered that within ourselves we could experience an inner tempo-rhythm and a different outer one at the same time and that the conflict of the two was evident from small hints in our actions. It gave power and reality to the character we were building. We discussed the tempo-rhythm of a whole play, of its through line of action, its subtle shiftings and yet its oneness of effect when successfully discovered and performed.

"All this was the tempo-rhythm of movement and action. Now we are going to apply the same discoveries to speech. I start with the fact that the voice sounds of syllables and words provide an excellent means of conveying the tempo-rhythm of the inner import of any play. As I said before, in the process of speech the line of words proceeds in time, and that time is broken up by the sounds of letters, syllables, words. This division of time makes rhythmic parts and groups.

"The nature of certain sounds, syllables and words requires a clipped pronunciation comparable to eighth and sixteenth notes in music: others must be produced in a more weighty, longer form, more ponderously, like whole or half notes. Along with this some sounds and syllables receive a stronger or a weaker rhythmic accentuation; a third group may be entirely without any accent.

"These spoken sounds, in turn, are interlarded with pauses, rests for breathing, of most variable lengths. All these are phonetic possibilities out of which to fashion an endless variety of the tempo-rhythms of speech. In making use of them an actor works out for himself a finely proportioned speech style. He needs this when he is on the stage and using words to convey both the exalted emotions of tragedy and the gay mood of comedy.

"To create a tempo-rhythm of speech it does not suffice to divide time into particles of sound; one must also have a beat to form speech measures.

"In the domain of action we produced this by means of the metronome and bell. What can we use for this problem? How shall we synchronize individual rhythmic stresses, the particular letters and syllables of the words in our text? Instead of a metronome we shall be obliged to make use of a mental count. We must constantly, intuitively keep ourselves attuned to it and its tempo-rhythm.

"A measured, resonant, well blended speech possesses many qualities akin to those of music and singing.

"Letters, syllables, words—these are the musical notes of speech, out of which to fashion measures, arias, whole symphonies. There is good reason to describe beautiful speech as musical.

"Words spoken with resonance and sweep are more affecting. In speech as in music there is a great difference between a phrase enunciated in whole, quarter or sixteenth notes, or with triplets or quintuplets thrown in. In one case the phrase can be solemn, in another the tripping chatter of a school girl.

"In the first instance there is calm, in the second nervousness, agitation.

"Talented singers know all about this. They stand in fear of sinning against rhythm. If the music calls for three quarter notes a true artist will produce three tones of exactly that length. If the composer has put a whole note, the true singer will hold it to the end of the bar. If the music calls for triplets or syncopations, he will sing them with the mathematical rhythm required. This precision has an irresistible effect. Art requires order, discipline, precision and finish. Even in cases where one is called upon to convey a rhythmic effect musically, one must do it with clear cut finish. Even chaos and disorder have their tempo-rhythm.

"What I have just said in regard to music and singers is equally applicable to us dramatic artists. There exists, however, a vast number of singers who are not real artists but just people who sing, with or without voices. They have an astonishing facility for jumbling eighth with sixteenth notes, quarter with half notes, three eighth notes of equal length into one and so on.

"Consequently their singing lacks all necessary precision, discipline, organization, finish. It turns into a disorderly, chaotic mess. It ceases to be music and becomes some sort of sheer vocal exhibitionism.

"The same thing can and does happen to speech. Take an actor, for instance, of the type of Vasya with an uneven rhythm in his speech. He switches it not only from clause to clause but in the middle even of a single phrase. Often one half of a sentence will be spoken in a slow tempo and the second half in a markedly rapid one. Let us take the phrase 'Most potent, grave and reverend signiors.' That would be spoken slowly, solemnly, but the next words 'my very noble and approved good masters,' would be, after a long pause, suddenly delivered with extreme rapidity.

"Many actors who are careless of speech, inattentive to words, pronounce them with such thoughtless slipshod speed, without putting any endings on them, that they end up with completely mutilated, half spoken phrases.

"Shifting rhythms are even more obvious in actors of certain national origins.

"In proper and beautiful speech there should not be any of these manifestations, except where a change of tempo-rhythm is called for on purpose for the characterization of a part. Obviously the splitting up of words must correspond to the rapidity or slowness of speech and must preserve the given tempo-rhythm. In quick conversation or reading the pauses are shorter and, conversely, longer in slow conversation or reading.

"Our difficulty lies in the fact that many actors lack a well-rounded training in two important elements of speech; on the one side there is smoothness, slowness, resonance, fluency, and on the other, rapidity, lightness, clarity, crispness in the pronunciation of words. We rarely hear in the Russian theatre speech which is slow, resonant, legato, or really rapid and light. In the vast majority of cases all we are aware of is long pauses and the words between them hurriedly rushed out.

"To achieve stately, slow speech we need first of all to replace silent pauses with sonorous cadences, the sustained singing tone of the words.

"It will help you to read aloud very slowly to the timing of a metronome, if you are careful to preserve the smooth flow of words in rhythmic measures and also if you provide yourselves with the right inner basis for your exercise. In this way you should be able to achieve slow, fluent speech.

"It is even more rare to hear good rapid speech on our stage, well sustained as to tempo, clear cut in rhythm, enunciated so as to be intelligible. We do not know how to rival the French and the Italian actors in their brilliant quick speech. Most of us cannot do real patter, we babble, spatter and spew out words. Real patter has to be learned and it begins with the mastery of very slow, exaggeratedly precise speech. By long and frequent repetition our speech apparatus becomes so trained that it learns how to execute the same words at the quickest possible rate of speed. This requires constant practice because dramatic speech at times requires this speed. So do not take the bad singers with their broken rhythms of speech as your models. Take the true artists, learn their ways of speech with all their clarity, right proportions and discipline.

"In speaking give the proper length to sounds, syllables, words, use a clean cut rhythm in combining their tonal particles; form your phrases into measures of speech, regulate the rhythmic relationship among whole phrases; learn to love correct and clear accentuation, appropriate to remembered emotions and also to the creation of a character image.

"A clear cut rhythm of speech facilitates rhythmic sensibility and the opposite is also true: the rhythm of sensations experienced helps to produce clear speech. Of course, all this occurs in the cases where precision of speech is thoroughly based on inner, suggested circumstances and the *magic if.*"

2

To-day's lesson began when Tortsov ordered the large metronome to be set going at a slow tempo. As usual Rakhmanov indicated the measures by the ringing of a bell.

Then another small metronome was started to indicate the rhythm of speech. Tortsov then asked me to speak to their accompaniment.

"What shall I say?" I asked, puzzled.

"Whatever you like," he replied. "Tell me about some episode in your life, what you did yesterday, what you are thinking about to-day."

I racked my brains and then told about what I had seen the previous evening in the movies. Meantime the metronome beat the accents, the bell rang, but they bore no relation to what I was saying. They worked along in their mechanical way, and I talked along in mine.

Tortsov laughed and remarked:

"The band is playing and the flag just flaps."

"It's not surprising because I don't understand how I am supposed to speak in cadence with a metronome," I retorted nervously in an effort to defend myself. "One can sing, or recite verses in time and in measures, and try to make the stress and scansion coincide with certain beats of the machine. But how can this be done with prose? Where should the stresses coincide—I don't understand," I said in a plaintive tone. But Tortsov would only tell me to continue.

Actually I was ahead or behind the accent, I dragged or I rushed the tempo unreasonably. In either case I missed the beat of the metronome.

Then suddenly and quite by accident I happened to coincide with the beat over and over again and this gave me an extraordinarily agreeable feeling.

But my joy was shortlived. The tempo-rhythm which I had accidentally hit on lasted only for several seconds, then it quickly vanished to be replaced once more by the previous disjunction.

I forced myself to achieve a new accord with the metronome. But the greater my effort the more confused I became in my rhythm and the more I was put out by the beat of the machine. I was no longer conscious of what I was saying and finally I stopped altogether.

"I can't go on! I have no sense of tempo or of rhythm," I concluded and I was almost on the verge of tears.

"That's not so! Don't you confuse yourself," was Tortsov's rejoinder. "It is only that you are too demanding in your tempo-rhythm in prose, consequently it cannot give you what you expect. Don't forget that prose cannot be scanned, any more than ordinary motions of the body can be danced. Rhythmic coincidence cannot be rigidly regular, whereas in verses and in dances this is carefully prepared in advance.

"People who possess a greater sense of rhythm will achieve more frequent coincidence of accents. Those in whom this sense is not so well developed will do this less often. That's all. What I am trying to discover is who among you belong in the first and who in the second category.

"You personally may be reassured," he said, "because I count you among the rhythmically endowed students. It is only that you are as yet not cognizant of one method which would help you to a control of tempo-rhythm. So listen attentively and I shall explain an important secret of speech technique to you.

"There is tempo-rhythm in prose as well as in poetry and music. But in ordinary speech it is accidental. In prose the tempo-rhythm is mixed: one phrase will be spoken in one rhythm, the next in an entirely different one. One phrase will be long, another short, and each will have its own peculiar rhythm.

"In the beginning one may be inclined to the sad conclusion that prose is not given to rhythm. But I would suggest this question: Have you ever had occasion to hear an opera, an aria, or a song, not written in verse but in prose? If so you heard a composition in which the notes, pauses, measures, accompaniment, melody, tempo-rhythm were integrated with the letters, syllables, words and phrases of the text. The whole combined to produce harmonious, rhythmic musical sounds with the underlying text of words. In that realm of mathematically proportioned rhythm simple prose appeared almost to be verse, it had gained all the harmony of music. Now let us try to follow this same path in our own prosaic speech.

"Let us recall first what takes place in music. The voice sings a melody with words; the spaces, where there are no notes with words, are filled out by the accompaniment, or rests are inserted to round out the rhythmic beats in each measure.

"We have the same thing in prose. Letters, syllables, words take the place for us of notes, and stops, pauses for breath are counts which fill the rhythm when there is no verbal text to round out the measure of speech.

"The sound of letters, syllables and words with pauses in between are excellent material, as you already know, for the creation of all sorts of different rhythms.

On the stage our prose speech can to a certain extent approach music and verse when the stresses on words fall constantly on the same beat as the accent in a given rhythm.

"We see something of this sort in 'poems in prose', and also in the work of some modern poets which might be called 'prose in verse' and which is so close to ordinary colloquial talk.

"The tempo-rhythm of our prose, then, is made up of alternating groups of stressed and unstressed syllables, interlarded with pauses, which naturally have a flow pleasing to the ear and which follow infinite patterns of rhythm. At the same time we must speak and be silent, move or be still in tempo-rhythm.

"Ordinary pauses and pauses for breath in spoken poetry or prose have an extreme importance not only because they are a component part of the rhythmic line but also because they play a significant and active role in the very technique of creating and controlling rhythm. Both types of pauses make possible the coincidence of the stresses in the rhythms of speech, actions, emotions with the accents of an actor's inner beat.

"This process of rounding out the blanks in a measure with rests and pauses for breath is called by some 'Ta-ta-ti-ra-reering!'

"The origin of the expression, incidentally, is drawn from the fact that when we are singing a melody and do not know the words we replace the beats with nonsensical syllables such as: ta-ta-ti-ra-ra.

"You were upset because the agreement of your stresses with the tick of metronome was accidental. Now I hope you will be less concerned about it, since you know that there are means to overcome this, and one, which will render your prose speech rhythmic."

3

"The crux of the matter is, of course, in knowing how to combine phrases of varying rhythms into one whole. It almost plays a part similar to that of a conductor and a chorus who are called upon to carry all the crowd of people listening to them from one part of a symphony written in 3/4 time to another in 5/4 time. This cannot be done immediately. People in general, and especially the mass of an audience, when accustomed in one part of a symphony to be attuned to a given rate of speed and measure, cannot easily shift to and accept an entirely different tempo and rhythm in another part of a symphony.

"A conductor is occasionally obliged to help both his performers and his audience over the obstacle of this transition. He does not accomplish his goal at once, he carries his performers and listeners through a series of transitional, rhythmic steps which lead in logical progression to the new rhythm.

"We must do the same in turning from one measure of speech with its tempo-rhythm to another of a different beat, of differing tempo and length of measure. The difference between the conductor and us lies in the fact that he accomplishes what he is after quite openly with his baton in hand, but we have to do it secretly, inwardly, with the help of a mental beat or 'tatatirareering'.

"The first purpose for which we actors need these transitional devices is to make a clear cut, definite entry into the new tempo-rhythm and be confident that we carry with us the person with whom we are engaged at the time and, along with that person, carry the whole audience.

"This 'ta-ta-ti-ra-reering' in prose is the bridge which links the most heterogeneous phrases or measures of most heterogeneous rhythms."

The rest of the lesson was spent in our talking to the tick of the metronome in a very much simplified way. We chatted normally, but now we tried to have our key words and syllables coincide wherever possible with the beat of the metronome.

Into the intervals between the beats we arranged a series of words and phrases so grouped that, without changing the sense of what we were saying, it was logically right to have the stresses coincide with the beats. We even succeeded in filling out the blanks in the verbal contents of our phrases with counts and pauses. Of course that kind of speaking is very arbitrary and haphazard. Neverthless it did produce a certain harmony and I derived some inner encouragement from the experiment.

It is to this effect of tempo-rhythm on the inner sensibilities that Tortsov ascribed great importance.

4

Tortsov opened with this small scene from Griboyedov's verse classic, *Woe From Too Much Wit*.

Famusov: What's this? . . . Molchalin, you?

Molchalin: I? . . .

Famusov: Here and at this hour? Why? . . .

After a brief pause Tortsov rephrased the speeches thus:

" 'Well, what is the occasion for your being here? Is that you, my friend Molchalin?' 'Yes, it's I.' 'How do you happen to be here at this hour?' "

He now spoke the phrases without rhyme or rhythm.

"The sense remains the same, but what a difference! In the prosy form the words spill all over, they lose their tautness, their clean cut, emphatic quality, their edge," explained Tortsov. "In verse every word is necessary, there are no superfluous ones. What we use a whole phrase to express in prose may often be said in a word or two in poetry. And with what finish, what control!

"You may say that the essential difference between the two contrasting versions I have used as examples of poetry versus prose lies in the fact that the former was written by the great Griboyedov and the second was unsuccessfully composed by me.

"That is, of course, true. Nevertheless I maintain that even if the great poet had written the very same thing in prose he would not have been able to convey the same exquisite quality as he did in his verse, the clean cut rhythm, the sharpness of the rhymes. For instance when Molchalin meets Famusov in the first act, in order to express the state of panic he is in, he is given only the one word to say: 'I'.

"The actor who plays Molchalin must have the same finish, edge, sharpness to his inner feelings as to his external conveying of all that lies behind the words: the terror, the embarrassment, the apologetic servility—everything that Molchalin is experiencing.

"Poetry arouses different emotions because of its different form from prose. But the converse is also true. Poetry has another form because we sense its subtext in a different way.

"One of the main differences between spoken prose and verse forms lies in their having different tempo-rhythms, in the fact that their measures differ in their influence on our sensations, memories, our emotions.

"On this basis we may reason as follows: The more rhythmic verse or prose is in speech, the more clearly defined should be our experience of the thoughts and emotions which underlie the words of the text. And conversely: The more clear, defined and rhythmic the thoughts and emotions we experience the more they call for rhythmic verbal expression.

"Here we have a new aspect of the effect of tempo-rhythm on emotion and of emotion on tempo-rhythm.

"Do you remember how you beat out and 'conducted' the tempi and rhythms of various moods, actions, even images suggested to your imaginations? Then the sheer beating of tempo-rhythm was sufficient to stimulate your emotion memories, your feelings and experiences.

"If that much could be brought about by ordinary tapping, how much more easily can you achieve the effect by means of the living sounds of a human voice, the tempo-rhythm of letters, syllables, words and their underlying implications.

"Yet even if we do not understand the meaning of words their sounds affect us through their tempo-rhythms. I recall, for instance, the soliloquy of Corado in the melodrama *Family of a Criminal* as played by Tommaso Salvini. This soliloquy described a criminal's escape from prison.

"I was ignorant of the Italian language, I had no idea what the actor was narrating, but I was deeply involved in all the detailed emotions he was experiencing. I was helped to this largely not only by the magnificent intonations of Salvini, but also by the remarkably clear cut, expressive tempo-rhythm of his speech.

"Think too of verses in which tempo-rhythm paints sound pictures, such as the ringing of bells or the clatter of horses' hooves. For example:

Hear the tolling of the bells—
Iron bells!
What a world of solemn thought their monody compels!

I sprang to the stirrup, and Joris and he:
I galloped, Dirck galloped, we galloped all three; . . ."

5

"You know that speech consists not only of sounds but also of pauses," Tortsov explained to-day. "Both of these must be equally impregnated with tempo-rhythm.

"Rhythm is inherent in an actor and manifests itself when he is on the stage, whether in his actions or when he is inactive, when he speaks or is silent. It is interesting now to trace the inter-relationship of these moments of tempi and rhythms in action and inaction, speech and silence. This is an especially difficult question when we are dealing with verse forms in speech. I shall begin with that.

"The difficulty lies in the fact that in verse there is a limit to the extent of any break or pause. One cannot with impunity prolong a pause because it breaks the tempo-rhythm of the spoken words. This causes both the speaker and the listener to lose track of the previous tempo and metre of the verse, they get out of control and must be re-established.

"That in turn causes a rift in the verse. Nevertheless there are circumstances when prolonged pauses are inevitable because of necessary actions. Take as an example that part of the first scene of Griboyedov's play *Woe From Too Much Wit*. Lisa knocks at Sophia's bedroom door, to put an end to an amorous interview between her mistress and Molchalin which has been prolonged to the early morning hours. The scene runs thus:

Lisa (at Sophia's door):
They hear but they refuse to listen. (A pause. She sees the clock, an idea strikes her.)
I'll set the clock ahead, although it means a scolding, I'll make the hour strike . . .
(Pause. Lisa crosses the stage, opens the clock case, turns the hands, causes them to play their chimes. She dances. Enter Famusov)
Oh, master!
Famusov: Your master, yes.
(Pause. Famusov goes over to the clock, opens the case, stops the chimes)
How frivolous,
You naughty girl. I know
I could not have imagined such a creature!

"As you see there are lengthy intervals imposed here between the lines by the nature of the action. It must be added that the difficulty of carrying over the verse is further complicated where there is the necessity of making the point of the rhymes. An excessively long interval between the rhymed lines makes one forget them, it kills them, and an all too short interval between them, which hurries and scamps the action called for, destroys one's belief in the credibility and truth of those actions. It is necessary to reckon a combination of timing, intervals between rhymed words and the feeling of truth in the action. In all these alternations of spoken words, pauses, wordless actions, 'ta-ta-ti-ra-reering' will support the inner rhythm.

"Many actors who play the parts of Lisa and Famusov are afraid of extended breaks in the spoken text, they rush too fast through the necessary business in order to get back as quickly as possible the words and the tempo-rhythm which has been interrupted. A choppiness results, it kills the audience's belief in the truthfulness of what is happening. Such undermining of the action and speech turns what is done on the stage into simple nonsense. It takes all life out of acting, and anything that is lifeless and has no under-lying basis is unconvincing. From every point of view it is boring, it cannot hold, it cannot even attract the attention of the public. This state of affairs not only does not shorten the pauses, on the contrary it makes them seem even longer. That is why the kind of actors I am describing defeat their own purposes by fussy movements, winding the clock, stopping the chimes. They betray their own powerlessness, their fear of pauses, their senseless fidgets and their lack of all the underpinnings to their lines. They should proceed quite differently: they should quietly, without undue pauses between lines, carry out the needed movements in accord-ance with the inner beat. And they should at all times be motivated by a sense of truthfulness and rhythm.

"When an actor begins to speak again after a long pause, he needs for a second or two to emphasize the accent of verse rhythm. This will help both him and the audience get back into the rhythm that has been interrupted and perhaps even lost track of.

"As you see an actor should know how to be rhythmic not

only in speech but also in silence. He must reckon the words together with the pauses and not take them as separate entities.

"It is because the measure of spoken words and the rhythmic quality of the intervals is most evident in verse that I have used that as the first demonstration.

"It is not my job to teach you versification or even how to read verse. That will be done by an expert. I am merely acquainting you with various discoveries of my own experience. They will help you in your work.

"From all I have said you can easily judge the all-important part tempo-rhythm plays in an actor's work. Together with the through line of action and the subtext it runs like a thread through all movements, words, pauses, the emotional experience of a part and its physical interpretation."

6

The next step was a review of tempo-rhythm. Leo was the first called up to be examined. He read the Salieri soliloquy (from Pushkin's *Mozart and Salieri*) and he acquitted himself very well. In recalling how unsuccessful Leo had been demonstrating tempo-rhythm in the exercise with the tray, Tortsov made the remark:

"Here is an example of the co-existence in one person of arhythmic physical action with rhythmic speech, even when this latter is rather dry and somewhat lacking in inner content."

Vasya was next, and in contrast to Leo he executed the old tray exercise excellently, although he did not come off so well with his spoken rhythms.

"There is the opposite state of affairs, a person who is rhythmic in his movements and at the same time arhythmic in speech," said Tortsov.

Grisha read next. Tortsov's comment on him was to class him with the actors who make use of one fixed tempo-rhythm in everything they do, their movements, words, silences, all in a monotonous pace and measure.

These actors suit their permanent tempo-rhythm to their type: the "noble father" has his fixed and always "noble" rhythm; the ingenue always warbles in a youthful restless, rapid rhythm, the comédienne, the hero, the heroine—each has his permanently established tempo-rhythm.

Although Grisha aspires to be a leading man, he has adopted the tempo and rhythm of a character actor, or what the French call a *raisonneur*.

"That is too bad," explained Tortsov, "because it has a dampening effect. It would be better for him to stick to his off-stage tempo-rhythm. That, at least, would not have frozen in one kind of pace, it would reflect the alternating rhythms of life."

For various reasons Tortsov did not have the others go through a demonstration. Instead he turned to the explanation of another aspect of this same problem of tempo-rhythm:

"There are many actors," he said, "who allow themselves to be carried away by the external form of poetry, its metre, and completely ignore the subtext and all the inner rhythm of living and feeling.

"They may be meticulous, even to the point of pedantry, in their rendering of the metre. They may stress, with careful articulation, each rhyme, and scan a poem with mechanical precision. They are extremely fearful of any divergence from the mathematically exact rhythm. They are also afraid of pauses because they sense the vacuum of subtext. Actually the subtext is non-existent with them, they cannot really love a poem without knowing that which illumines it from within. All that is left is an empirical interest in rhythms and rhymes produced for their own sake, and hence a mechanical reading.

"These same actors have a similar attitude towards tempo. Having fixed this or that rate of speed they stick to it throughout a whole reading, never realizing that the tempo must go on living, vibrating, to a certain degree changing, but not remain frozen at the one rate of speed.

"There is little to choose between this attitude towards tempo, this lack of sensitiveness, and the soulless grinding out of a melody on a hand organ, or the tick of a metronome. Just compare this conception with that of a gifted conductor.

"For musicians of that sort an andante is not an inflexible andante, an allegro is not an absolute allegro. The first may at any time impinge on the second, or the second on the first. This life-giving oscillation does not exist in the mechanical tick of a metronome. In a good orchestra the tempi are constantly, almost imperceptibly, shifting and blending like the colours in a rainbow.

"All this applies to the theatre. We have directors and actors who are just mechanical craftsmen, and others who are splendid artists. The tempo of speech of the first is boring, monotonous, formal, whereas that of the second is infinitely varied, lively and expressive. Need I stress the fact that actors who take a cut and dried attitude towards tempo-rhythm never can really handle verse forms?

"We are familiar with the other extreme of reading on the stage in which the verse is all but turned into prose.

"This often is the result of excessive, exaggerated, over-intensified attention to the subtextual content, out of all proportion to the verse. It becomes burdened down by psycho-technique in the pauses, involved and muddled psychology.

"All this produces a heavy-footed inner tempo-rhythm and a psychologically over complex subtext which because of its involutions seeps into the verbal verse.

"A dramatic Wagnerian soprano with her rich, powerful voice is not chosen to sing the light, ethereal coloratura arias.

"In the same way one cannot weigh down the lightly rhyming verse of Griboyedov's play with an unnecessarily deep emotional subtext.

"This does not mean, of course, that verse cannot have deep emotional content. On the contrary. We all know that writers use the verse form when they want to convey edifying experiences or tragic emotions. Yet actors who overburden it with unduly ponderous subtextual content never really know how to handle poetry.

"There is a third type of actors who stand midway between the first two. They have an equal interest in the subtext with its inner tempo-rhythm and with the verbal verse text with its external tempo-rhythm, its sound forms, its measures and its definite outline. Actors of this type handle verse in quite a different way. Before they begin to recite they immerse themselves in waves of tempo-rhythm, and they remain soaked in it. In this way, not only their reading, but also their movements, their gait, their emanations and even the springs of their emotional experiences are constantly being flooded by these same waves of tempo-rhythm. They do not cut themselves off from them while they are speaking, nor when they are silent, in either logical or psychological pauses, when they are in action or when they are motionless.

"Actors of this type, who are inwardly permeated with tempo-rhythm, are perfectly at ease in pauses because these are not blank, dead places in the role, but lively intervals full of meaning; they have an inner glow of feeling and of imagination.

"These actors are never without an inner metronome; it provides an ever-present mental accompaniment to each word, act, reflexion, emotion.

"It is only under such circumstances that the verse form not only presents no embarrassments to the actor and his emotions, but even helps him to a full freedom of inner and outer action. It is only under such circumstances, when the inner process of an actor who is living his part is fused with its external incarnation, that a common tempo-rhythm is created and there is a complete union of the text and the subtext.

"When actors have an innately right comprehension of what they are conveying to the public they instantly fall into a more or less rhythmic pattern of verbal and physical expression. This happens because the bond between rhythm and feeling is so very close. Yet these same people, if their feelings do not respond spontaneously and they have to resort to rhythm to arouse them, are utterly helpless.

"So it is a great advantage to have a natural sense of tempo and rhythm. In any case it is something one should work to develop from one's earliest youth. Unfortunately there are many actors in whom it is scarcely developed at all."

7

Our class to-day was devoted to a summing up by Tortsov:

"The time has come to look at the results of our prolonged efforts. Let us check rapidly over what we have accomplished. Do you remember how we clapped hands to stimulate a mood in which feelings would correspond to the rhythm? Do you remember how we clapped out anything that came to mind, a march, a train's noise, various conversations? This clapping evoked a mood and feelings, if not in the listeners, at least in the person who was doing it. Do you remember the various tempi suggested by the departure of a train and all the real excitement felt by the passenger? And how we amused ourselves by evoking all kinds of feelings with a make-believe metronome? Then there was the exercise with the tray and all your outward and inward metamorphoses from the president of a sporting club into a drunken waiter in a small town railroad café. And do you recall acting to music?

"In all these sketches and exercises in action it was the tempo-rhythm in each case which created the mood and stimulated the corresponding emotional experiences.

"We made analogous experiments with words. You remember the influence on your feelings of the words recited in quarter notes, eighth notes, etc.

"Then we tried out ways of combining verse with

rhythmic intervals of silent action. Here you discovered the help to be derived from 'ta-ta-ti-ra-reering'. It served to keep the general rhythm of the verse form and the proportions of clear cut action, thereby effecting the union of words and acts.

"In all these exercises which I have enumerated there is one result which emerges, in greater or lesser degree. A state of inner experience, of inner sensation is created.

"This makes it possible for us to accept the fact that *tempo-rhythm, whether mechanically, intuitively or consciously created, does act on our inner life, on our feelings, on our inner experiences.* The same is true when we are in the very process of creative action on the stage.

"For what I have to say now I shall ask your most serious attention because I shall speak about something of deepest import not only in the field of tempo-rhythm, in which we have just been working, but in the wider field of our whole creative effort."

Tortsov made a significant pause here before he disclosed what was on his mind.

"Everything we have discovered about tempo-rhythm leads us to the conviction that it is the closest ally and adjunct óf feeling because it *often appears as a direct, immediate or else sometimes even an almost mechanical stimulus to emotion memory and consequently to innermost experience.*

"From this it follows that we cannot truly feel in the presence of the wrong or inappropriate tempo-rhythm. And further that we cannot find the true tempo-rhythm unless we simultaneously are moved by the feelings that are appropriate to it.

"There is an indissoluble interdependence, interaction and bond between tempo-rhythm and feeling and, conversely, between feeling and tempo-rhythm.

"If you will examine closely what I am saying you will realize the full extent of what we have discovered. It is extraordinarily important. We are considering the effect, direct or often only mechanical, of external tempo-rhythm on our capricious, arbitrary, intractable, shy feelings; on those feelings subject to no commands, frightened off by the least exhibition of force into the inaccessible well springs of our beings, those same feelings which up to now we have succeeded in affecting only by indirect, magnetic means. Here suddenly we find a direct, an immediate approach!

"This is indeed a great discovery! And if it really is the case then the *correctly established tempo-rhythm of a play or a role, can of itself, intuitively (on occasion automatically) take hold of the feelings of an actor and arouse in him a true sense of living his part.*

"Ask any singer what it means to him to sing under the direction of a talented musician who knows how to gauge the right tempo-rhythm, the one which is true, exact and characteristic of a given piece of music. He will tell you he scarcely recognizes himself.

"Imagine by contrast what happens to the singer who has prepared his role the right way and then comes out on the stage to be met with a wrong tempo-rhythm which clashes with his own. It is bound to undermine completely his feelings, his part, his inner creative state which is essential to his work.

"Exactly the same thing happens to actors when there is a clash of tempo-rhythm between their feelings and their physical interpretation of them in words and acts.

"Where does this lead us in the end? To the inescapable conclusion offered us by the wide possibility inherent in our psycho-technique, namely that we possess a direct, immediate means to stimulate every one of our inner motive forces.

"*The direct effect on our mind is achieved by the words, the text, the thought, which arouse consideration. Our will is directly affected by the super-objective, by other objectives, by a through line of action. Our feelings are directly worked upon by tempo-rhythm.*

"This is an all important acquisition for our psycho-technique."

13

STAGE CHARM

"DO YOU remember," Tortsov began to-day's class, "how when we did the exercise we called a 'masquerade' I took Sonya to task for depending on the natural appeal of her voice, mannerisms, eyes, face?

"I think I pointed out then that there are certain actors who have only to step on the stage and the public is already enthralled by them. Why? Is it because of their good looks? Yet very few of these actors possess this quality. Is it their voices? But exceptional voices are often lacking in these actors. Talent? On this score many do not deserve the delight they provoke.

"What then is the basis of the fascination they exercise? It is an indefinable, intangible quality; it is the inexplicable charm of an actor's whole being; it transforms even his deficiencies into assets. His idiosyncrasies and shortcomings become things to be copied by his admirers.

"Such an actor can permit himself anything—even bad acting. All that is required of him is that he come out on the stage as frequently and remain as long as possible, so that his audience can see, gaze upon and enjoy its idol.

"Still it often happens that when they meet this same actor off the stage even his warmest admirers are disillusioned. 'Oh, how unattractive he is in real life!' they say. Evidently it is the lighting or the scenery or the proscenium which bring out qualities that never fail to win admiration. It is no wonder that the quality is called stage and not natural charm.

"It is a great advantage for an actor to possess it because it guarantees in advance his hold on the audience, it helps him to carry over to large numbers of people his creative purposes. It enhances his roles and his art. Yet it is of utmost importance that he use this precious gift with prudence, wisdom and modesty. It is a great shame when he does not realize this and goes on to exploit, to play on his ability to charm. Behind the scenes such actors are dubbed 'prostitutes' because they exhibit their charms, trade on them for their own gain rather than make use of this power to fascinate, to enhance the character they have created.

"This is a dangerous mistake. We know of many cases when this gift has brought ruin to an actor because in the end he devoted all his interest and technical equipment to the sole purpose of self-exhibition.

"It is almost as though nature revenges herself on an actor for his inability to make the right use of her gifts, because self-admiration and exhibitionism impair and destroy the power to charm. The actor becomes the victim of his own splendid, innate endowment.

"Another angle to the danger inherent in this stage charm is that of making actors who possess it monotonous because of the temptation constantly to make use of it in their own persons. If they hide themselves in a characterization they hear their admirers remonstrate, 'How awful! Why does he disfigure himself so?' Whereupon the fear of displeasing his public, above all his feminine admirers, pushes him as soon as he appears on the stage to re-establish his saving charm and bend every effort to reveal it through the make-up and costume of a part which may not call for his own particular qualities.

"There are also actors who possess another variety of stage charm. In contrast to the first type they must not show themselves as they are, for in that aspect they are completely lacking in the power to attract. Yet they have only to put on wigs, a make-up which entirely masks their own personalities and they exercise a great stage magnetism. They draw the public not through personal but through artistically created charm. Behind this creation may lie tenderness, subtlety, grace, or boldness, vividness, or even insolence and sharpness—and it all adds up to an ability to allure.

"Now I come to the unlucky actor who lacks theatre attractiveness, who has on the contrary an inherent quality which influences the public against him when he is on the stage. On the other hand he has the advantage in ordinary life of making people exclaim, 'How nice he is!' And then they add in dismay, 'I wonder what makes him so unattractive on the stage?' Yet such actors are often far more intelligent, gifted, more conscientious about their art than those blessed with stage charm and to whom, because of it, all is forgiven.

"We should therefore take especial note of and accustom ourselves to these actors who are slighted by nature. It is only in that way that we are able to appreciate to the full their true artistic merits. This may take time and the recognition of their talents may be delayed.

"This raises the question: Is there no method by which on the one side it is possible to develop a certain degree of stage charm when an actor is not endowed with it, or on the other side can he not overcome the repellent quality which is foisted on him?

"This can be done, but only to a limited extent. It is accomplished not so much by the development of charm as by toning down unattractive shortcomings. Naturally the actor must first understand, or rather sense what they are, and then, when he has reached that realization, learn to wrestle with his own problem. This is not easy. It requires close observation, a knowledge of himself, great patience and systematic work aimed at extirpating natural qualities and everyday habits.

"As for acquiring that indefinable something which attracts an audience—that is even more difficult and perhaps it is even impossible of attainment.

"One of the most important helps in this field is habit.

A spectator can become accustomed to the shortcomings of an actor and they may even take on the aspect of a certain attractiveness through the very fact that he no longer is aware of qualities which may in the first instance have shocked his sensibilities.

"To a certain extent one may even create stage charm through the use of an excellent, well-bred manner in acting as that in itself is attractive.

"Indeed we often hear people say, 'How such-and-such an actor has mellowed! One would scarcely know him now. He used to be so unattractive!'

"In rejoinder to such remarks one might say that it is work and recognition of his art that have brought about this change.

"Art lends beauty and nobility, and whatever is beautiful and noble has the power to attract."

14

TOWARD AN ETHICS FOR THE THEATRE

"THE time has now come to speak of one more element," Tortsov began to-day, "contributing to a creative dramatic state. It is produced by the atmosphere surrounding an actor on the stage and by the atmosphere in the auditorium. We call it ethics, discipline, and also the sense of joint enterprise in our theatre work.

"All these things taken together create an artistic animation, an attitude of readiness to work together. It is a state which is favourable to creativeness. I do not know how else to describe it.

"It is not the creative state itself but it is one of the main factors contributing to it. It prepares and facilitates that state.

"I shall call it ethics in the theatre because it plays an important part in preparing us in advance for our work. Both the factor itself and what it produces in us and for us are significant because of the peculiarities of our profession.

"A writer, a composer, a painter, a sculptor are not pressed for time. They can work when and where they find it convenient to do so. They have the free disposal of their time.

"This is not the case with an actor. He has to be ready to produce at a fixed hour as advertised. How can he order himself to be inspired at a given time? It is far from simple.

"He needs order, discipline, a code of ethics not only for the general circumstances of his work, but also and especially for his artistic and creative purposes.

"The first condition towards the bringing about of this preliminary state is to follow the principle I have aimed at: Love art in yourself and not yourself in art.

"The career of an actor," Tortsov went on, "is a splendid one for those who are devoted to it and understand and see it in the true light."

"What if an actor does not do this?" one of the students asked.

"That is unfortunate because it will cripple him as a human being. Unless the theatre can ennoble you, make you a better person, you should flee from it," Tortsov replied.

"Why?" we asked in chorus.

"Because there are a lot of bacilli in the theatre, some are good and some are extremely harmful. The good bacilli will further the growth in you of a passion for what is fine, elevating, for great thoughts and feelings. They will help you to commune with the great geniuses such as Shakespeare, Pushkin, Gogol, Molière. Their creations and traditions live in us. In the theatre you will also meet modern writers and representatives of all branches of art, science, of social science, of poetic thought.

"This select company will teach you to understand art and the essential meaning at its core. That is the principal thing about art, therein lies its greatest fascination."

"Exactly in what?" I asked.

"In coming to know, in working on, studying your art, its bases, methods and technique of creativeness," explained Tortsov.

"Also in the torments and joys of creation, which we all feel as a group.

"And in the joys of accomplishment, which renew the spirit and lend it wings!

"Even in the doubts and failures, for in them also lies a stimulus to new struggles, strength for new work and fresh discoveries.

"There is too an aesthetic satisfaction which is never altogether complete and it provokes and arouses new energy.

"How much of life there is in all this!"

"What about success?" I enquired rather shyly.

"Success is transient, evanescent," answered Tortsov. "The real passion lies in the poignant acquisition of knowledge about all the shadings and subtleties of the creative secrets.

"Meantime do not forget the bad, the dangerous, corrupting bacilli of the theatre. It is not surprising that they thrive there; there are too many temptations in our theatre world.

"An actor is on view every day before an audience of a thousand spectators from such and such an hour to such and such an hour. He is surrounded by the magnificent trappings of a production, set against the effective background of painted scenery, dressed often in rich and beautiful clothes. He speaks the soaring lines of geniuses, he makes picturesque gestures, graceful motions, produces impressions of startling beauty—which in large measure are brought about by artful means. Always being in the public eye, displaying his or her best aspects, receiving ovations, accepting extravagant praise, reading glowing criticisms—all these things and many more of the same order constitute immeasurable temptations.

"These breed in an actor the sense of craving for constant, uninterrupted titillation of his personal vanity. But if he lives only on that and similar stimuli he is bound to sink low and become trivial. A serious minded person could not be entertained for long by such a life, yet a shallow one is enthralled, debauched, destroyed by it. That is why in our world of the theatre we must learn to hold ourselves well in check. We have to live by rigid discipline.

"If we keep our theatre free from all types of evil we, by the same token, bring about conditions favourable to our own work in it. Remember this practical piece of advice: Never come into the theatre with mud on your feet. Leave your dust and dirt outside. Check your little worries, squabbles, petty difficulties with your outside clothing—

all the things that ruin your life and draw your attention away from your art."

"Excuse me for pointing this out," interrupted Grisha, "but no such theatre exists in the world."

"Unfortunately you are right," admitted Tortsov. "People are so stupid and spineless that they still prefer to introduce petty, humdrum bickerings, spites and intrigues into the place supposedly reserved for creative art.

"They do not seem to be able to clear their throats before they cross the threshold of the theatre, they come inside and spit on the clean floor. It is incomprehensible why they do this!

"It is all the more reason why you should be the ones to discover the right, the high minded significance of the theatre and its art. From the very first steps you take in its service train yourselves to come into the theatre with clean feet.

"Our illustrious forbears in acting have summed this attitude up in the following way:

"A true priest is aware of the presence of the altar during every moment that he is conducting a service. It is exactly the same way that a true artist should react to the stage all the time he is in the theatre. An actor who is incapable of this feeling will never be a true artist!"

2

A great deal of discussion was caused in the theatre by a scandal in connection with one of the actors. He was severely reprimanded and warned that he would be dismissed if he repeated the intolerable offence.

Grisha had as usual a lot to say on the subject:

"I for one don't think the management has any right to mix into an actor's private life!"

Whereupon some of the others asked Tortsov to explain his point of view to us.

"Does it not seem irrational to you to tear down with one hand what you are trying to build up with the other? Yet many actors do that very thing. On the stage they make every effort to convey beautiful and artistic impressions and then, as soon as they step down from the boards, almost as though they had been intent on spoofing their spectators who a moment ago were admiring them, they do their best to disillusion them. I can never forget the bitter pain caused me in my youth by a famous visiting star. I shall not tell you his name because I do not want to dim his glory for you.

"I was present at an unforgettable performance. The impression he made on me was so tremendous I did not feel I could go home alone. I felt the necessity to discuss my experience with someone. So a friend and I went together to a restaurant. When we were in the midst of an excited conversation who should come in but our genius. We could not restrain ourselves, we rushed up to him and unloosed the floodgates of our enthusiasm. The great man invited us to join him at supper in a private room and there before our very eyes he proceeded to drink himself into a bestial state. Under the gloss was hidden such human corruption, such revolting boastfulness, deceit, gossip—all the attributes of a vulgar show-off. On top of that he refused to pay his bill for the wine he had consumed. It took us a long, long time to pay off this unexpected debt. And all the pleasure we got out of it was the privilege of conducting our belching and roaring host to his hotel where they were most unwilling to receive him in that disreputable drunken state.

"Mix together all the good and all the bad impressions which we received from that extraordinarily gifted man and try to determine what result you get."

"Something like the hiccoughs you get from drinking champagne," suggested Paul brightly.

"Well, mind you don't have the same thing happen to you when you get to be famous actors," said Tortsov.

"It is only when an actor is behind closed doors at home, in his most intimate circle, that he can let go. For his part

is not played out when the curtain goes down. He is still
bound in his everyday life to be the standard bearer of what
is fine. Otherwise he will only destroy what he is trying to
build. Remember this from the very beginning of your term
of service to art and prepare yourselves for this mission.
Develop in yourselves the necessary self-control, the ethics
and discipline of a public servant destined to carry out into
the world a message that is fine, elevating and noble.

"An actor, by the very nature of the art he serves, becomes
a member of a large and complex organization—the theatre.
Under its emblem and hall-mark he represents it daily to
thousands of spectators. Millions read daily in the papers
about his work and activity in the institution of which he
is a part. His name is so closely bound up with that of his
theatre that it is scarcely possible to distinguish between
them. Next to his family name that of this theatre belongs
to him. In the mind of the public his artistic and his personal
life are inextricably linked together. Therefore if an actor
from the Art Theatre, the Maly, or another, commits a
reprehensible act, any crime, is involved in any scandal, no
matter what alibi he may offer, no matter what denial or
explanation may be printed in the papers, he will be unable
to wipe away the stain, the shadow, he has laid on his whole
company, his theatre. This, therefore, obligates an actor to
conduct himself worthily outside the walls of his theatre
and to protect his good name both on the boards and in his
private life."

3

"One of the measures calculated to insure order and a
healthy atmosphere in the theatre is to reinforce the
authority of the people, who for one reason or another, have
been put in charge of the work.

"Before they are chosen and appointed you may argue,
wrangle, and protest against one candidacy or another but
once that person has been elected to a post of leadership or

management it is up to you to support him in every possible way. That is only fair from the point of view of the common good. And the weaker he is the more you should support him. For if he does not enjoy any authority the main motive force of the group will become paralyzed. What becomes of a collective if it is deprived of the leader who initiates, pushes, and directs the common work? We love to decry, discredit, humiliate those whom we have raised to high 'places, or if a gifted person climbs above us we are ready to use all our strength to beat him down and yell at him: How dare you presume to stand over us, you climber! How many talented and useful people have been destroyed that way. A few, in spite of all obstacles, have achieved general recognition and admiration. But on the whole the brazen ones, who usually succeed in bossing us, have all the luck. And we growl to ourselves and stand it because we find it hard to arrive at any unanimity and we are afraid to overthrow those who terrorize us.

"In theatres, with few exceptions, this is vividly exemplified. The struggle for priority among actors, regisseurs, jealousy of each other's success, divisions caused by differences in salaries and types of parts—all this is strongly developed in our line of work and constitutes its greatest evil. We cloak our ambition, jealousy, intrigues with all kinds of fine sounding phrases such as 'enlightened competition', but all the time the atmosphere is filled with the poison gases of backstage back-biting.

"Out of fear of all competition and because of its narrowminded envy actors meet any newcomer in their midst with fixed bayonets. If he can stand the test he is lucky. Yet how many are terrified, lose all faith in themselves, and go under?

"How close to animal psychology all this is!

"Once when I was sitting on the balcony of a house in a small provincial town I had an opportunity to watch some dogs. They also have their own limits, lines of demarcation which they are keen to maintain. If an outsider dares to overstep a certain boundary he is met by the combined curs of that particular district. If he succeeds in giving a good account of himself he wins recognition in the end and is accepted in the district into which he had intruded. Or he turns tail and flees, wounded and maimed, from his own fellow creatures.

"And it is this very form of brute psychology which is rampant, alas, in all theatres with few exceptions, and which must be destroyed. It is in force not only among newcomers but also among the groups of old timers. I have heard two great actresses going for each other not only backstage but during performances and in terms that a fishwife would envy. I have been witness to the conduct of two famous and talented actors who refused to enter the stage through one and the same wing or door. I have been told about two celebrated stars, a man and a woman, who for years played opposite each other without being on speaking terms. During rehearsal they communicated with one another through a third person. He would say to the man directing the play: 'Tell her that she is talking nonsense', and she would reply through the same channel: 'Tell him that he is acting like a boor'.

"Why is it that such talented people are willing to destroy the fine work which they themselves originally built up? For the sake of personal, trivial, petty insult and misunderstandings?

"Such are the suicidal depths to which actors sink if they are not able to overcome in time their bad professional instincts. I hope this will be an example and vivid warning to you."

4

"Let us suppose that one actor in a well and carefully prepared production, either through laziness, neglect or inattentiveness, departs so far from the true performance of his part as to act in a purely routine, mechanical way. Has he the right to do this? After all, he was not alone in producing the play, he is not solely responsible for the work put in it. In such an enterprise one works for all and all for one. There must be mutual responsibility and whoever betrays that trust must be condemned as a traitor.

"In spite of my great admiration for individual splendid talents I do not accept the star system. Collective creative effort is the root of our kind of art. That requires ensemble acting and whoever mars that ensemble is committing a crime not only against his comrades but also against the very art of which he is the servant."

5

Our class was to meet for a rehearsal in one of the green-rooms backstage where the regular actors of the theatre company met their friends. Afraid of disgracing ourselves before them we asked Rakhmanov to give us some advice about how to act there.

To our surprise the Director himself appeared. He said that he had been much touched to hear of our serious attitude toward the rehearsal.

"You will realize what you need to do and how you should conduct yourselves if you bear in mind that this is a collective enterprise," he said to us. "You are all going to be producing together, you will all be helping one another, all be dependent on one another. You will all be directed by one person, your regisseur.

"If there is orderliness and proper distribution of work, your collective effort will be pleasant and productive because it is based on mutual help. But if there is chaos and a wrong atmosphere for work then your collective enterprise can become a torture chamber, you will be getting in each other's way, pushing each other around. It is clear therefore that you must all agree to establish and support discipline."

"How do we support it?"

"First of all, you arrive at the theatre on time, a half hour or a quarter of an hour before the rehearsal is called, in order to go over the elements which are necessary to establish your inner state.

"If even one person is late it upsets all the others. And if all are late your working hours will be frittered away in waiting instead of being applied to your job. That makes an actor wild and puts him in a condition where he is incapable of work. But if on the contrary you all have the right attitude towards your collective responsibilities and come to your rehearsal with proper preparation you will create a splendid atmosphere which will challenge and encourage you. Your work will go along hummingly because you are all helping each other.

"It is also important that you take the right attitude towards the object of each individual rehearsal.

"The great mass of actors have quite a wrong idea about their attitude toward rehearsals. They believe that they need work only at rehearsals and that they can be idle at home.

"Whereas this is not the case at all. The rehearsal merely clarifies the problems that an actor needs to work on at home. That is one reason why I place no confidence in actors who chatter a lot at rehearsals and do not make notes on planning their home-work.

"They pretend that they can remember everything without notes. Nonsense! Do they think that I do not know that they cannot possibly remember everything because, in the first place, the regisseur mentions so many details both major and minor that no memory could retain them, and, in the second place, they are dealing for the most part not with definite facts but with feelings stored up in emotion memory. To understand, to comprehend and recall them, the actor must find the appropriate word, expression, example, some means of description with the aid of which he will be able to evoke, to fix the sensation under discussion.

"He will have to think about it at home before he will be able to find it again and call it forth from his inner being.

That is a tremendous piece of work. It requires great concentration in his work both at home and also at rehearsal when the actor first receives the comments of the regisseur.

"We, the regisseurs, know better than anyone else what credence to give to the assertions of inattentive actors. We are the ones who are obliged to repeat the same things to them over and over again.

"That kind of an attitude on the part of certain individuals toward a joint piece of work acts as a great brake. Seven will not wait for one. Remember that. Therefore work out for yourselves the right kind of artistic ethics and discipline. This will force you to prepare yourselves properly at home in advance of each rehearsal. Let it be a source of shame and badge of disloyalty to you before your whole group if you are the cause of making the regisseur repeat something he has already explained. You have no right to forget the regisseur's remarks. You may not comprehend them all at once, you may have to return to them in order to study them more thoroughly, but you may not merely take them in one ear and send them out of the other. That is a crime against all the other workers in the theatre.

"Therefore, in order to avoid that misdemeanour, you must teach yourself how to work independently at home on your part. This is no easy task but it is something you must learn how to do thoroughly and well while you are in training here. Here I can take all the time which may be necessary to go into the details of that work but at rehearsals I cannot come back to these things without running the risk of their being turned into lessons. Out on the stage the demands made on you will be far stricter than in the class room. Bear this in mind and prepare yourselves for it."

6

"How does a singer, a pianist, a dancer, start his day?" Tortsov asked at the beginning of to-day's class.

"He gets up, bathes, dresses, has breakfast and at a time appointed for this purpose he begins his exercises. The singer vocalizes, the pianist plays his scales, the dancer hurries to the theatre, to his practice bar in order to keep his muscles in trim. This is done day after day, winter and summer. A day omitted is a day lost and a detriment to the art of the performer.

"Tolstoy, Chekhov and other great artists considered it a necessity to sit down every day at a given hour to write, if not on a novel or short story or play, at least in a diary, to record thoughts and observations. The main point was day by day to cultivate the most delicate and precise ways of rendering all the subtle intricacies of human thoughts and feelings, visual observations and emotional impressions.

"Ask any artist and he will tell you the same thing.

"Nor is that all: I know a surgeon (and surgery is also an art), who devotes all his free time to playing with the most delicate kind of oriental jackstraws. After tea, while conversing with others, he cleverly fishes out some item underneath a complicated pile of little sticks just to keep his hand in.

"And it is only the actor who, when he has gotten up in the morning, dressed and breakfasted, hurries out into the street or calls on friends or does other personal errands, because that is his free time.

"That may well be. But the singer, the concert pianist, the dancer do not have any more time. They have rehearsals, lessons, performances too.

"Nevertheless it is always the excuse of the actor, who neglects his home-work on the technique of his art, that he has 'no time'.

"What a pity! As I have said before, an actor, more than any other special artist, is in need of that work at home. Whereas a singer has to be concerned only with his voice and breathing, a dancer with his physical apparatus, and a pianist with his hands or an instrumentalist with his breathing and lip technique—an actor is responsible for his arms, his legs, his eyes, his face, the plasticity of his whole body, his rhythm, his motion and all the programme of our activities here in the school. These exercises do not stop with graduation, they go on through your whole lives as artists. And the older you get the more necessary it will be for you to point up your technique and consequently to maintain a system of regular work-outs.

"But since the actor has 'no time' for such practice his art at best will mark time or at worst run down hill because it consists of only an accidental technique drawn by necessity from unthinking, false, untrue, mechanical rehearsing or badly prepared public appearances.

"And yet an actor, especially the ones who complain most about lack of time, those who play roles of second or third in importance, actually have more freedom than anyone else active in various artistic professions.

"Just look at the schedule. Take an actor who plays in the mob scenes in, let us say, *Tsar Fyodor*. He must be ready by 7.30 p.m. He appears in the second scene (the reconciliation of Boris with Shuiski). Then there is an intermission. Do not think that the actor needs to use all of it to change his make-up and costume. No, indeed! Most of the actors keep the same make-up and change only their outer garments. Let us assume that ten out of the fifteen minutes normally assigned to an intermission is used up.

"Following that is the short scene in the garden, a two minute wait and then the long scene in the Tsar's chamber. It plays not less than half an hour, therefore if you add that to the intermission you have approximately thirty-five plus ten—forty-five minutes.

"Then come the other scenes which you can calculate for yourselves and arrive at a general sum total.

"That is how the matter stands for our colleagues who play in the mob scenes. There are also a number of actors who play bits or even larger parts which are episodic in character. After his episode is finished the actor is either free for the rest of the evening or he waits for another five

minute appearance in the last act and the whole time i.
loafing around the dressing-room and being bored.

"That is the way actors divide their time when engaged
in one of the more complicated and large productions, like
Tsar Fyodor.

"And now what about the large number of others who
are not playing on this particular evening? They are free
and they spend their time appearing in pot boiler performances. Let us make a note of that.

"So much for the evening occupations. What happens
during the day-time at rehearsals? In some theatres, take
ours for instance, rehearsals are called for eleven or twelve
o'clock. Until then our actors are free. And that is only
right for various reasons that are connected with the
peculiarities of our lives. An actor's performance finishes
late, he is wrought up and it takes some time for him to
calm down sufficiently to go to sleep. At an hour when most
people are sound asleep our actor is playing the last and most
difficult act of a tragedy. When he comes home he takes
advantage of the quiet to concentrate, without being
interrupted, on the new part he is preparing.

"So what is surprising about the fact that on the following
morning when everyone else is already up and at work our
tired actor is sound asleep after his long hours of wear and
tear on his nerves?

"He has probably been on a spree—is what many say
about us.

"And there are theatres, which pride themselves on keeping their actors on their toes with their iron discipline and
model order—so-called. They have rehearsals at 9 a.m
(incidentally after finishing a Shakespearean tragedy at
11 p.m. the previous evening).

"Such theatres, which boast of their organization, do not
take their actors into consideration and in a way they are
quite right. Actors in those theatres can die three times a
day with utmost comfort and they can rehearse three
different plays every morning.

" 'Tra-la-la. . . . boom, boom. . . .' the leading actress trills in a low voice to her partner in a scene, and adds: 'I cross to the sofa and sit down!'

"To which the leading man replies in half tones: 'Tra-la-la. . . . boom, boom. . . .' etc., and then: 'I cross to sofa, drop on one knee and kiss your hand!'

"If often happens when we are on our way to a rehearsal at noon that we meet an actor from one of those other theatres who is strolling around after a whole morning of rehearsals.

" 'Where are you off to?' he asks. 'To rehearsal.' 'What? At noon! At such a late hour!' he exclaims not without irony and venom and obviously thinking to himself: 'What a sleepyhead and shiftless creature!' and then he says aloud: 'What a way to run a theatre! Why, I have already finished my rehearsal. We ran through a whole play! We begin work at nine a.m.!' This last is said with a touch of boastfulness by the mechanic-artist who measures with condescending eye our belated actor.

"But I have said enough. I already know in that instance what so-called 'art' is in question in those theatres.

"And now here is my problem: there are many managers in good theatres who are seriously trying to achieve a degree of genuine artistry who really believe that the so-called iron discipline and order of the mechanical actors is right and even ideal. How can such people, who judge the product and conditions of work of a real artist according to standards established by book-keepers, cashiers, and accountants, be put in charge of the direction of artistic accomplishment or even understand how it is to be carried on, how much nervous energy, life, and the highest spiritual outbursts are laid on the altar of their beloved art by true actors who 'sleep until noon and are the cause of endless disorder in the schedules set up by the repertory office!'

"How can we get away from such managers with petty tradesman or bank clerk mentalities? Where are we to find people who understand and, above all, who sense what the main object of true artists is and how to deal with them?

"Meanwhile I am putting more and more pressure on these already over-burdened real artists, regardless of whether they are playing long or short parts: I am asking that they take their last remaining free time—the intermissions and the waits between their entrances and the hours between rehearsals—to work on their technique.

"For such work, as I proved to you by figures, there is plenty of time."

"But you want to exhaust the poor actor, and take away his last breathing spell!"

"No, indeed, I assert. The most exhausting thing for an actor is to loaf around his dressing-room waiting for his next entrance."

7

"There are many actors and actresses who do not take creative initiative. They do not prepare their roles outside the theatre by letting their imaginations and subconscious play on the character they are to portray. They come to the rehearsal and wait around until they are led along a path of action. After a great effort the regisseur can sometimes succeed in striking sparks in such passive natures. Or these lazy persons may catch fire from watching others take hold, they may follow their lead and become infected with their feelings about the play. After a series of such vicarious sensations, if they have any gift at all, they may be able to arouse their own feelings and acquire a real grasp on their parts in their own right. Only we regisseurs know how much work, inventiveness, patience, nervous strength and time it takes to push such actors of weak creative impulse ahead, away from their dead centre. Women, in such cases, are apt to excuse themselves charmingly and coquettishly by saying: How can I help it? I cannot act until I feel my part. As soon as the impulse comes everything will turn out all right.

They say this with a touch of pride and boasting as though that procedure were a sure sign of inspiration and genius.

"Need I explain that all such drones, who profit by the work and creativeness of others, are an infinite drag on the accomplishment of the whole group? It is because of them that productions are often delayed for weeks before they can be released. They not only are slow in their own work but the cause of delay in that of others. Indeed the actors playing opposite them have to exert themselves to the utmost in order to overcome their inertia. This in turn produces overacting, ruins their parts especially if they are not any too secure in them anyway. When they do not get the right cues the conscientious actors make violent efforts to stir the initiative of the sluggish actors, thereby impairing the true quality of their own playing. They get themselves into an impossible state and instead of facilitating the performance they clog it up by making it necessary for the regisseur to deflect his attention away from the general to their particular needs. Consequently we see not only the one passive actress contributing exaggerated, false acting to the rehearsal instead of lifelike, true emotions, but also the men who are playing opposite her as well. It takes no more than two actors straying down the wrong path to deflect a third or even a fourth. In the end one actor can derail a whole performance that was running smoothly and send it tumbling down hill. Poor regisseur! Poor actors!

"You may say that it would have been better to dismiss those actors with undeveloped creative initiative and corresponding technique, but it is unfortunately true that among them there are a great many with talent. Less gifted actors would not dare to be so passive, whereas the more gifted ones, feeling unimpeded, allow themselves more leeway; they sincerely believe that they are in duty bound and indeed have the right to wait for the favourable wind, the rising tide of inspiration.

"From all of which it should be clear to you that no actor has a right to take advantage of the work of others during a rehearsal. He must provide his own living emotions with which to bring his own part to life. If every actor in a production would do that he would be helping not only himself but the work of the whole cast. If on the contrary each actor is going to depend on the others there will be a complete lack of initiative. The regisseur cannot do the work of everyone. An actor is not a puppet.

"So you see every actor is obliged to develop his own creative will and technique. He, along with all the others, is bound to do his own productive share of work at home and at rehearsal, always playing his part in the fullest tones of which he is capable."

8

"The problem for our art and consequently for our theatre is—to create an inner life for a play and its characters, to express in physical and dramatic terms the fundamental core, the idea which impelled the writer, the poet, to produce his composition.

"Every worker in the theatre from the doorman, the ticket taker, the hat-check girl, the usher, all the people the public comes into contact with as they enter the theatre on up to the managers, the staff, and finally the actors themselves—they all are co-creators with the playwright, the composer, for the sake of whose play the audience assembles. They all serve, they all are subject to the fundamental aim of our art. They all, without exception, are participants in the production. Anyone who in any degree obstructs our common effort to carry out our basic aim should be declared an undesirable member of our community. If any of the staff out front greets any member of the audience inhospitably thereby ruining his good humour, he has struck a blow against our general objective and the goal of our art. If it is cold, dirty, untidy in the theatre, if the curtain is late in rising, if the performance drags—then the mood of the public is depressed, they are not receptive to the main thoughts and feelings offered to them through the joint efforts of the playwright, the regisseur, the company and the actors. They feel they had no cause to come to the play, the performance is spoiled, and the theatre loses its social, artistic and educational significance.

"The playwright, the composer, the cast, all do their share to create the necessary atmosphere on their side of the footlights, and the administrative staff does its part in creating an appropriate mood in the audience and backstage where the actors are getting ready for a performance. The spectator as well as the actor is an active participant in a performance and therefore he too needs to be prepared for his part, he must be put in the proper mood in order to be receptive to the impressions and thoughts the playwright wishes to impart to him.

"This absolute dependence of all the workers in the theatre on the ultimate aim of our art remains in force not only during performances but also during rehearsals and even at other hours of the day and night. If for any reason a rehearsal is unproductive those who obstructed the work were undermining our general purpose. Artists can operate successfully only under certain necessary conditions. Anyone who upsets those conditions is being disloyal to his art and to the society of which he is a part. A bad rehearsal does harm to a part and a distorted part prevents an actor from conveying the thoughts of the playwright, in other words from accomplishing his main job."

15

PATTERNS OF
ACCOMPLISHMENT

I

TO-DAY I had occasion to call on Rakhmanov in his home.
He was in the midst of some rush preparations. He was
gluing, cutting, designing, painting. The room where he
was at work was in great disorder to the horror of his
wife.

"What are you getting ready for?" I asked with interest.

"A little surprise. You may be sure I am not doing all
this for fun. It has its pedagogic purpose. By to-morrow
I have to make not just one, but a whole mass of banners,"
he explained with great zest, "and they must be not just
any old banners; they must be beautiful so we can hang them
on the walls in our school. What a job! And Tortsov is
coming himself to see them. Then we'll hang them and
they will show very effectively just what our whole system
of acting is about. You know, if you really want to get a
good idea of things, my boy, you have to see them with your
eyes. This is an important fact and it is also a useful one.
Through drawings and through what you look at you are
better able to take in the whole thing and also the relations
between the different parts of the system."

After that Rakhmanov began to explain to me the reason
for the arrangement he planned. We had now reached the
high point in our school course.

"Of course, we have gone through the work only in the
most general terms," Rakhmanov hastened to remind me.
"We shall come back a hundred times, in fact all our lives,
to review what we have learned. So far so good. And

to-morrow we shall cast up our accounts and see how far we have progressed. That's what you will see!"

He pointed with pride and an almost childlike glee at the pile of material lying in front of him.

"Everything we prepare here to-day we shall install to-morrow at the school. It will all be in absolute order and it will be clear as day to-morrow what we have accomplished in these two years."

A constant flow of talk helped Rakhmanov work.

Two property men from the theatre came in to help. I was drawn into the work and stayed on until late in the night.

2

To-day Rakhmanov announced to us that all the flags, banners, streamers would be exhibited on the right wall of the auditorium. That entire wall would be given up to the dual representation of an actor's internal and external preparation.

"So you see, my friends, on the right you have the preparations of an actor and on the left the preparations of a part. Our job is to find the proper place in the scheme for each flag, banner, streamer so that everything will be in order according to what you have been taught and attractive to the eye."

After he had finished speaking our attention was centred on only the right wall and we saw that it had been divided into two parts. According to Rakhmanov's plan one was to be devoted to the factors that go into the preparations of an actor's inner qualities and the other to the preparations of his physical attributes.

"Art loves order, my friends, so let us place on the shelves of your memory all that you have taken in during your time here and which is now floating around inside your heads in an unsorted mass."

The flags were all carried over to the right side of the

auditorium, with Vanya taking a lively part in the work. He had removed his coat and taken up a large and beautiful streamer on which were inscribed the words of the Pushkin aphorism—"Sincerity of emotions, verisimilitude of feelings in given circumstances, that is what our mind requires from the playwright". With his usual impetuousness he was already on top of a ladder and preparing to nail the banner in the upper left-hand corner. But Rakhmanov hastily checked him.

"Good gracious, what are you doing?" he cried. "You can't hang that up there for no reason at all! That's not the way to act!"

"But it looks fine there! I swear it does!" declared Vanya with enthusiasm.

"It doesn't make any sense, my boy," said Rakhmanov in an attempt to convince him. "When do you ever put your foundations on top? What are you thinking of? After all the Pushkin saying is the basis of everything. Our whole system is built on it. Don't forget that! It is what you might call our creative basis. That's why we have to put the banner with our motto down below, and in the most prominent place, and not just under the one part, but across both parts of the wall as it is equally a factor in the process of *living a part* and that of clothing a part in *physical terms*. Let's see, where is the place of honour? Down here right in the very centre of the wall. Hang the words of Pushkin here!"

Paul and I helped Vanya stretch the banner out across the space indicated and we were getting ready to nail it on the very bottom of the wall, but Rakhmanov again interrupted. He explained that at the very bottom, across both halves of the wall we should place a long narrow streamer of a dark colour and with the words *An Actor Prepares*. As it bore on everything else on this wall it must run all across it.

"This banner should encircle all the other banners. Think what that means!"

While Vanya and one of the property men tacked the banner in its rightful place Rakhmanov and I watched Nicholas, whom we had appointed official draughtsman to draw the plan of the grouping and artistic arrangement of the flags.

"But you, Nicholas, my boy, you have taken part of the ground work, the basic floor plan, that banner with the inscription *Action*, and put it way up at the top! What in the world are you thinking of! It must go down right beside the Pushkin motto, it is on a par with that in importance in our work."

"Gee, I can't tell these things apart. They're all the same colour," Vanya called out as he struggled with another long banner.

"That is also a motto, it is what you might call the third fundamental, *The Subconscious via the Conscious*," said Rakhmanov designating its place down at the bottom of the wall to the right of the Pushkin axiom.

"That's fine. Now we have the fundamentals all lined up for both sections of this wall. Now we have to choose what goes on the right and on the left of the upper part. To the left let us put *Psycho-Technique*, and to the right *External Technique*. There are the banners. They each represent one half of how an actor prepares. Isn't that a big job! And now you may be sure you'll find all the rest of the details here. Look at that flock of little flags. They are all made of the same colour and in the same shape. They are the elements that go into the make-up of the *Inner Creative State*. Look, there is the *Sense of Truth, Emotion Memory, Attention, Units and Objectives*.

"But hold on there," Rakhmanov's face clouded. "You can't put them up yet, you are missing a step."

"What have we missed?" several of us asked.

"An important, very important factor in both parts of an actor's preparations is the triumvirate with which you are already familiar: *Mind, Will, Feelings*. These flags are of prime importance as you will come to realize in good time,"

Rakhmanov went on as he supervised the placing of the three flags in a line over the banners which indicate the two aspect's of an actor's training.

Now the large number of smaller pennants bearing the names of all the elements we had studied in our course were left over.

"Hang them in a row, next to each other to look like a striped awning!" ordered Rakhmanov.

Without further reflection we began to hang all the element pennants relating to psycho-technique (*Imagination, Attention, Sense of Truth*, etc.) in the order in which we had worked on them, but when we came to those having to do with external technique we stopped, not knowing where to begin.

"You made your start in that with the *Relaxation of Muscles*," Rakhmanov suggested helpfully. "As long as a person's muscles are as taut as wet ropes he is incapable of action. Tense muscles are taut cables, engendered emotions are of spider-web consistency. A spider web cannot break a cable. So hang *Relaxation of Muscles* as the first element in external technique."

Next to it we placed *Expressive Body Training*, which included gymnastics, dance, acrobatics, fencing (foils, rapiers, daggers), wrestling, boxing, carriage, all aspects of physical training. *Plasticity* was put on a separate flag, and then came *Voice* (to include breathing, voice placing, singing).

Speech filled the next spot. Under this heading were included enunciation, pauses, intonation, words, phrases— the whole speech technique. Following this came *External Tempo-Rhythm*. Other flags were hung in the same order as on the left side and corresponded in physical terms to the elements in psycho-technique.

Just as we had hung over the *Logic and Coherence of Feelings* we now put up a pennant for *Logic and Coherence of Physical Actions*. And *External Characterization* balanced *Inner Characterization*.

On the side of external technique there followed *External*

Stage Charm, Restraint and Finish, Discipline, Ethics, Sense of Ensemble.

All there was now left to do was to add three flags: one above each group of elements—on the left *Inner Creative State*, on the right *External Creative State*, and then the third above these two entitled *Over-All Creative State*. Topping them we had left one long pennant without any inscription on it.

Next Rakhmanov had us get a roll of tape to lead from flag to flag indicating the inter-relationship of the various parts of the technique.

The three flags indicating the triumvirate of inner motive forces—*Mind, Will, Feeling*—had to be taped upwards to each and every one of the small pennants in the upper row, the elements of inner and external technique. Just as these in turn had to have their tapes leading upwards to, on the left, the inner creative state and, on the right, the external creative state, both of which were united by tapes to the over-all creative state above them.

Actually this produced such a labyrinth of lines that the import of the main design was lost. So it was decided to sacrifice the minor lines and, for the sake of clarity, let a few indicate the general relationship.

"What a mess you do make!" fussed the old porter who came in to sweep after us while Nicholas copied down the final plan of our design.

3

Tortsov walked in accompanied by an elated Rakhmanov. He examined our arrangement of flags and pennants and exclaimed:

"Wonderful, Rakhmanov! It's clear and pictorial. Even a stupid person would get the idea. You have really produced a picture of the ground we have covered in two years. It is only now that I can explain in systematic form what I should have said to all the students at the beginning of our common work.

"After I pointed out to you the three main directives of dramatic art we began our closer examination of how to live a part, to study hard to prepare ourselves for it. Our two years' course has been devoted to just that." As he spoke he pointed to the long banners across the bottom of the whole wall.

"From my passing comments throughout you have learned the fundamentals on which our so-called system of acting is based.

"The first of these," Tortsov explained, "is, as you know, the principle of activity, and indicative of the fact that we do not play character images and emotions but *act in the images and passions of a role.*

"The second is the famous saying of Pushkin which points out that the work of an actor is not to create feelings but only to *produce the given circumstances in which true feelings will spontaneously be engendered.*

"The third cornerstone is the organic creativeness of our own nature which we express in the words: *Through conscious technique to the subconscious creation of artistic truth.* One of the main objectives pursued in our approach to acting is this natural stimulus to the creativeness of organic nature and its subconsciousness.

"We do not however study the subconscious, but only the paths leading up to it. Remember the things we have discussed in class, which we have been searching for throughout our work together. Our rules have not been founded on any unsteady, uncertain hypotheses concerning the subconscious. On the contrary, in our exercises and rules we constantly based ourselves on the conscious and we tested it out hundreds of times on ourselves and others. We took only incontrovertible laws as the foundation of our knowledge, our practice and our experiments. It was they alone that did us the service of leading us to the unknown world of the subconscious which for moments came alive inside of us.

"Although we knew nothing of the subconscious we still sought contact with and reflex approaches to it.

"Our conscious technique was directed on the one side towards putting our subconscious to work and on the other to learning how not to interfere with it once it was in action."

Tortsov then pointed to the left half of the wall and spoke of its being devoted to the whole *process of living a part.*

"This process is of such importance in acting because every step, every movement in the course of our creative work must be enlivened and motivated by our feelings. Whatever we do not actually experience in our own emotions remains inert and spoils our work. *Without experiencing a role there can be no art in it.* That is why we began with this when we initiated our course.

"Does this mean that you are fully cognizant of all this implies and that you can put it into practical form?

"No. That would be an improper conclusion. For this process is something we continue throughout our working careers as actors.

"Your classes of drill have helped and will help you. But the rest can come only from future work on roles and experience on the stage.

"Our second year was devoted to the external aspect of acting, the building of our physical apparatus. To this you have assigned the right half of the wall.

"When I am in a theatre I want first of all to understand, to see, to know, and at the same time to feel with you all the infinitesimal shades and changes of your emotion in your part. So you must make your invisible inner experience visible to my eyes.

"It often happens that an actor has all the fine, subtle, deep feelings necessary to his part and yet he may distort them beyond recognition because he conveys them through crudely prepared external physical means. When the body transmits neither the actor's feelings to me nor how he experiences them I see an out of tune, inferior instrument on which a fine musician is obliged to perform. The poor man! He struggles so hard to transmit all the shadings of his emotions. The stiff keys of the piano do not yield to his touch, the unoiled pedals squeak, the strings are jangled and out of tune. All this causes an artist great effort and pain. The more complex the life of the human spirit in the part being portrayed, the more delicate, the more compelling and artistic should be the physical form which clothes it.

"This makes an enormous call on our external technique, on the expressiveness of our bodily apparatus, our voice, diction, intonation, handling of words, phrases, speeches, our facial expression, plasticity of movement, way of walking. To a supreme degree sensitive to the slightest twist, the subtlest turns and changes in our inner lives while on the stage, they must be like the most delicate barometers, responsive to imperceptible atmospheric changes.

"Your immediate objective then has been to train your physical apparatus to the limits of your natural, inborn capacity. You must still go on developing, correcting, tuning your bodies until every part of them will respond to the predestined and complex task assigned them by nature of presenting in external form your invisible feelings.

"You must educate your bodies according to the laws of nature. That means a lot of complicated work and perseverance!"

4

To-day Tortsov continued his review using the chart on the wall of the school auditorium.

"You are aware of the fact that we have not one single, but three motive forces in our inner life—*Mind, Will* and *Feelings*—three virtuoso performers," he said as he indicated the three flags.

"They are like three organists before their instruments, and above them hang the little pennants like the pipes of an organ, to give out resonance through all the various elements which are included in the make-up of an inner and outer creative state."

Before continuing Tortsov made certain rearrangements in the order of the little pennants. He pointed out that they should be in the sequence in which they come into play in the broader phases of our work.

The way he explained this was:

1. The creative process starts with the imaginative invention of a poet, a writer, the director of the play, the actor, the scene designer and others in the production, so the first in order should be *Imagination and its Inventions, The Magic If, Given Circumstances.* (These and many others of the terms used are defined and described in *An Actor Prepares*—EDITOR.)

2. Once the theme is established it must be put into an easily handled form, consequently it is broken up into *Units* with their *Objectives.*

3. The third phase comes with the concentration of *Attention* on an *Object* with the help of which, or for the sake of which the objective is achieved.

4. To bring life to the objective and the object an actor must have a *Sense of Truth*, of *Faith* in what he is doing. This element is fourth in the series. Where truth exists there is no room for conventional routine, for lying pretence. This element is inextricably bound up with the extermination of all artificiality, all cliché and rubber-stamp acting.

5. Next comes desire, which leads to *Action.* This follows spontaneously on the creation of an object, objectives, in the validity of which an actor can really believe.

6. Sixth place goes to *Communion,* that intercourse in various forms for the sake of which action is taken and directed towards an object.

7. Where there is intercourse there is of necessity *Adaptation* so they must hang side by side.

8. To help stir his dormant feelings an actor has recourse to *Inner Tempo-Rhythm.*

9. All these elements release *Emotion Memory* to give free expression to *Repeated Feelings* and to create *Sincerity of Emotions.* Therefore these are in ninth place.

10. *Logic and Continuity* were last. Of these Tortsov said:

"In every phase of our work, whether we were speaking of inventions of the imagination, proposed circumstances, objects of attention, units and objectives and the other steps, we constantly had occasion to speak of *logic* and *continuity*. I can only add that these are elements of prime importance in relation to all the others and to many gifts which actors possess and which we have not been able as yet to study in detail.

"Can we do without logic and continuity in anything we do?" asked Tortsov. "Let me see you do this problem: Lock that door and then go through it into the next room. You cannot do it? In that case try to answer this question: If it were absolutely dark in here now, how would you put on this light? Cannot do that either?

"If you wanted to impart to me your most cherished secret, how would you yell it out to me?

"In many plays the hero and the heroine do all in their power to come together; they suffer every trial and torture, they struggle desperately with obstacles; yet when the desired end is achieved and the lovers embrace, they immediately assume a chilly attitude towards each other, as if everything were over and the play already finished. How disappointed the public is to find that, after believing all evening in the sincerity of his and her emotions, it is disillusioned by the coldness of the principal actors, because they had not planned their parts with logic and coherence.

"At all other points creativeness must be logical and with continuity. Even illogical and incoherent characters must be represented within the logical plan and framework of a whole play, a whole performance.

"I have spoken at length to you about logic and continuity, of action, the imagination, given circumstances and other kindred phases of our work.

"If I were now to speak of logic and coherence as applied to thought and speech I should be only repeating much of what we have been working on in our second year's course.

"Yet what disturbs me is that I am so far unable to talk to you about the most important aspect of all in this subject: *the logic and continuity of feelings.*

"Not being a specialist I dare not approach this topic from the scientific angle. Even from the practical angle. I must frankly confess myself still insufficiently prepared to give you anything properly tested out in my own experience.

"All I can do is share with you the results of certain very elementary means which I use in my own work as an actor.

"My method is this: I set up a list of actions in which various emotions spontaneously manifest themselves."

"What sort of actions, what sort of list?" I asked.

"Take, for example, *love*," Tortsov began. "What incidents go into the make-up of this human passion? What actions arouse it?

"First, there is a meeting between 'her' and 'him'.

"Either immediately or by degrees they are attracted to each other; the attention of either or both of the future lovers is heightened.

"They live on the memory of every moment of their meeting. They seek pretexts for another meeting.

"There is a second meeting. They have the desire to involve one another in a common interest, common action which will require more frequent meetings, and so on. . . .

"Later:

"There is the first secret—an even greater bond to draw them together.

"They exchange friendly advice about various matters and this makes for constant meetings and communication. So it develops.

"Later:

"The first quarrel, reproaches, doubts.

"Fresh meetings, explanations to dissipate the disagreement.

"Reconciliation. Still closer relations.

"Later:

"Obstacles to their meetings.

"Secret correspondence.

"Secret rendezvous.

"The first present.

"The first kiss.

"Later:

"Friendly lack of constraint in their manners towards each other.

"Growing demands on each other.

"Jealousy.

"A break.

"Separation.

"They meet again. They forgive each other. So it goes on. . . .

"All these moments and actions have their inner justification. Taken as a whole they reflect the feelings, the passion, or the state which we describe by the use of the one word *love*.

"If you will carry out in your imagination—with the right basis of detailed circumstances, proper thinking, sincerity of feeling—each step in this series of actions, you will find that first externally and then internally you will reach the condition of a person in love. With such preparations you will find it easier to take on a role and a play in which this passion figures.

"In a good and amply worked out play all or most of these moments will be in evidence in some degree. The actor will look for and recognize them in his part. Under these circumstances we will execute a whole series of objectives and actions on the stage, which in their sum total will add up to the state known as being in love. It will be brought about step by step, not all at once or in general terms. The actor in this case performs actions, he does not simply put on an act: he experiences what he does as a human being, he does not indulge in theatrical pretence, he feels instead of imitating the results of feelings.

"Most actors do not penetrate the nature of the feelings they portray. For them *love* is a big and generalized experience.

"They try immediately to 'embrace the unembraceable'. They forget that great experiences are made up of a number of separate episodes and moments. These must be known, studied, absorbed, fulfilled in their entirety. Unless an actor does this he is destined to become the victim of the stereotype."

5

Tortsov opened his remarks to-day by suggesting the following:

"Suppose you have just waked up. You are still drowsy, your body is stiff, you have no desire to move, to get up; you feel a slight morning chill in your bones. But you make yourself get out of bed, you do some setting up exercises. They warm you, limber up the muscles not only of your body but of your face as well. Proper circulation starts up in all your limbs down to the extremities.

"With your body in supple order you begin on your voice. You tune it up. The sound comes full, clear, resonant; it is placed forward in the mask of your face and floats freely out to fill the whole room. Your sounding surfaces are beautifully vibrant, the acoustics of your room throws your tones back to you, tempting you to further efforts, more energy, activity, greater liveliness.

"Clear diction, the clean cut phrase, vivid speech seek thoughts to produce, to round out, express with power.

"Unexpected inflections, rising spontaneously from within, are ready to form more incisive speech.

"After this you move into cycles of rhythm and sway back and forth in all kinds of tempi.

"Throughout your whole physical nature you sense order, discipline, balance and harmony.

"All the parts which contribute to your external, physical technique are now flexible, receptive, expressive, sensitive, responsive, mobile—like a well oiled and regulated machine in which all the wheels, rollers and cogs work in absolute co-ordination with one another.

"You find it difficult to stand still, you have the urge to move, to perform some act, to fulfill and express the dictates of the human spirit inside you.

"Your whole body is poised ror action, your steam is up. Like children you do not know what to do with your excess energy, so you are ready to use it up in anything that may happen along.

"You need an objective, an inner urge or order which calls for embodiment. If it comes you will throw your whole physical organism into its fulfillment, and do it with all the passionate energy of a child.

"This is the physical readiness which an actor should be able to evoke when he is on the stage. It is what we call the *external creative state.*

"Your apparatus of physical technique must not only be highly trained but also perfectly subordinated to the inner dictates of your will. This bond between the inner and outer aspects of your nature and their reciprocal action must be developed in you to the point of an instantaneous, unconscious, instinctive reflex.

"When our three musicians—the Mind, the Will, the Feelings—have taken their places and begun to perform on their two instruments on the left and on the right side of our wall, then the *external* and the *inner creative state* will proceed to act as sounding boards to catch the tones of all the individual elements.

"What is now left to be done is the gathering of them all into one whole. When this is accomplished we describe it as the *general creative state*, combining as it does the double aspect of inner psycho-technique with external physical technique.

"When you are in this state every feeling, every mood that wells up inside you is reflexively expressed. It is easy to react to all the problems the play, the director and finally you yourself put forward for solution. All your inner resources and physical capacities are on call, ready to respond to any bid. You play on them as an organist on the keys of his instrument. As soon as the tone fades away on one of them you pull out another stop.

"The more immediate, spontaneous, vivid, precise the reflection you produce from inner to outer form, the better, broader, fuller will be your public's sense of the inner life of the character you are portraying on the stage. It is for this that plays are written and the theatre exists.

"No matter what an actor is doing in the creative process he should at all times be in this overall state, of inner and outer co-ordination. He may be saying his lines for the first or the hundredth time, he may be studying his part or reading it over, working on it at home or at rehearsal, searching for tangible or intangible materials for a part, thinking about its inner or outer aspect, its passions, emotions, ideas, acts, its general outer appearance, his own costume or make-up—in all these major or minor contacts with a part an actor should without fail put himself into the general creative state which embodies both sides of his technique.

"Unless we do this we have no approach to a role. These things should be permanently established as normal, natural attributes of our second nature.

"This is the culminating point of our second year of work together and the general course of how an actor prepares himself.

"Now that you have learned how to achieve this creative state we can go on to the next step of how an actor prepares a whole part.

"All the knowledge you have acquired in these two years will be crowding your minds and hearts. You may find it difficult to settle it all into the right niches.

"Yet when all is said and done these various elements of an actor's make-up which we have been studying constitute nothing but the natural state of human beings and they are familiar to you from actual life. When we go through an experience in our own lives we naturally find ourselves in this state, which we seek to re-create when we are on the stage.

"In both cases it consists of the selfsame elements. Unless we are in this state we cannot, in our own lives, give ourselves up to the experience of our inner emotions or their external expression.

"The amazing thing is that this familiar state which is produced by normal means under natural conditions, vanishes without a trace the instant an actor sets foot on the stage. It takes a great effort, much study, the development of habits and a technique to bring to the stage the life of every human being.

"That is why we actors are obliged to engage in unflagging, systematic exercises and training. We must have patience, time and faith. It is to this that I summon you. The saying that habit is second nature is nowhere more pertinent than in our work. Habit is such an absolute necessity that I shall ask you to signify it by putting up two final pennants with the words *Habit*, and *Training* (both inner and outer). Let them hang on this wall where you have put the other elements which constitute the creative state.

"For all its many components this state is a very simple human thing. Amid the material surroundings of canvas backdrops, flies, wings, paint, glue, cardboard props it is this state that breathes life and truth into the stage.

"We have not finished the whole survey of an actor's preparation, but when that time comes and the first entire role is ready the walls will be covered with flags right up to the ceiling."

"But you have made no mention at all of the huge streamer with no inscription on it which hangs across the whole top of this wall," I said.

"Oh, that is the most important, most impelling reason why we do all our work on the physical truths and the ultra-real and ultra-natural components of our nature."

"Excuse me, please," broke in Grisha, "but then why have we been bothering about all these lower factors if the important object does not lie in them, but in this something or other higher up?"

"Because you cannot climb to the top at once," answered Tortsov. "You need a ladder, or steps. It is by means of them that you reach the top. I give you these steps. They are here before you in the guise of these illustrative flags. But they are only preparative steps leading to that all important, loftiest region of all art—the subconscious. Before, however, we can come to the edifying part we have to learn the simple things of right living."

As Tortsov was leaving and had already reached the door of the auditorium, it opened and in came Rakhmanov with the two pennants he had just mentioned: *Inner* and *External Habit* and *Training*.

6

"You have now reached the status, more or less, of specialists," Tortsov began, "and this gives me the opportunity to speak of something of capital importance—the subtlety of nature, its way of working in the theatre.

"You may ask what we have been doing up to now if not this. I shall illustrate what I mean by an example.

"When you want to make a rich, nourishing bouillon you prepare the meat, all kinds of soup greens, you add water, put the pot on the stove and give it a chance to simmer for a long time, so that the juices can be extracted, or else you will not have any bouillon.

"Yet this will all be to no purpose if you have not lighted a fire. Without it you will have to eat the contents of your pot separately and in their raw state, and drink the plain water.

"The super-objective and the through line of action constitute the fire which does the cooking.

"In ordinary life our creative nature is indivisible, its component parts cannot exist of and for themselves. Yet on the stage they fall apart with extraordinary ease and it is very difficult to reassemble them. That is why we must work out the means of reuniting all these parts we have been studying and harness them in common action.

"This is the great work that lies ahead of you when you come to prepare an entire role. The elements you have prepared must be transfixed by a through line of action carrying them along to the common goal of the overall objective of that role. Off the stage this happens in normal fashion, even if we are entirely unaware of such things as separate elements, through actions, super-objectives.

"How do we accomplish on the stage this process of prime importance?

"Under these *elements* we group, on the one side, natural capacities—talents, endowments, attributes, assets—and on the other side we put the means which are favourable to our technique as actors.

"You already know that we use the word super-objective to characterize the essential idea, the core, which provided the impetus for the writing of a play. You know too that the through or unbroken line of action is made up of the minor objectives in the life of a character in a play, on the stage.

"So choose as deep, firm, and well grounded a line of action as possible for your part, play or sketch (if this last is substantial enough to have an overall objective). As if you had a threaded needle in your fingers now pass it through the elements already set up inside you, the objectives you have prepared in the detailed score of your part, and string them on the unbroken line leading to the supreme goal of the play being produced.

"You will perfect this process and the practical means of accomplishing it as you work on a role."

16

SOME CONCLUSIONS ON
ACTING

I

ALTHOUGH our course had come to an end we felt that
we were still far from having achieved a practical mastery
of the so-called "system" even if we had a theoretical grasp
of it. In answer to the doubts we expressed Tortsov gave
this answer:

"The method we have been studying is often called the
'Stanislavski system'. But this is not correct. The very
power of this method lies in the fact that it was not con-
cocted or invented by anyone. Both in spirit and in body
it is a part of our organic natures. It is based on the laws
of nature. The birth of a child, the growth of a tree, the
creation of an artistic image are all manifestations of a
kindred order. How can we come closer to this nature of
creation? That has been the principal concern of my whole
life. It is not possible to invent a system. We are born with
it inside us, with an innate capacity for creativeness. This
last is our natural necessity, therefore it would seem that we
could not know how to express it except in accordance with
a natural system.

"Yet strangely enough, when we step on to the stage we
lose our natural endowment and instead of acting creatively
we proceed to perform contortions of pretentious proportions. What drives us to do this? The condition of having
to create something in public view. Forced, conventional
untruthfulness is implicit in stage presentation, in the foist-
ing on us of the acts and words prescribed by an author, the
scenery designed by a painter, the production devised by a
director, in our own embarrassment, stage fright, the poor

taste and false traditions which cramp our natures. All these impel an actor to exhibitionism, insincere representation. The approach we have chosen—the art of living a part— rebels with all the strength it can muster against those other current 'principles' of acting. We assert the contrary principle that the main factor in any form of creativeness is the life of a human spirit, that of the actor and his part, their joint feelings and subconscious creation.

"These cannot be 'exhibited'; they can only be produced spontaneously or as the result of something that has gone before. One can only feel them. All you can 'exhibit' on the stage is the artificial, contrived results of a non-existent experience.

"There is no feeling in that; there is only conventional artificiality, cliché acting."

"But it can also be effective. The public is impressed by it," remarked one of the students.

"I admit that," agreed Tortsov, "but what kind of an impression does it make? The quality of one impression must be distinguished from that of another. Our approach to acting in this theatre is extremely clear on this point.

"We are not interested in hit and run impressions, here to-day and gone to-morrow. We are not satisfied merely with visual and audible effects. What we hold in highest regard are impressions made on the emotions, which leave a lifelong mark on the spectator and transform actors into real, living beings whom one may include in the roster of one's near and dear friends, whom one may love, feel one's self akin to, whom one goes to the theatre to visit again and again. Our demands are simple, normal, and therefore they are difficult to satisfy. All we ask is that an actor on the stage live in accordance with natural laws. Yet because of the circumstances amid which an actor has to do his work it is much easier for him to distort his nature than to live as a natural human being. So we have had to find means to struggle against this tendency toward distortion—that is the basis of our so-called 'system'. Its purpose lies in destroying inevitable distortions and in directing the work of our inner natures to the right path which is carved out by stubborn work and the proper practices and habits.

"This 'system' should restore the natural laws, which have been dislocated by the circumstances of an actor's having to work in public, it should return him to the creative state of a normal human being.

"But you will have to be patient," Tortsov went on. "It will take several years even if you watch yourself carefully for these things you have been striving for to mature and blossom. By then, when you have the opportunity to go off in a false direction, you will find that you cannot do it, the essentially right way will be so firmly rooted in you."

"But great artists act by the grace of God and without all these elements of a creative state!" I objected.

"You are mistaken," countered Tortsov instantly. "Read what it says in *My Life In Art*. The more talent the actor has the more he cares about his technique, especially with regard to his inner qualities. A true creative state while on the stage, and all the elements that go to compose it, were the natural endowment of Shchepkin, Ermolova, Duse, Salvini. Nevertheless they worked unremittingly on their technique. With them moments of inspiration were almost a natural state. Inspiration came to them by natural means almost every time they repeated a role, yet all their lives they sought an approach to it.

"There is all the more reason why we, of more meagre endowments, should seek it. We ordinary mortals are under the obligation of acquiring, developing, training in ourselves and by ourselves each one of the component elements of a creative state on the stage. It takes us a long time and much hard work. Still we must never forget that the actor who has nothing more than capacity will never be a genius, whereas those whose talents may be more modest, if they will study the nature of their art, the laws of creativeness, may grow into the class of those who are akin to the geniuses. The 'system' will facilitate that growth. The preparation it gives an actor is not something to be laughed at: its results are very very great!"

"But, oh, how hard it all is!" I groaned. "How can we ever take it all in!"

"Those are the doubting reactions of impetuous youth," said Tortsov. "To-day you learn something. To-morrow you think you can already be letter perfect in technique. But the 'system' is not a hand me down suit that you can put on and walk off in, or a cook book where all you need is to find the page and there is your recipe. No, it is a whole way of life, you have to grow up in it, educate yourself in it for years. You cannot cram it into yourselves, you can assimilate it, take it into your blood and flesh, until it becomes second nature, becomes so organic a part of your being that you as an actor are transformed by it for the stage and for all time. It is a system that must be studied in parts and then merged into a whole so that it can be understood in all its fundamentals. When you can spread it all out before you like a fan you will obtain a true grasp of its entirety. You cannot hope to do this all at once. It is like going to war: you must conquer the territory bit by bit, consolidate your gains, keep in contact with your rear communications, expand, make further gains before you can speak of final conquest.

"In the same way we go about conquering our 'system'. In our difficult task the gradual quality and the training in it are of enormous help. They allow us to develop each new means we learn to a point of automatic habit, until it is organically grafted into us. In its initial stages each new factor is an obstacle, it draws off all our attention from other more important matters," Tortsov continued his description. "This process does not wear away until it is quite assimilated, made our own. Here again the 'system' is of great assistance. With each new means once conquered a part of our burden is eased and our attention is freed for concentration on more essential matters.

"Piecemeal the 'system' enters into the human being, who is also an actor, until it ceases to be something outside of him and becomes incorporated in his own second nature. To begin with we find this difficult, just as a year old baby finds it difficult to take his first steps, and is appalled by the complicated problem of controlling the muscles in his still wobbly legs. But he no longer thinks of this a year later when he has already learned to run, play and jump.

"A virtuoso on the keyboard also has his moments of difficulty and is aghast at the complexity of a certain passage. A dancer finds it extremely taxing in his early training to distinguish among all the various complicated, involved steps.

"What indeed would happen should he, when he comes to a public performance, still be obliged to be conscious at every movement of hand or foot, of his exact muscular action? If that is the case then the pianist or the dancer has proved he is not capable of doing the required work. It is out of the question to recall each touch of the fingers on the keys during a long piano concerto. Nor can a dancer be consciously aware of the movements of all his muscles throughout a whole ballet.

"S. M. Volonski stated this felicitously when he said: 'The difficult should become habitual, the habitual, easy, the easy, beautiful.' To accomplish this requires unrelenting, systematic exercise.

"That is why the virtuoso pianist or dancer will hammer away at a passage or a 'pas' until it is fixed forever in his muscles, until it has been converted into a simple, mechanical habit. Thereafter he never needs to give another thought to what in the beginning was so difficult to learn.

"The unfortunate and dangerous part of it, however, is that habits can also be developed in the wrong direction. The more often an actor appears on the stage and acts in a theatrical, untrue way and not according to the true dictates of his nature, the farther he will move away from the goal we seek to achieve.

"It is an even sadder fact that this false state is so much easier to acquire and make a habit of.

"I should like to hazard a guess as to the relative results of this fact. I should say that for every performance an actor gives of the wrong sort it takes him ten performances on the right basis to rid himself of its deleterious effects. Nor should you overlook the fact that public performance has still another effect, it tends to fix a habit. So that I should add: ten times of rehearsing in the wrong creative state equal in their bad influence one public performance.

"Habit is a two-edged sword. It can do great harm when badly used on the stage and be of great value when proper advantage is taken of it.

"It is essential to work on the system step by step when you are learning to establish the right creative state by forming trained habits. This is not so difficult in practice as it seems in theory. You must, however, not be in a hurry.

"There is also something worse which obstructs an actor's work."

This brought fresh fears to our minds.

"It is the inflexibility of the prejudices some actors have. Almost as a rule, since there are few exceptions to it, actors do not admit that laws, technique, theories, much less a system, have any part in their work. Actors are overwhelmed by their 'genius' in quotation marks," Tortsov said, not without irony. "The less gifted the actor the greater his 'genius' and it does not allow him to make any conscious approach to his art.

"Such actors, in the tradition of the handsome matinee idol Mochalov, gamble on 'inspiration'. The majority of them believe that any conscious factor in creativeness is only a nuisance. They find it easier to be an actor by the grace of God. I shall not deny that there are times when, for unknown reasons, they are able to have an intuitive emotional hold on their parts and they play reasonably well in a scene or even in a whole performance.

"But an actor cannot gamble his career on a few accidental successes. Because they are lazy or stupid these actors of 'genius' convince themselves that all they have to do is 'feel' something or other in order to have the rest take care of itself.

"But there are other occasions when for the same inexplicable and capricious reasons 'inspiration' does not turn up. Then the actor, who is left on the stage without any technique, without any means of drawing out his own feelings, without any knowledge of his own nature, plays not by the grace of God well, but by the grace of God poorly. And he has absolutely no way of getting back on to the right path.

"The creative state, the subconscious, intuition—these are not automatically at one's beck and call. If we can succeed in developing the right approaches to them, they can at least protect us from making the old mistakes. It seems obvious where we should start.

"But actors, like most people, are slow to see where their real interests lie. Think how many lives are still lost from sickness, although talented scientists have discovered specific cures, inoculations, vaccines, medicines! There was an old man in Moscow who boasted that he had never ridden in a train or spoken over a telephone. Humanity searches, it undergoes unspeakable trials and tribulations to discover the great truths, to make great discoveries, and people are so reluctant even to stretch out their hands and take what is freely offered them. That is an absolute lack of civilization!

"In the technique of the stage, and above all in the domain of speech, we see the same sort of thing. Peoples, nature itself, the best brains of the scholars, poets who rank as geniuses, have over the centuries contributed to the formation of language. They did not invent it, like Esperanto. It sprang from the very heart of life. It has been studied for generations by scholars, it has been refined, polished by poetic geniuses like Shakespeare and Pushkin— the actor has only to take what is prepared for him. But he will not swallow even a predigested food.

"There are some lucky ones who, without benefit of any study, have an intuitive sense of the nature of their language, and they speak it correctly. But they are the few, the rare cases. The overwhelming majority of people speak with scandalous slovenliness.

"Look at the way musicians study the laws, the theory of their art, the care they take of their instruments, their violins, 'cellos, pianos. Why do dramatic artists not do the same? Why do they not learn the laws of speech, why do they not treat their voices, their speech, their bodies with care and respect? Those are their violins, 'cellos, their most subtle instruments of expression. They were fashioned by the greatest genius of all craftsmen—the magician Nature.

"Most people in the theatre are unwilling to understand that accident is not art, that you cannot build on it. The master performer must have complete control of his instrument, and that of an artist is a complex mechanism. We actors have to deal not just with a voice the way a singer does, not just with hands like a pianist, not just with the body and legs like a dancer. We are obliged to play simultaneously on all the spiritual and physical aspects of a human being. To gain mastery over them requires time and arduous, systematic effort, a programme of work such as we have been pursuing here.

"This 'system' is a companion along the way to creative achievement, but it is not a goal in itself. You cannot act the 'system': you can work on it at home, but when you step out on to the stage cast it aside, there only nature is your guide. The 'system' is a reference book, not a philosophy. Where philosophy begins the 'system' ends.

"Reckless use of the 'system', work that is done according to it but without sustained concentration, will only drive you away from the goal you seek to reach. This is bad and can be overdone. Unfortunately this is often the case.

"A too emphatic, exaggerated care in the handling of our psycho-technique can be alarming, inhibiting, can lead to an over-critical attitude, or result in a technique used for its own sake.

"To insure yourselves against falling into these undesirable bypaths you should do your initial work only under the constant, careful supervision of a trained eye.

"You are perhaps disturbed that you have not yet learned

to make practical use of the 'system', yet what basis have you for concluding that what I have said to you in class should be instantly assimilated by you and put into action? I am telling you things that must remain with you all your life. Much that you hear in this school will be fully understood by you only after many years, and as the result of practical experience. It is only then that you will recall that you were told about them long since, but they did not penetrate into your consciousness. When that time comes, compare what experience has taught you with what you were told in school, then every word of your classes will spring to life.

"When you have mastered the creative state necessary to your artistic work you must learn to observe, evaluate your own feelings in a role and criticize the image you naturally portray and live in.

"You should expand your knowledge of art, literature, and other aspects of learning and show that you can improve your natural talents.

"You should develop your bodies, your voices, your faces into the best physical instruments of expression capable of rivalling the simple beauty of nature's creations."

2

"I want to devote our last class together to the praise of the greatest artist we know.

"And who can that be?

"Nature, of course, the creative nature of all artists.

"Where does she live? Where should we address all our laudatory remarks? I do not know.

"She is in all the centres and parts of our physical and spiritual make-up, even those of which we are not aware. We have no direct means of approaching her, but there exist oblique ones which are little known and scarcely practicable as yet.

"We call this thing that fills me with such enthusiasm genius, talent, inspiration, the subconscious, the intuitive. Yet where they are lodged in us, I cannot tell. I feel them in others, sometimes even in myself.

"Some believe that these mysterious and miraculous things are sent from above, that they are gifts from the Muses. But I am not a mystic and do not share this belief, although in moments when I am called on to create, I wish I might. It fires one's imagination.

"There are others who say that the seat of the thing I am searching for is in our hearts. But I only feel my heart when it pounds or swells or aches, and that is unpleasant. What I am talking about is, on the contrary, extraordinarily agreeable, enthralling to the point of self oblivion.

"A third group asserts that genius or inspiration is lodged in the brain. They compare consciousness with a light thrown on a particular spot in our brains, illuminating the thought on which our attention is concentrated. Meanwhile the remainder of our brain cells remain in darkness, or receive only some reflected light. But there are times when the whole cranial surface is illumined in a flash and then all that was in darkness is, for a brief period reached by the light. Alas, there is no electrical mechanism which would know how to make use of that light, so it continues to be inactive, only flaming out when it happens to wish to. I am ready to concede that this example gives a successful idea of just how things operate in the brain. But does that advance the practical side of the matter at all for us? Has anyone learned how to control this flashing light of our subconscious, our inspiration or intuition?

"There are scientists who find it extraordinarily easy to juggle with the word 'subconscious', yet whereas some of them wander off with it into the secret jungles of mysticism and utter beautiful but most unconvincing phrases about it, the others scold at them, laugh them to scorn and proceed, with great self-assurance to analyze the subconscious, set it forth as something quite prosaic, speak of it in the way we describe the functions of our lungs or livers. The explanations are simple enough. It is only too bad that they do not appeal to our heads or hearts.

"But there are still other learned people who offer us certain thoroughly worked out, complex hypotheses, although they admit that their premises are not yet proved or confirmed. Therefore they make no pretence of knowing the exact nature of genius, talent, the subconscious. They merely look to the future to achieve the findings they are still meditating on.

"This admitted lack of knowledge based on deep study, this frankness, is the outgrowth of wisdom. Such confessions arouse my confidence and convey to me a sense of the majesty of the searchings of science. To me it is the urge to attain, with the help of a sensitive heart, the unattained. And it will be attained in time. In the expectation of these new triumphs of science I have felt there was nothing for me to do except to devote my labours and energy almost exclusively to the study of Creative Nature—not to learn to create in her stead, but to seek oblique, roundabout ways to approach her, not to study inspiration as such but only to find some paths leading to it. I have discovered only a few of them, I know that there are a great many more and that they will eventually be discovered by others. Nevertheless I have acquired a sum of experience in the course of long years of work and this is what I have sought to share with you.

"Can we count on anything more since the realm of the subconscious is still beyond our reach? I do not know of anything I can offer you: *Feci quod potui—feciant meliore potentes* ('I have done what I could, let him who can do better').

"The advantage of my counsels to you is that they are realistic, practical, applicable to the work in hand, they have been tested out on the stage over decades of acting experience, and they produce results.

"We have learned certain laws concerning the creativeness

of our nature—that is significant and precious—but we shall never be able to replace that creative nature by our stage technique, no matter how perfect it is.

"Technique follows logically, admiringly on the heels of nature. Everything is clear, intelligible and intelligent: the gesture, the pose, the movement. The speech too is adapted to the part; the sounds are well worked out, the pronunciation is a joy to the ear, the phrases beautifully shaped, the inflections musical in form, almost as though they were sung to notes. The whole is warmed and given a basis of glowing truth from the inside. What more can anyone desire? It is a great satisfaction to see and hear such acting. What art, what perfection! Alas, how rare are actors of this kind!

"They and their performances leave behind wonderfully beautiful, aesthetic, harmonious, delicate impressions of forms completely sustained and perfectly finished.

"Do you believe that such great art is to be had for the mere studying of a system of acting, or by learning some external technique? No, this is true creativeness, it comes from within, from human and not theatrical emotions. It is towards this goal that we should strive.

"Even so there is for me still one lack in such acting. I do not find in it that quality of the unexpected which startles, overwhelms, stuns me. Something that lifts the spectator off the ground, sets him in a land where he has never walked, but which he recognizes easily through a sense of foreboding or conjecture. He does, however, see this unexpected thing face to face, and for the first time. It shakes, enthralls, and engulfs him.

"There is no room here for reasoning and analyzing—there can be no doubt about the fact that this unexpected something has surged up from the well springs of organic nature. The actor himself is overwhelmed and enthralled by it. He is carried away to a point beyond his own consciousness. It can happen that such an inner tidal wave will pull an actor away from the main course of his part. That is regrettable, but nevertheless an outburst is an outburst and it stirs the deepest waters. One can never forget it, it is the event of a lifetime.

"And when this storm travels along the main course of a part it enables the actor to reach heights of the ideal. The public is given the living creation it came to the theatre to see.

"It is not just an image, although all images taken together are of the same kind and origin; it is a human passion. Where does the actor get this technique of voice, speech, movement? He may be awkward, but now he is the embodiment of plastic ease. Usually he mumbles and mouths his words, but now he is eloquent, inspired, his voice is vibrant and musical.

"Good as the actor of the preceding type may be, brilliant and fine as his technique is, can he yet be compared with this last? Such acting is stunning in the very audacity with which it brushes aside all ordinary canons of beauty. It is powerful, yet not because of the logic and coherence we admired in the first type of acting. It is magnificent in its bold illogicality, rhythmic in its unrhythmicness, full of psychologic understanding in its very rejection of ordinarily accepted psychology. It breaks through all the usual rules, and that is what is good and powerful about it.

"It cannot be repeated. The next performance will be quite different, yet no less powerful or inspired. One wants to call out to the actor: Remember how you did it! Don't forget we want to enjoy it again! But the actor is not his own master. It is his nature which creates through him, he is only the instrument.

"There is no estimate that we can put on such works of nature. We cannot say: why is it thus, and not otherwise? It is thus because it is and cannot be anything else. We cannot criticize lightning, a storm at sea, a squall, a tempest, dawn or sunset.

"Nevertheless there are those who think that nature often works poorly, that our dramatic technique can improve on her, give proof of greater taste. To some aesthetically-minded people taste is of more consequence than truth. But in the instant when a crowd of thousands is being moved, when they are all swept by one great feeling of enthusiasm, no matter what the physical shortcomings of the actors or actresses who cause this emotional storm—is it a matter of taste, conscious creation, technique, or is it that unknown something which is possessed by and possesses the genius, who has no power over it?

"At such times even a deformed person becomes beautiful. Then why does he not make himself beautiful more often, as and when he wishes, merely by his technique and without recourse to that unknown power which gives him his beauty? Yet those all knowing aesthetes do not know how to bring this about, they do not even know how to confess their lack of knowledge, and they continue to praise cheap, technical acting.

"The greatest wisdom is to recognize one's lack of it. I have reached that point and I confess that in the realm of intuition and the subconscious I know nothing, except that these secrets are open to the great artist Nature. That is why my praise is for her. If I did not confess my own powerlessness to achieve the greatness of creative nature I should be feeling my way like a blind man, in paths from which there is no issue, believing that I was surrounded by an endless expanse of space. No, I prefer to stand on the heights and from there look out to the limitless horizon, trying to project myself for a little distance, a few miles, into that vast region still inaccessible to our consciousness, which my mind cannot grasp even in its imagination. Then I shall be like the old king in Pushkin's poem who

> . . . *from the heights*
> *could scan with gladdening eye*
> *The valley studded with white tents*
> *And, far beyond, the sea*
> *and scudding sails. . . ."*